MATERIAL CULTURE IN THE SOCIAL WORLD ▪

MATERIAL CULTURE IN THE SOCIAL WORLD

VALUES, ACTIVITIES, LIFESTYLES

TIM DANT

OPEN UNIVERSITY PRESS
BUCKINGHAM · PHILADELPHIA

Open University Press
Celtic Court
22 Ballmoor
Buckingham
MK18 1XW

e-mail: enquiries@openup.co.uk
world wide web: http://www.openup.co.uk

and

325 Chestnut Street
Philadelphia, PA 19106, USA

First Published 1999

A catalogue record of this book is available from the British Library

ISBN 0 335 19821 X (pb) 0 335 19822 8 (hb)

Library of Congress Cataloging-in-Publication Data
Dant, Tim. 1951–
Material culture in the social world: values, activities, lifestyles / Tim Dant.
p. cm.
Includes bibliographical references.
ISBN 0-335-19822-8. – ISBN 0-335-19821-X (pbk.)
1. Material culture. 2. Social interaction. I. Title.
GN406.D36 1999
306–dc21 99–14375
CIP

Typeset by Type Study, Scarborough, North Yorkshire

Printed and bound in Great Britain by
Marston Lindsay Ross International Ltd,
Oxfordshire

FOR MOLLIE AND JO

CONTENTS

ACKNOWLEDGEMENTS ■

There are a number of people who have helped in the writing of this book whom I would like to thank. My colleagues in the Department of Sociology, Manchester Metropolitan University have provided useful comments and discussion as well as supporting a sabbatical term and conference trips. Earlier versions of Chapter 3 were presented at the British Sociological Association (BSA) annual conference in Preston in 1994 and subsequently published in *Sociological Review* 44(3): 495–516. Earlier versions of Chapter 6 were presented at the American Sociological Conference annual meeting in New York in 1996 and subsequently published in the *Journal of Material Culture* 3(1): 77–95. I am grateful to the editors, Blackwell Publishers and Sage Publications Ltd for permission to reprint this material here.

I am also grateful to a number of individuals who have helped in many different ways, with key references, comments, criticisms, personal information or allowing me to read their unpublished work. I would like to mention in particular Graeme Gilloch, Ian Heywood, Jon Hindmarsh, Lee Lloyd, Ian Roderick, Paul Rosen, Jason Rutter, Seamus Simpson, Paul Sweetman, Paul Taylor, Belinda Wheaton, Val Woodward and Derek Wynne. Mollie Foxall and Jo Foxall Dant helped in a wide range of unspecifiable ways, which included being unintentional informants and critics.

1

INTRODUCTION: THE CAIRN AND THE MINI-STRIP ▪

So I squeeze it a little bit, I can hear she's special, Papa, you gonna like the sound of this instrument, and she's got a big long bellows, plenty of squeeze in her, a crying voice. Oh she's a nice little girl accordeen, lonesome for the pine trees in the north.

(Buddy explaining to his father why he bought another accordion to add to the family's collection in *Accordion Crimes*, by E. Annie Proulx, 1996: 288)

Humans stand apart from other animal species not only because of their upright posture, the size of their brains, their use of language and the opposition between thumb and forefinger, but also because of the way they create, use and live with a wide variety of material objects. This world of man-made things modifies the natural world to provide a material environment as the context in which social interaction takes place. Things, both natural and man-made, are appropriated into human culture in such a way that they re-present the social relations of culture, standing in for other human beings, carrying values, ideas and emotions – Buddy's accordion has the crying voice of a lonesome girl. But unlike images, ideas, talk and text, things are not just representations, but also have a physical presence in the world which has material consequences – the size of the bellows means that the accordion has the capability to produced a well sustained note that any animal nearby would hear.

The things of the world are incorporated into social interaction and provide an embodiment of social structures reflecting back the nature and form of our social world. As archaeologists and anthropologists have long recognized, material culture provides evidence of the distinctive form of a society. It provides this evidence because it is an integral part of what that society is; just as the individual cannot be understood independently of society, so society cannot be grasped independently of its material stuff. And yet sociology has taken a largely agnostic view of the role of material objects in the life of societies.

This book is an attempt to argue that sociology needs to begin to attend to the ways in which interaction with objects is part and parcel with the social interaction which gives rise to social forms. We express ourselves as part of *this* society through the way we live with and use objects. Material culture ties us to others in our society providing a means of sharing values, activities and styles of life in a more concrete and enduring way than language use or direct interaction. But material culture is never distinct from language or interaction; things are often the topic of talk or the focus of action and they often facilitate interaction or mediate by providing a means of interaction rather like language. Social human beings establish what we might call 'quasi-social' relationships with objects in which they live out in a real, material form the abstract relationships they have with the wider society in which they live. It is through this quasi-social relationship with things that individuals both express their social identity and experience their location within society. It is a *quasi*-social relationship in that the object stands in for other social beings. The things that we relate to have embodied within them the social relations that gave rise to them through their design, the work of producing them, their prior use, the intention to communicate through them and their place within an existing cultural system of objects. It is in these ways, I wish to argue, that material culture is an important component of the social world we live in that affects our values, our actions and our lifestyles.

This book looks at a number of different ways of thinking sociologically about objects and how our interactive relationships with objects arise out of social relationships. Rather than attempt to build up a comprehensive picture of one material culture, I shall attempt to ground ideas about the nature of our quasi-social relationships with things by practical illustrations. To begin with I want to describe two different types of objects that embody two different extremes of the sorts of social meanings that are part of material culture in modern, western societies.

MATERIAL CULTURE IN NATURE – THE CAIRN

As you climb up hills and mountains in the United Kingdom, as in most countries, you find a falling away of human society that is marked by a change in material culture. In the valleys, stretching up into the lower hills, are roads for vehicles, fields with crops, plantations, collections of farm buildings and houses, telephone wires, fences and walls. As you go higher, the socially provided amenities that support modern material life disappear and are replaced by septic tanks, soakaways, calor gas, diesel powered electricity generators and fresh water wells and springs. Buildings become more isolated, the land less cultivated, crops give way to grazing animals, roads are a layer of aggregate rather than tarmac. A 'tree line' marks the point above which production on the land ceases. In England this point is usually reached at about 450 metres where the grouse moors and open land begin. Once the dry-stone walls have ended, often the only buildings are occasional lines of rough shooting butts.

Over the high ground, besides the Land Rover tracks and shooters' paths, there are some ancient roads between cities used by walkers, horse-riders and packhorses before the coming of the railways. A different type of path leads up the hill to the top. This is the rambler's path, the route taken by someone who is going nowhere, for no other purpose than to get to the top of a hill. On the tops, material culture has all but disappeared – one of the reasons for going there. Reaching the very top gives access to views across the countryside that take in the distant, toy-like form of the settlements down in the valleys and may stretch as far as a person can walk in a day. The perspective is that of a bird; the sky, clouds and sunsets are on a level with the eyes uncluttered with the material of buildings, streets and the plethora of things that they contain. The distance of the horizon allows a vision of openness, space and depth in contrast to the visual focus on detail and foreground in an everyday material environment. The optical experience of the high point is a reward for having climbed upwards. There is nowhere else to go but back, down into the cultivated and built environment. But having climbed beyond the production and construction of human societies, humans often mark their having been there with a cairn.

The cairn is a mess of stones which builds to a rough mound, usually on the highest point of a mountain. It marks the crest, the best view, ideally an all around panorama. It is a crude pyramid that points skywards, mimicking the mountain on which it is built; humans constructing a monument to themselves and their places, which stands atop whatever nature has managed to build. For some, their visit to the top is marked by adding another stone to the top of the cairn, for others simply to touch the top is enough. Still others resent the arrogance of the cairn and may kick it to pieces, spreading the stones over the land from whence they were gathered. There can be no productive purpose in being in the place where the mountaintop cairn is built; it is not a place of work or activity, but a place of leisure or contemplation.

The cairn is a building which has little practical use; the highest point is obvious to any human with a sense of balance, provided the view is not obscured by low cloud. Some cairns do become substantial enough to provide shelter, but most do not even provide anywhere comfortable to sit. The main use of the cairn is symbolic and sociocultural. They are landmarks, signs indicating the highest point, although sometimes used to indicate a boundary or a path, which is especially useful on stony tops where clouds can easily make it impossible to identify the safe way down. Sometimes they are raised as a memorial to a person, someone killed at a spot or who was a regular visitor. Cairns mark, like graffiti or the scratchings on a tree, the previous presence of people – someone was here. But the mark of the cairn is more self-effacing than the carved initials or the sprayed logo or moniker. Each stone speaks of an arrival of at least one, unnamed, undated human being. The building of the cairn is a collaborative enterprise between a group of people who are dispersed in time and may never meet. Their common purpose is expressed materially and specified in space; stones laid with similar meaning and intent may be separated by a century or more. The building of the cairn has a design that follows a standard pattern of a mound that may evolve into some other form. The material of the cairn is 'natural' in that each contribution is found, not formed. No one makes or shapes the stones – at the most they are chosen. And in the choosing, simple constraints apply – easily lifted and placed, flat surfaces for steadying the new rock on the pile and making a place for the next.

An unintended effect of cairn building can be to 'clear up' an area, neatly removing to a tidy pile stones that would otherwise be strewn about.

At first glance, the cairn may appear to be a natural feature, as when a stone outcrop on a mountaintop is rendered into a pile of stones through weathering or a pile of stones is left by the morainic droppings of a glacier. But the cairn provides a marker between nature and culture. The human work which makes the cairn is, by and large, not waged labour, but symbolic labour, undertaken to mark human presence, not to create wealth. Each contribution is made voluntarily and without direct or negotiated collaboration with other contributors at other times. Whatever else it may be, the cairn is not a commodity and has no exchange-value; its value is entirely symbolic. On the top of a mountain it is inaccessible and insubstantial. It is not made with the care and skill of a dry-stone wall, which uses similar materials; it is not so useful since it only marks the land rather than providing a barrier. There is no articulated tradition of cairn making, no factory, no apprenticeship, no guild. No machines or tools are employed, no signs or symbols other than the pile itself. Each cairn is unique and particular. To copy it would be to produce a different object, since the stones, the location and the sequence of human builders all contribute to its particularity. While such a simple construction can endure the ravages of elements over sufficient time to become as much a part of the landscape as a natural feature, it may be dispersed to re-merge with the surroundings, leaving no trace or waste.

MATERIAL CULTURE AS COMMODITY – THE MINI-STRIP

The cairn has no commodity status, unlike the soccer team 'mini-strip' which hangs in the back of the supporter's car. It is also a product of material culture that symbolizes non-work activity, but is a modern artefact, produced *en masse* through highly sophisticated manufacturing techniques by waged labour working at machines with entirely manufactured materials. It is a commodity that precisely replicates another in miniature, is bought and inserted within a material world, coded to signify allegiance to a cultural grouping and advertise corporate brands.

Supporters of soccer teams have always declared their allegiance through a series of objects, some of which have had a certain usefulness (the warmth of a woolly hat and scarf in team colours) and others (pennants, badges, flags) which are simply waved, attached to clothing, stuck on walls or hung in cars. In recent years a variant of this supporter's equipment has appeared – the mini-strip. Replicating the players' clothing, it appears in public suspended on a mini-hanger from a hook on a plastic suction cup stuck in the rear window of the supporter's car. Though made of material, with an inside and an outside, in doll size proportions, and sold like Barbie and Sindy clothes on little hangers, the mini-strip has no limb holes so that it could not actually be used to dress a doll. It has replaced the more traditional triangular pennant, that used to be displayed in supporter's cars, showing the club emblem and colours. Informants told me that the mini-strip is a bit 'naff', a part of the commodity culture of modern football's merchandising. Real supporters are interested in the game and those who drive to away matches would not leave any sign of team allegiance on display in their parked car, for fear of attack by rival supporters.

In the days of televised matches, sponsorship and merchandising, strips change frequently. Different home and away strips, varying colour schemes, patterned and textured effects, collars and shaped necks, the advertisements of sponsors and annual changes have all become features of the team strip. High definition colour television means that more subtle colours and design features are visible to viewers who see much of the action closer than those at the football ground. The mini-strip mimics not only the real team's strip but also the full-size kit that a supporter may buy and wear proudly (at least the shirt) to the match, to the pub or even to play football with friends. It also mimics the child-sized versions of strips that can be bought for younger fans and supporters. But the mini-strip cannot be worn and has no use-value other than its symbolic value; it simply shows allegiance to the team it stands for. The visual code of the mini-strip cannot vary because it is rigidly fixed to replicate the team's strip. Unlike the pennant, flag or scarf, which merely display colours and emblems, the form of the mini-strip claims a verisimilitude with something that is a real part of the team – the clothes worn when the team plays. When the team strip is redesigned, so is the mini-strip, even when colours and club badge stay the same.

This is one of the mini-strip's messages: it is a true likeness of the original in all except its usefulness. It represents not only the original strip but also the representation of the original in the news photograph or the television picture. Indeed, the reduced proportions of the mini-strip when seen from a distance of a few yards match those of these two-dimensional presentations of footballers. As it hangs on its little hanger, the three dimensionality of the mini-strip, collapsed to two dimensions, reproduces the way that material culture is so often appropriated in contemporary culture through the two dimensions of still or moving images. There are variations on the mini-strip theme with some even smaller versions designed to hang from the rear-view mirror and some with the reverse of the shirt to show the name of a particular team member.

An effect of exactly reproducing the team strip is to carry over the sponsor's logo and brand name, which are much larger than the club's emblem. So the mini-strip hung in the back window of the family car not only shows support for a team such as England's 'Manchester United' but also for 'Sharp' and 'Umbro'. The flag of allegiance has become an advertisement for a multinational company whose connection with the team supported is money and the sportswear manufacturer who make the strip. The goods advertised including the strip and the mini-strip are made in the Far East – not in Manchester. People who display the mini-strip actually pay to advertise a brand name that they have not directly chosen. Even the non-football fan, who could not identify the team by the colour and design of the strip, can easily decode from a distance the brand name and logo of the sponsor.

MATERIAL CULTURE – ARTEFACTS, THINGS AND LIVING WITH THEM

These two types of objects, the cairn and the mini-strip, have been chosen and described in general terms to indicate some of the ways that we live with and through things. The tradition of sociology has attended to the form of society – its structure and its institutions – and to the ways in which we live together through social relations, interaction and culture. The emphasis has tended to fall on the ways in which we form ourselves into social groups, achieving distinction from other groups and recognizing affiliation. The traditional concerns with class, status and party have in the middle of the twentieth century been overlain with issues of race, gender, age and physical ability. The traditional focus on economic relations, religion and class politics have been overlain with contemporary concerns with identity, the body, nationality and globalization. Culture has always been one of the ways of referring to how we live as a society; how we share values and experiences, how we create, produce and communicate. From large scale attention within the sociologies of knowledge, religion, science, art, communication and education to more local attention to the interactions that constitute work, the family, deviance and community, the form of culture has been a topic always close to the centre of sociology.

But unlike the disciplines of archaeology and anthropology, material culture has largely been a marginal aspect of sociology. As sociology has focused on how human social relations are developed, sustained and changed, it has tended to overlook the importance of the material environment in the form of these relations. For archaeology there is nothing else but the sedimented material remains of past cultures from which to reconstruct an account of long-dead historical social formations. In its comparative study of living cultures, anthropology has responded to the visible and concrete elements of those cultures. In the anthropological ethnographic tradition there are photographs and drawings of pots, huts, beads, weapons, clothes, ornaments, canoes and so on, which seem necessary to describe those cultures adequately. Anthropology explores distinctions between material culture (pots, carvings) and mythological culture (stories, beliefs), explores the economics of the exchange of objects (shells, leaves) and the importance of gifts. In anthropology the idea of social relations being embodied in objects is well established:

> Things possess a personality, and the personalities are in some way the permanent things of the clan. Titles, talismans, copper objects and the spirits of the chiefs are both homonyms and synonyms of the same nature and performing the same function. The circulation of goods follows that of men, women, and children, of feasts, rituals, ceremonies, and dances, and even that of jokes and insults. All in all, it is one and the same. If one gives things and returns them, it is because one is giving and returning 'respects' – we still say 'courtesies'. Yet it is also because by giving one is giving *oneself*, and if one gives *oneself*, it is because one 'owes' *oneself* – one's person and one's goods – to others.
>
> (Mauss 1990 [1950]: 46)[1]

Within sociology, which has its own urban ethnographic tradition, there is remarkably little attempt to incorporate a description of material culture. With few exceptions, which will begin to emerge in later chapters, sociology has not established materiality as part of the social relations that it describes.

There are, I think, two reasons for this. First, the familiarity of material culture has meant that sociologists do not tend to record or respond to it: they do not take photographs, drawings, film or video recordings (see Becker 1986; Smith and Ball 1992) nor do they gather or collect artefacts. Detailed descriptions of material objects are most unusual (for some exceptions see Riggins 1994a). The conditions of social existence of, say, the poor or the rich, can apparently be achieved by words which make generalized reference to material forms which are so familiar that they do not need to be described in detail or photographed or represented in other ways. One of the pleasures of writing this book was to stray into those parts of the library that were concerned with designing, building and using objects now and in the past, that were illustrated with drawings and photographs as well as detailed descriptions. These were not, by and large, sociological texts and, on the whole, I do not regret the absence of photographs in such a general text as this. Encountering these texts which foreground the stuff of material culture brought into relief how readily sociology ignores the content of material relations. Even in studies of production, of the transformatory effects of machine processes and mass production, the object is taken for granted in its effects. However, for a sociology of objects to develop empirically, there is a need for sociologists to become more visually and technically acute and to develop methods of research that adequately represent objects as they interact with people – anthropology clearly has a head start here.

Second, Marx has had an enormous impact not only on the central concerns of sociology but also on its ethos. Georg Simmel (as we shall see in Chapters 5 and 7) had a broad interest in culture and his 'sociological impressionism' identified the importance of cultural changes that were connected to changes in material culture. Marx had a very different focus on the political consequences of economic changes that came about with the development of capitalism. Put simply, the realm of the object was not one to which the human subject should be subordinate. Marx was of course writing in a Kantian–Hegelian philosophical tradition in which the relationship between humans and things was taken as a categorial distinction between subject and object. This distinction involves a valuation that is very difficult not to simply take for granted; subjects have a higher status and significance in the processes of the world than do objects. Subjects apprehend objects through the operation of reflective consciousness out of which arises the order of social relations and subjective distance from the material world. In Marx's analysis this is no longer a mere philosophical distinction but one that begins to have a bearing on how the practical world is understood. In his critique of Hegel, what were abstract concepts to do with the forms of consciousness are transformed into concepts that refer to the material existence of people under capitalism. So, 'objectification' becomes a process of the estrangement and alienation of human beings rather than their coming to consciousness. The very practical and material business of producing goods leads to specific consequences:

> The *devaluation* of the human world grows in direct proportion to the *increase in value* of the world of things . . . The product of labour is labour embodied and made material in an object, it is the *objectification* of labour . . . In the sphere of political economy this realization of labour appears as a *loss of reality* for the worker, objectification as *loss of bondage to the object*, and appropriation as *estrangement*, as *alienation.*
>
> (Marx 1975 [1844]: 323–4)

Marx's ideas were a response to material and social structural changes that had, and continue to have, an overarching impact on the form of western societies, including its material culture. But Marx directed the emphasis firmly towards the sphere of production, and even there, focused not on how work was done but on the political economic consequences of the way work was done. In Chapter 3 I shall address the issue of the fetishism of commodities to show the deconstructive effect of the critique from Sahlins, Baudrillard and others on the orientation of a Marxist influenced sociology towards the object as something that is produced as a commodity. Here it is sufficient to note that Marx's analysis resists an alternative view which recognizes the liberation of human existence through the transformation of the material world. This transformation, which might be achieved only through social processes of oppression and exploitation, brings about a society in which most needs for the material of shelter, clothing and food can be met. It also brings about the characteristic material complexity of modern culture with its vast array of different objects, which become available to an ever widening faction of society. Modern social formations, while undoubtedly the product of capitalism with all its social ills, are realized partly through a material culture in which forms of life are shaped by the things that we live with.

MATERIAL CULTURE

The idea of material culture that this book explores is simple. In a practical sense, that which is *material* is that which we can see, touch and smell but which is not human or animal. The *culture* is the set of common human practices that surround material objects – the ways of using material, of sharing it, of talking about it, of naming it and of making it. This culture is, however, dynamic and variable such that individual responses will adapt and alter those common practices. *Artefacts* that are made by humans may be distinguished from natural forms which would be there whether or not human beings were. But this distinction begins to break down when found natural objects are constituted socially by the culture that names, describes and incorporates mountains, rivers, stones, plants and so on.

Things are objects that are available to our senses as discrete and distinct entities which do not count as other beings or other objects. Even in this practical sense there are categorial difficulties because some living forms seem to be treated by us as if they are things – bugs, pests, vermin. Beings that are dead seem to become things yet they never lose their being-like quality. Food, especially meat, provides a particularly difficult anomalous form that is both material and yet not. Once eaten, the material becomes part of its consumer and cannot be distinguished as separate and material. Some things are not distinct from other things (where does one road end and another begin?) often because there are problems over boundaries or margins. Most things are made of other things which can be distinguished if it is appropriate for practical purposes (chairs have legs, which may become important when identifying a chair as broken and unsafe).

If the meaning of the phrase 'material culture' is unproblematic, at least for practical purposes, this is because common sense makes a distinction between material and human/animal that works for most everyday purposes. But the argument of this book is that the everyday distinction is taken too seriously by sociology, which concerns itself with social relationships and the structure of society while ignoring the impact of material forms on the topics and issues that sociology addresses. The aim of bringing material culture into the centre of sociology is to make the claim that the distinctions between that which is social and that which is material are not as easily made as the social sciences traditionally assume.

The argument being put forward here is that social forms are not only contingent on human activities but also contingent on the material environment of those activities. That material environment is not natural or given, it is itself a social product and as such it feeds back on the development of social forms – institutions, rituals, practices, modes of interaction, activities, beliefs. The things we make, appropriate and use are a manifestation of social forms while also shaping them. This is the idea that I want to develop with the concept of *material culture*; not only are things our products, designed to help us fulfil basic animal needs, but also they are an expression of who and what we are that shapes how society can proceed.

The cairn and the mini-strip are both available within the sphere of material culture. Different practices will appropriate these different types of objects. The cairn is not a commodity and cannot be 'consumed' in the sense of being purchased, possessed or used up. Its production and its cultural appropriation remain public and shared through simple practices of noticing, touching and building that may have ritual and symbolic significance. The mini-strip is a commodity that can be bought in a shop and can be understood in terms of consumption; who buys it, where from, what pressures led them to the purchase? But the mini-strip is also involved in other practices of cultural appropriation; where it is put, what other objects it competes with, how it is referred to and how long it is kept are all practices that involve adapting rituals. Unlike the cairn, it is not an object that lends itself to *bricolage* (see Chapter 4) or to the maintenance rituals that might for example be applied to real clothes (see Chapter 5). This is not because the mini-strip is a commodity but because such a simple object does not lend itself to much material appropriation beyond being hung somewhere. On the other hand, unlike the cairn, it is a mediating object (see Chapter 8), a vehicle for a series of iconic, graphic and linguistic signs that are presented on the surface of the object. The meanings derived from a particular mini-strip – which at least include the support of a particular team at a particular time – have to be 'read' in the light of a code or series of codes.

THE SHAPE OF THINGS TO COME

I began to think about material culture because of the emerging centrality of computers in social relations of knowledge (Lyotard 1984) and the debate about artificial intelligence that led to questions about the agency of computers (Dreyfus and Dreyfus 1986; Bloomfield 1987; Woolgar 1987; Collins 1990). Impressed by the rapid development of the functional capacity of computers, many commentators were keen to find something distinctive in this 'new' type of object. But as I thought about these issues in relation to the sociology of knowledge (Dant 1991) it became clear that computers were tools and as such much like other objects; they had a limited capacity to be 'delegated' a certain amount of agency, as Latour (1992) might put it (see Chapter 6). Computers are no more than a development of other types of objects. They are complicated inside, they process and manipulate discourse but at best they translate; they never grasp meaning or discover value.

All objects are social agents in the limited sense that they *extend human action* and *mediate meanings* between humans. It is this double dynamic of objects that I want to explore. Whether an object is produced by the application of a craft skill, the mechanical operations of a factory or the *bricolage* of the unskilled with what is to hand, objects are shaped by a culture which defines what certain types of things can *do*. It is the culture that specifies how we make sense of shapes, colours, textures, strengths and channelling of energy and so determines how we make use of and live with things. Many objects are embedded with function and style and a given object may contain a large number of interconnected objects, each of which contributes to the experienced function and style of the object. The car is a familiar example of a complex of subsidiary objects that add up to a thing which contains a multiplicity of functions oriented to the overarching function of transport and of aesthetic statements that add up to the overall style of the car. Both the functional capacity and the style of the car are emergent from the interaction of the various components that constitute it – wheels, bodywork, suspension, engine and so on. The complexity of many objects, their capacity for many different uses and their production by many different intentions means that they cannot be reduced to *a* function or *an* aesthetic. Even the simplest object such as a paperweight (see Chapter 7) is treated as a complex object by those who establish a relationship with it.[2]

The process of cultural appropriation of material things is not reducible either to production or consumption (see Chapter 2) but is to do with a series of types of interactions between people and objects. These interactions with things – touching, making, looking at, talking and reading about, using, storing, maintaining, remaking and so on – are social in that they are learnt and shared within the culture. Material objects are physically formed within a culture but are also socially constructed in the ways that they are fitted into routine, everyday practices and ways of life. Culture is embedded and disembedded throughout the life of the object while the processes of production and consumption are organized around economic exchange.

Picking up and playing a button accordion that was made at another time in another place, for another person and another type of music, can release potentials stored within it that were never intended or anticipated by its maker. The picking up and playing disembeds something – a tone, a harmonic sequence, a volume, a voice – which is distinctively cultural. The embedding was achieved by particular ideas, imagination, technology and practical skills in manufacture and the object makes certain demands on the user (dexterity, body size, 'ear'). Its use is not simply a 'using up' of the 'good' but a releasing of what has been embedded; it is not a consumption so much as a reproduction. The process of embedding and disembedding culture through using and living with things I shall call appropriation.

In this book my aim is to shift thinking in the cultural and social sciences about the nature of material objects from treating them as 'products', 'commodities' or 'technology' to thinking about them as allies, as artefacts and meaningful objects that make up a substantial part of the context of our social lives. Things are useful in a variety of ways; they allow us to do what we need and want to do, they allow us to communicate and they enable us to express our sense of cultural togetherness as well as our individuality within that collectivity.

I have tried to think about different ways in which we live with things and draw on previous discussions by others who are anthropologists, historians, psychologists, design theorists, political theorists, philosophers, cultural critics and a few sociologists. I would have liked to have included far more empirical work that explored how we live with things – such empirical work remains to be done. I would also have liked to say more about processes of making things but decided that the economic and social relations of production are of too complex a nature to deal with in a book of this scope. I have also avoided discussing the tension between nature and culture that is raised by ecology. This is a complex perspective on material culture that again I have avoided rather than deal with too briefly.

The absence of an empirical sociology of things is perhaps because we live so closely with things; we take them for granted, and do not regard our relationship with the washing machine or the chair as in any way important or problematic. Once acquired, we often do not notice these objects until they break or are commented on by someone else. Until they are put in a museum or turn up in a strange context, we do not notice that they are culturally distinctive, that they are part of *our* lives alongside the people we live with. Much more of our daily lives is spent interacting with material objects than interacting with other people. Even when not actually handling them, our contact with objects is often continuous and intimate in comparison with our contact with people (think of the chair you are sitting on and the range of objects in sight, within a short reach that are there, ready for when you need them). As well as supporting us they serve our needs, entertain us and act as a go-between in our interactions with others.

Chapters 2 and 3 tackle largely theoretical issues to do with consumption and the idea of material objects as fetishes. This leads to a new approach that treats the social value of objects as emergent in the way we use and live with them. The remaining chapters look at different areas of social life in which material objects play a part. This approach begins in Chapter 4 with the idea of home, where the organization of material objects provides a context for social organization and where the interaction with those objects is inextricable from interaction with other people within the home. In Chapter 5 we move from the material context of social interaction to thinking about the intimate interaction between people and the clothes they wear. In Chapter 6 I look at the idea of playing with things using as an example the activity of windsurfing. What is interesting here is the complexity of a relationship between the individual and an object that is simply for pleasure, which reveals a complex web of social meanings that are embedded in the object and the mode of interaction with it. In Chapter 7 I raise some of the issues about how material culture emerges in the context of its own history – the history of aesthetics, design and production, and how temporality is reflected in the biographies of things. Chapter 8 reflects on objects that are specifically intended to mediate culture and asks how their form and the attention they demand influences the culture they do mediate. Chapter 9 explores the boundaries between the human body as an object and other objects that are introduced to replace or supplement it. In Chapter 10 I draw some tentative conclusions on the significance of material culture for understanding the social world.

NOTES

1 Emphases in quotations are always in the original text unless otherwise stated.
2 Baudrillard (1998 [1970]: 112) regards the paperweight as a residual function for objects, 'the function reserved for all absolutely useless objects!'

2

CONSUMING OR LIVING WITH THINGS? ■

All unnoticed, the articles of everyday use act upon man.
(Giedion 1969 [1948]: 360)

In contemporary social theory the approach which has brought material culture into focus takes consumption to be a key feature of late modernity. This approach has its roots in responses to Marx's analysis of the relations of production and the importance of material culture identified by Mauss and the tradition of anthropology. In this chapter I want to critically overview the concept of consumption in sociology and anthropology to suggest that at its most economic it overlooks the importance of relations with material objects in sustaining the flow of social life by concentrating on the selling of goods and the moment of their exchange for money. At the same time, I want to draw from this literature some of the social relations with material things that are not reduced to economic relations, the practices of living with things that contribute to the character of social life.

CONSUMPTION AND STATUS

If Marx situates material objects within social and political life as commodities that are produced and exchanged within capitalist class relations, it is Veblen who situates those objects within a cultural life that distinguishes those classes. His theory of the conspicuous consumption of the leisure class (Veblen 1953 [1899]) offers a way of responding to the social significance of material objects. Veblen set in train a view of consumption as concerned with excess and waste that continues to have impact. However, there is an implied philosophical anthropology that underlies his politico-economic concepts of class, productive work, leisure, waste and use. Although these are intended as technical terms and Veblen is clear that he is not making moral judgements on individual choices, there is none the less a valuation that lies behind these binarily opposed concepts.

For example, his concept of 'leisure' is defined in terms of a class who display their status by non-useful activities – conspicuous leisure – by which it can be seen that they do not have to work productively. The leisure and consumption of the leisure class is conspicuously wasteful 'because this expenditure does not serve human life or human well-being on the whole' (Veblen 1953: 78). Use for Veblen is derived from the 'instinct for workmanship' which is deemed to be directed towards 'net gain in comfort or in the fullness of life' (Veblen 1953: 79). In contrast 'waste' is expenditure for the purposes of 'pecuniary comparison'. These concepts are all underpinned by values of a particular sort – equalitarian, communitarian, utilitarian – that inform an ethics of work and rigour while denigrating the significance of difference both in the flow of individual experience and between the experiences of different people. While these values are highly commendable they are based on concepts of 'need', 'use' and 'waste' that are oriented to the individual and not to the social.

C. Wright Mills (1953: xvi) points out that Veblen had no sense of the sociological function of a system of consumption in which actions such as taking collective decisions, marrying, making alliances and training the young bring about an effective social structure. It is difficult not to see Veblen as stuck within a rather narrow ethical view of individual human needs and how actions conserve and sustain human well-being. His argument draws our attention to the work that material culture does in indicating social distinctions but his identification of distinctions deriving from consumption is specific to his historical period and the values that he brought to his analysis (Miller 1987: 147).

The value of Veblen's work might be greater if his analysis provided a model of how objects were incorporated into and reflected social status, but sadly there is little detail. For example, his discussion of the hand-wrought silver spoons versus machine-made aluminium spoons attempts to undermine the higher economic value of the former but does not describe the spoons in any detail or how they are lived with (i.e. where they come from, on what occasions they are used, and with what other cutlery, crockery, tableware and so on). His complaint is that the silver spoons are 'felt to be serviceable somewhat in proportion as they are wasteful and ill adapted to their ostensible use' (Veblen 1953: 94). His argument is that the aluminium version is at least as effective as a spoon although it gives away its cheapness by its somewhat lighter weight. That the silver spoon is one hundred times more expensive is not warranted by its being more beautiful or tasteful because the aluminium version is such a good copy and of such similar material that it would be almost as pleasing to the eye. Here the very familiar argument of taste versus utility in relation to cost is set out with a quite clear orientation towards maximizing 'value for money' – the continuing plot of *Which?* consumer magazine and endless other claims to assess relative value. Implied is a 'rational economic individual' who would make rational consumption judgements if only they were not confused by the status implied by the price tag. The difficulty with such arguments is that human beings in cultural contexts cannot be represented by a reduction to 'rational economic man' – an argument that is dealt with by anthropologists who have tackled consumption and which I shall return to below. For Veblen, the cultural impact of the material object once it is purchased is presumed to be no more than a sign of its purchaser's capacity to purchase. He shows little interest in the formation of social relationships that include specific objects or the ways in which those material objects are themselves constitutive of culture.

Despite the limitations of Veblen's categories for sociological purposes, his concepts of 'leisure class' and 'conspicuous consumption' do have a resonance with contemporary culture. While not the distinct and elite class that he described, there is a 'leisure class' of people who can afford to spend money on leisure. It is also clear that much consumption is at least partly conspicuous, designed to show off the capacity to consume. However, although Veblen recognized that much consumption is for use as well as ostentation, his economic concepts are unable to grapple with the nature of use. So his account of 'leisure', for example, does not explore what leisure does for someone other than ascribe them status. Conspicuous consumption involves complex processes of comparison and distinction that need to be acquired and exercised, practices that have much greater social effect than simply displaying 'pecuniary advantage'.

A more recent attempt to articulate the relationship between social structure and cultural difference is the influential work of Pierre Bourdieu. In *Distinction* (Bourdieu 1984 [1979]) he explores how people's tastes in the French culture of the 1960s were related to their social standing. Drawing on a wealth of conceptual tools (habitus, field, practice, cultural capital, trajectory) he teases out the tension between 'taste' as an innate sensibility – the effect of taste on tastebuds – and 'taste' as a set of cultural preferences and aesthetic judgements. This tension gives rise to the production of the taste of various social classes through their consumption choices about cultural goods. For Bourdieu, cultural practices of consumption are a function of the class habitus of agents combined with their capital – both economic and cultural – engaging with a field of cultural production (music, art, political ideas and so on). The habitus is a network of social determinants that specify the particular orientation of an individual to the culture. Through cultural practices of consumption people differentiate themselves in a multiplicity of ways that complicate simple socio-economic class structure. Cultural orientation, which is the expression of taste, is embedded in the routine practices of social being, such as

> automatic gestures or the apparently insignificant techniques of the body – ways of walking or blowing one's nose, ways of eating or talking – and engage the most fundamental principles of construction and evaluation of the social world, those which most directly express the division of labour (between the classes, the age groups and the sexes) or the division of the work of domination, in divisions between bodies . . . the sexual division of labour and the division of sexual labour.
>
> (Bourdieu 1984: 466)

Bourdieu's fascinating theoretical evocation of the relationship between taste as consumption practice and habitus as social location is woven around an empirical account that includes quantitative studies as well as 'vignettes' of French life. But these succeed only in telling us the obvious; that taste and therefore consumption practices vary with occupational group, education, age and sex. Unlike Veblen, who suggested that there was a 'trickle down' effect of taste from those who had power and wealth to those who did not, Bourdieu describes a system of cultural distinction in which taste expresses the precise position of the individual in the networks of power relations. The consequence is that taste is not ultimately a matter of individual choice nor is it a pure and abstract aesthetic standard. By describing the interaction of economic and cultural capital (the learnt capacity to make distinctions) he describes a system of inclusion and exclusion that maintains social distinctions.

Bourdieu's is a dynamic theory in the sense that the form of taste is constantly changing in response to changes in the field of cultural production and changes in the particular trajectories of habitus. But it is a surprisingly static theory in relation to history. Large scale shifts in class structure will of course be reflected in patterns of consumption that achieve distinction but Bourdieu does not discuss either how the particular distribution of tastes and class positions emerges in modernity or the particular changes in train in French culture at the time of the study. This is particularly frustrating as there are a number of cultural fields which seem to be linked to dramatic changes in social and cultural form that Bourdieu does not engage with at all. Television as a developing cultural field is virtually ignored and the field of popular music is also overlooked. Recently his attention has turned towards television but as a field of cultural production rather than as a site of consumption (Bourdieu 1998a, 1998b). In fact, any attempt to scrutinize the cultural fields that Bourdieu does address in *Distinction* reveals a startlingly parochial perspective. 'Legitimate' music for example (i.e. that legitimized by academic recognition) is dealt with in terms of a very narrow range of composers and pieces. Taste is represented in the most crude form through knowing the composers of sixteen named works and giving a list of three favourites from among them. Cultural practice is indicated by having an opinion, listening to music on the radio or playing a musical instrument. The use of surveys inevitably both determines the field to which they refer and necessarily limits it to a cartoon-like representation. But Bourdieu's survey sits most uncomfortably with the paraphernalia of his theoretical account of the formation of habitus. The presentation of 'correspondences' between a multiplicity of variables mapping taste dispositions onto class fractions produces unsurprising results in which the amount of cultural capital and economic capital available to a particular occupational grouping is related to their taste. The limitations of his approach have been subjected to critical modifications especially by those who have concentrated on the play of other forces such as cultural intermediaries who influence the forms of taste from within urban cultures (Wynne and O'Connor 1998).

Bourdieu's focus of concern is *taste* and the social formations with which taste is associated, rather than the objects that might attract taste. The concept of consumption is used in his work to refer to cultural engagement which covers a wide range of activities and ways of doing things. He neither uses the term in its economic sense of 'using up' nor has he much to say about material culture as such. 'Goods' or commodities are not as important as experiences and services and where they are, Bourdieu's interest is in the social basis of choice between equivalent items rather than in the forms of use of things.

ANTHROPOLOGICAL CONSUMPTION

Anthropologists have shown an interest in the process of consumption and have linked it to symbolic meanings. Marshall Sahlins (1976) carefully draws the concept of consumption out of Marx's analysis of the mode of production (see Chapter 3) and then connects it to what he calls 'practical reason' which assigns symbolic value to things in the flow of social life. The value of objects does not lie in their material form but neither can it be judged in relation to abstract human needs. For Sahlins, material culture is based on exchange within a system of symbolic meaning whose distinctions have correlates in the social order of age, gender, time, work and leisure. Ultimately however, Sahlins follows Marx in putting production prior to consumption in understanding the meanings of culture which are a 'reflection, direct or indirect but always essential, of the relations of production' (Sahlins 1976: 216).

Mary Douglas and Baron Isherwood (1996 [1979]) also relate the social value of 'goods' to symbolic meanings but, unlike Sahlins, they do not see the key to the meaning structure of goods in the relations of production. They argue that consumption is more than an economic process and involves more than the purchase of goods in the market place:

> Consumption is the very arena in which culture is fought over and licked into shape . . . choices express and generate culture in its general sense . . . Ultimately they are moral judgements about what a man is, what a woman is, how a man ought to treat his aged parents, how he himself should grow old, gracefully and disgracefully and so on.
>
> (Douglas and Isherwood 1996: 37)

They set out some of the ways in which consumption choices are made which rely on social customs and practices rather than rational economic decisions. Goods are chosen in a variety of ways: as gifts; to express or confirm familial relationships; to follow social conventions; for ritual practices. Their argument is against the sovereignty of the individual economic agent acting in their own rationally calculated best interests. Instead, consumption choices about goods such as food, space, clothing, transport and sanitation are 'heavy with meaning' and choice 'continuously creates certain patterns of discrimination, overlaying or reinforcing others' (Douglas and Isherwood 1996: 44). Goods provide a fixed and visible meaning system by which culture is realized through a series of distinctions between time, place, activity, social location, inclusion and exclusion. However, once meaning has been added to the abstract concept of utility in goods, then Douglas and Isherwood's attention returns to the principally economic concern with the processes of *buying* goods – the impact of incomes on demand, the fluctuations in demand for new commodities, the periodicity in the replacement of goods and so on.

Rather than focus on meaning in the circulation of goods, Arjun Appadurai (1986) argues that exchanging value through the exchange of commodities is political. Buyer and seller, even though they may not share the same system of values, find a point of agreement where an exchange is made. Commodities can be exchanged across different cultural perspectives when the only common point between the culture of buyer and seller might be the terms of trade. This leads Appadurai (1986: 3) to suggest that commodities have social lives; things may actually be inert and lifeless but, to understand the way that they gain and lose value, we need to think of them as if they had a life. Objects do not have a commodity status built into them but they may become commodities, their commodity status may vary over time and they may cease to have a commodity status (see also Chapter 7; Thompson 1979; Kopytoff 1986). Types of objects have a cultural history and individual objects have their own biography so that their value lies in provenance (e.g. of a religious relic), the history of those who have possessed it (e.g. with the circulating shells of the Trobriand kula exchange) and ritual practices of exchange (Appadurai calls them 'tournaments of value': 1986: 21). Appadurai's approach to consumption goes a long way to disentangle value from the intrinsic object and the means of its production. It is the history and the politics of an object's association with humans that determine its commodity value at any point in time. The object in this perspective is a vehicle through which social value is expressed as a trace of the people, occasions and cultural contexts that inscribed value in the object.

Appadurai focuses attention on luxury goods 'whose principal use is *rhetorical* and *social*, goods that are simply *incarnated signs*' (Appadurai 1986: 38). As well as identifying the social status of their possessors that Veblen described, he suggests that they carry two types of knowledge. First, each commodity expresses the current state of technological, aesthetic and social knowledge of the culture that went into its production. Second, a different kind of knowledge is required to consume it appropriately, to know what the commodity is good for. These two systems of knowledge may not be equal or the same although they will interconnect through the process of exchange; both consumers and producers need to know something of the market and the ways that others enter it.

These anthropological accounts of consumption begin to address the symbolic value of goods but do not explore how material culture is formed through practices of living with things, except through the economic processes of production, exchange and circulation.

CONSTRUCTING NEEDS

Arising from the critical analyses of Marx and Veblen, the issue of consumption becomes linked to the idea of 'need'. Crudely, human beings only 'need' certain things to reproduce labour power, anything more is the product of surplus labour creamed off for the ostentatious display of a class whose needs are more than met. However, the discussion of human needs and how they relate to the consumption of commodities within a capitalist mode of production is notoriously complex. Any idea of 'basic needs' against which 'excessive needs' can be judged begs the question of culture (see the discussions by Leiss 1978: 59–83 and Slater 1997: 2–5, 133–6). The content of culture may not directly meet individual basic needs but none the less provides the social conditions necessary for those basic needs to be met. Needs which appear to be excessive, such as the conspicuous consumption of Veblen's leisure class, may sustain a set of distinctions and differentiations that enable society to operate. As William Leiss remarks, following Marx: 'the perception of the usefulness of things related to needs such as food and clothing is . . . conditioned by cultural and symbolic mediations' (Leiss 1978: 87). Slater comes to a very similar conclusion, suggesting that the 'important point is how modern societies go about defining people's needs and their relative importance' (Slater 1997: 136).

The cultural and symbolic mediations of society can of course construct needs, creating a demand for goods which fuels capitalism. Some commentators on consumption have focused on the mechanics of signs that compete for our attention as forms. Haug (1986) for example argues that late capitalism is characterized by a commodity aesthetics in which the appearance or form of commodities becomes detached from the objects themselves in processes such as advertising and sales talk. Innovations in form which can be described in aesthetic terms to promote the product, appear to arise from within the object, as if it is evolving independently of human manipulation. Similarly Ewen and Ewen (1992) provide an account of the development of a 'technology of discourse' in which the

> ability to accumulate, package, and disseminate knowledge represented the formation of new networks of understanding, prefiguring the slow abolition of autonomous and indigenous popular forms of 'culture'.
> (Ewen and Ewen 1992: 3)

In these accounts, the sensibility to form has been progressively appropriated by capitalism to extend and exploit our desire for goods. Material culture is not, apparently, about engagement with the objects themselves but about uncritically accepting ideas and values about them.

What is unclear from commentators like Haug and the Ewens is quite how the discourse of advertising relates to material culture. If we are sold the aesthetic in order to sell us the goods, does that leave us bereft of other critical resources with which to judge whether we want the goods? The description of modern culture offered by commentators such as Bourdieu, Baudrillard and Featherstone is more subtle, allowing for aestheticization to arise in cultural and social structural experience. They suggest that as culture is transmitted, taste can be passed on but that it is not a fixed orientation to things. There are of course certain circumstances where taste may be affected much more radically by political and economic circumstances than the availability of cultural and economic capital. Gronow describes the strange phenomenon of 'democratic luxury' in the former Soviet Union that consisted of such products as 'champagne, cognac, caviar sandwiches, assorted chocolates, two specific types of cakes, chocolate and fruit, and perfumes' (Gronow 1997: 49). State planning of production and distribution of these goods made them available to all; taste for such items was regarded as universal. But of course there was a new form of desired luxury in the foreign goods, such as nylon stockings and denim jeans, that could be bought only with foreign currency – economic capital – even though they were mass goods in their country of origin not associated with taste, distinction or luxury.

CONSUMER SOCIETY

A key source of the idea that consumption is more indicative than production of the form of modern societies is Jean Baudrillard's early work on *The Consumer Society* (1998 [1970]; see also some of the essays in Baudrillard 1981 [1972]). Following his description (Baudrillard 1996 [1968]) of contemporary culture as one in which the acquisition of material objects is oriented to a system of meanings (Perec 1992 [1965] provides a contemporary novelistic account of this world), Baudrillard describes late modernity as distinctive:

> Strictly speaking, the humans of the age of affluence are surrounded not so much by other human beings, as they were in all previous ages, but by **objects**.
>
> (Baudrillard 1998: 25)

The age of affluence is one in which the success of capitalism has resulted in a profusion of objects of great variety epitomized by American society with its packaging, drugstores and hypermarkets. Baudrillard recognizes that it is a historical process, related to but different from the one Marx described in *Capital*, which has brought consumption to the fore:

> The same process of rationalization of productive forces, which took place in the nineteenth century in the sector of *production* reaches its culmination in the twentieth century in that of *consumption*. The industrial system, having socialized the masses as labour power, had much further to go to complete its own project and socialize them (that is, control them) as consumption power.
>
> (Baudrillard 1998: 81–2)

His critique is not here directly of Marx but of the American commentators on capitalist development in the west, in particular Galbraith and Riesman, who had emphasized the importance of shaping the consumer and creating demand. But their economic individualism conceived of an average individual with a set of calculable and predictable needs and desires that had become perverted by the attentions of capitalism. Baudrillard ironically refers to this reified being as '*homo oeconomicus*' and argues that the needs, motivations and pleasure orientations of humans are not prior to but emergent in history. Baudrillard's sociologistic response borrows much from early structuralism to grasp consumption as 'an order of significations, *like language*, or like the kinship system in primitive society' (Baudrillard 1998: 79). This system is part and parcel of the system of production, inseparable from it ('consumption . . . is *a function of production*': Baudrillard 1998: 78). One of the powerful images Baudrillard gives us is of consumption as 'social labour', in which the individual is conscripted into the work of consumption by late capitalism just as much as into the work of production (Baudrillard 1998: 84). As capitalism develops mechanized production, an increasing number of people are cast out from productive work but are still recruited for the work of consumption through the circulation of signs about objects. But consumption work is isolated and alienating and there is an inherent contradiction between a collective political response to the consequences of overconsumption (e.g. of pollution by cars) and the individual responsibility to continue to consume.

Baudrillard offers a corrective to the individualistic appeals to 'the consumer' or 'the customer' that knows his or her own mind or, at the very least, what gives her or him pleasure. He describes the mythology of late modernity which focuses on the individual as a consumer who has a body to be beautified, made fit, slimmed, leisured, dressed, perfumed and sexualized to be ready for joining the consumer society. The mythology is articulated through the discourse of advertisements and newspaper features in which ideal, personalized social beings are described in the series of signs that create the culture of consumption. The mythology becomes entrenched through incorporating its own critique – the objections of politicians and intellectuals – in the discourse. Advertisements and newspaper features become ironic, self-parodying and knowing.

The consumer society is not primarily about material culture but about the dispersal of discourse at a certain stage of modernity. As Baudrillard says, 'What characterizes consumer society is the *universality of the news item* in mass communication' (1998: 33). He has very little to say in *The Consumer Society* about the way material objects are actually appropriated into people's lives. His argument develops some of the themes of Barthes's *Mythologies* (1973) to confront the economic sociology of Galbraith and Riesman and, in doing so, treats material culture as equivalent to a system of signs that are given value in the discourse of advertising. This is of course a rather reductive view of social life in which what people do or say is overlooked on the assumption that they concur with the way they and their culture is described by advertisers and journalists. For Baudrillard, consumption is a language, a system of signs that circulate, distinct from symbolic meanings and lived relations. Objects have double lives as functions and as signs:

> Thus the washing machine *serves* as equipment and *acts* as an element of prestige, comfort, etc. It is strictly this latter field which is the field of consumption. All kinds of objects may be substituted here for the washing machine as signifying element.
>
> (Baudrillard 1998: 77)

The limitation with Baudrillard's theory of consumption is the separation of the two aspects of material objects, function and sign value, and the reduction of the social relationship with the object to the exchange of signs that is involved in buying it as a commodity. As commentators like Genosko (1994) and Levin (1996) recognize, Baudrillard's work does not follow a single method or build into a comprehensive system. His analysis of the form of consumer society leaves open, for example, the function of objects that itself leads to a social relationship through which the object becomes incorporated into people's lives. As we shall see in later chapters, Baudrillard does more than swivel sociological attention from production, class, economy and power to consumption, signs, simulacra and ambivalence.

LIFESTYLE, IDENTITY AND AESTHETICS

Bourdieu is rather dismissive about considering consumption practices as 'lived experience' (1984: 100) but has much to say about the importance of lifestyles in which consumption practices are combined to sustain individuals within the habitus. He makes distinctions, for example, between bourgeois lifestyles (for example characterized by rich, heavy food and formality in eating practices) and working class lifestyles (characterized by plenty of plain food and free-and-easy meals) (Bourdieu 1984: 185–96). Bourdieu's interest is in the social trajectory of class fractions in terms of economic and cultural capital and how this is reflected in lifestyle (Robbins 1991: 126). Although the precise link between lifestyle and economic class is not clearly articulated since it is always modulated by cultural capital, Bourdieu's interest in lifestyle and consumption has become a theme in much modern writing on consumption.

One response by social psychologists such as Lunt and Livingstone (1992) and Dittmar (1992) is to connect consumption practices to the shaping of personal identity as realized through lifestyles. In this work, issues to do with the way the purchase and possession of various objects enhance individuals' perceptions of their social being, are intertwined with the functionality of such objects. The meaning of objects is not staticly determined by the form and function of the object but is woven into an individual's life course, varying in significance over time (Csikszentmihalyi and Rochberg-Halton 1981). These studies show that objects are marked for gender and age and as such are instrumental in achieving and sustaining relationships as well as personal identities through the place of objects in everyday activities. For example Lunt and

Livingstone (1992: 115) point out that goods are acquired according to people's personal and social requirements that are connected to their stage in the life course. They argue from survey data that 'hi-tech' goods like hi-fi and compact disc players are associated with young people while goods such as dishwashers, microwave ovens, cars and computers are associated with families. Of course such age differences could be cohort effects rather than life-course effects and are at least partly a function of income. The broad focus of Lunt and Livingstone's study is on consumption, rather than on objects or material culture as such; they discuss money, debt, saving, shopping and attitudes to luxury goods and necessities.

Bourdieu's concept of cultural capital indicates that there is an aesthetic dimension to consumption practices that gives them sufficient coherence to amount to a lifestyle rather than merely a sign of status or of personal identity. The aesthetics of lifestyles, of the everyday life of social groups, has become a recurring theme in understanding modernity since Simmel responded to Kant's discussion of aesthetics. Like Bourdieu some half a century later, Simmel noticed how the individual experience of taste paradoxically feels as if it was founded on something universal (Frisby 1992: 137). But within Kantian aesthetics, 'art' was abstracted from everyday life in a realm where forms could be explored in and for themselves without being confronted with the exigencies of reality. For Simmel this was realized as an aesthetic *distance* between the object and its appreciation – the distance that resulted in an impression or the retention of a mere fragment. Simmel argued that the mediating effect of money in the modern economy created a distance between object and consumer. This made possible an aesthetic of the material stuff that is consumed as part of life although Simmel draws a distinction between things that are merely useful and those that are beautiful and therefore 'have a unique individual existence' (Simmel in Frisby 1992: 146; see also Chapter 8).

From Simmel's concept of modern aesthetics Mike Featherstone (1991) explores the way that aesthetic sensibility shifts in late modernity from the world of art, separated from the 'reality' of everyday life, towards the routine, mundane stuff of life whose form begins to be treated as valuable in itself, beyond its usefulness. He points to the twentieth century art movements that have incorporated the stuff of commodity and consumer culture into art, to the treating of lifestyles as a form of art and to the massive increase in the flow of signs and images (Featherstone 1991: 66–7). The contents of everyday life take on an aesthetic significance:

> Simmel and Benjamin can be used to direct us towards the way in which the urban landscape has become aestheticized and enchanted through the architecture, billboards, shop displays, advertisements, packages, street signs etc., and through the embodied persons who move through these spaces: the individuals who wear, to varying degrees, fashionable clothing, hair-styles, make-up, or who move or hold their bodies, in particular stylized ways.
>
> (Featherstone 1991: 76)

The emergence of the modern sensibility to material culture is explored in Chapter 7 where the roots of aestheticization in Baudelaire, Benjamin and Simmel are discussed. But Featherstone fits the concepts of aestheticization and lifestyle around Bourdieu's theory of consumption as the basis of distinction. This draws him into describing the ways in which 'goods' are consumed to achieve lifestyles and to emphasize the social resistance to transforming goods that are high in cultural capital into economic capital – a resistance that is finally broken down by a new class of cultural intermediaries (Featherstone 1991: 87–92). As with Bourdieu, Featherstone's interest in consumption is as a series of practices – of learning, of gaining knowledge as well as goods – that ultimately inscribe themselves on the bodies of the new petite bourgeoisie. The way in which material culture contributes to these practices is ancillary to the practices themselves.

CONSUMPTION AS SUBLATION

Within the field of sociology, Colin Campbell's (1987) compelling account of consumerism as a cultural force that emerges at the level of ideas as much as economics has given way recently to more general accounts of consumption. Material culture in these accounts remains tied to consumption as an economic process of exchange that is surrounded by ideas, advertisements and meanings which are oriented to leading the imagination towards making a purchasing choice. Bocock

(1993) provides a broad introduction to the topic while Lury (1996) explores the place of consumption in defining various social locations and identities. Slater (1997) explores the relationship of social theory to the field of consumption and Corrigan (1997) articulates the field of consumption as including objects, advertising, magazines, food and drink, tourism and the settings for consumption as being the body, the home and the department store. These writers comment on material culture but they adopt a view of consumer culture as incorporating material culture; the way that people interact with objects is largely shaped by the discourse, the circulation of signs and values about consumption.

A similar position is reached by Daniel Miller (1987) although his interest in consumption develops from Hegel's concept of 'objectification', via Marx, Munn and Simmel, into a perspective that draws on a range of human sciences including anthropology, economics and cultural studies. His theory of consumption centres on the recovery of objects from the alienated process of production:

> The authenticity of artefacts as culture derives, not from their relationship to some historical style or manufacturing process – in other words, there is no truth or falsity immanent in them – but rather from their active participation in a process of social self creation in which they are directly constitutive of our understanding of ourselves and others. The key [criterion] for judging the utility of contemporary objects is the degree to which they may or may not be appropriated from the forces which created them, which are mainly, of necessity, alienating. This appropriation consists of the transmutation of goods, through consumption activities, into potentially inalienable culture.
>
> (Miller 1987: 215)

This is a sophisticated response to the emphasis that Marx places on the alienating effect of objectification through the labour of capitalist production. Miller begins to provide a way of responding to the 'quantitative advance in the material forms' (1987: 214) of modern societies by recovering the Hegelian concept of 'sublation' (reabsorption) (Miller 1987: 12, 28) as a strategy for self-creation in the face of alienation.

Whereas for Hegel sublation was a philosophical practice of consciousness, for Miller it is a praxis based in the practical activities that he associates with consumption. These practices of everyday consumption achieve this transformation of alienated commodities into inalienable culture by means that are not visible to a traditional academic approach to design or aesthetics. Two of these practices he discusses briefly as 'play' (1987: 93) and 'framing' (1987: 100).

While there is much that I wish to adopt from Miller's theory of consumption – and indeed 'play' is one of the ways of living with things that I specifically discuss in Chapter 6 – one of the aims of this book is to unhook the link between material culture and consumption. Strangely, Miller has moved away from looking at material culture as a set of practices of sublation towards treating consumption as the 'vanguard of history', claiming a role for consumption in shaping the global as well as the local social order. He argues that it is the discipline of economics that has traditionally emphasized the centrality of production and of capital as the basic dynamic forces in modern history and politics. His anthropological perspective replaces production with consumption by studying the role of the supermarket, retailing, the market and shopping in modern culture. Miller challenges 'myths' that equate consumption with homogenization, loss of sociality and authenticity arguing that it is an 'attempt by people to extract their own humanity through the use of consumption' (1995: 31) from the alienating institutions of modern society. In late modernity the political importance of the 'male' productive worker is replaced by the 'housewife' as consumption worker acting on behalf of the moral economy of the household. Miller sees purchase as a form of 'voting', not only for goods but also for the social systems that deliver those goods. Consumption involves choice and the operation of imagination. Consumers express their will through exercising choice, within the constraints of the options of goods and services available for sale. They also have to imagine the consequences of goods – in terms of use, functionality, style, identity, status and so on – before these are purchased. For Miller, consumers, acting as a series of individuals in a 'relatively autonomous and plural process of cultural self-construction', shape the social worlds in which they live because purchase is 'the point at which economic institutions have direct implications for humanity' (Miller 1995: 41).

This approach claims a particular status for the actions of people as consumers but does not necessarily allow for the more complex interactions between people and objects that constitute material culture without direct economic consequences. To treat the consumer as an agent of political power is to re-emphasize the sphere of economics, of exchange mediated by money, as well as to emphasize the coherence of self and the location of agency within the individual, acting on the basis of will.

In laying such emphasis on consumption as shopping Miller is restating the social significance of material culture as being primarily economic. By taking the housewife as the archetypal consumer, he is emphasizing the role of the individual in the attempt to wrest the experience of modernity from the alienation of social institutions – a new form of *homo oeconomicus*. But what he overlooks is the complexity of the relationship between individuals with the objects that they acquire which extends far beyond the operation of choice and imagination prior to purchase. He also has little to say about the emergence of such relationships from social contexts – the learning of what Bourdieu and Featherstone treat as taste and lifestyles. There seems to be a drift from philosophical subtlety of his earlier writing (Miller 1987) and from the powerful evocation of material culture in constructing social lives in earlier empirical work (Miller 1988; see Chapter 4). In his most recent work, it is unequivocally shopping as a routine cultural activity that is centre stage rather than consumption as a developing relation between human beings and material objects (Miller 1998).

Like Miller, Grant McCracken (1990) is an anthropologist who writes with an interdisciplinary audience in mind. He adopts a cultural studies orientation that leads to a view of consumption as a social process of distributing meaning – a much broader perspective than Miller's increasing focus on shopping. McCracken describes two stages in this process; advertising and fashion transfer meanings ('ideas and values': 1990: 76) from the world to goods, rituals transfer the meanings from goods to people. The rituals are those of exchange, possession, grooming and divestment (1990: 83–7). The work invested in these rituals is *producing* the thing in a living relationship with a person, after the choice and purchase of economic consumption that Miller focuses on. Divestment grooming for example is the work of cleaning and repairing and redecorating that is undertaken before the sale of an object such as a car, caravan or house or after its purchase from a previous owner.

The exchange of goods is central to economic process;

goods that are produced must be bought but it does not matter what happens to the goods after purchase; they may be misused, unused or abandoned. Much of the social scientific analysis of consumption draws attention to consumption as buying in which the desire for goods is stimulated or managed through discursive processes that attribute social values and meanings. This economic model of consumption emphasizes the individual as using information and their imagination to make choices, which may affect their sense of identity and the perception of their social location. It is the success of selling ideas about things that are for sale that has led to the debate about consumption – the development of the department store, the shopping arcade and the shopping experience (Shields 1992; Miller 1998) as well as the impact of advertising (Leiss 1978; Haug 1986; Jhally 1987; McCracken 1990; Ewen and Ewen 1992; Corrigan 1997). These processes are of sociological importance and they are part of the context in which material culture emerges. But to focus too closely on them is to be pulled towards the economic relationship with objects and assume that the seller's ideas about objects are what constitutes their meaning or how human beings interact with them.

SOCIAL LIFE BEYOND CONSUMPTION

Many of those who discuss consumption emphasize that it does not end with purchase: 'What happens to material objects once they have left the retail outlet and reached the hands of the final purchasers is part of the consumption process' (Douglas and Isherwood 1979: 36). In his early work, Miller also makes an argument for the understanding of consumption as

> the start of a long and complex process, by which the consumer works upon the object purchased and recontextualizes it, until it is often no longer recognizable as having any relation to the world of the abstract and becomes its very negation, something which could be neither bought nor given.
>
> (Miller 1987: 190)

Some work on consumption has moved attention away from the act of purchase or acquisition as consumption to consider its consequences and the social contexts in which they might be felt. Alan Warde (1994) criticizes theorists of late modernity/postmodernity (Beck, Giddens and Bauman) for treating the practices of consumption as the modal form of social action in the current epoch that affirm individual identity. He argues that the selection of an item for consumption can be careless and of no significance for identity. It might of course be chosen with care and consideration for its identity-forming consequences but then it will be chosen with reference to a social context of advice and help (peer example, consultation with family and friends, as well as advertisements and inducements to buy). Colin Campbell (1996) follows a similar line by pointing to the confusion between the meanings ascribed to objects and the meanings of actions of consuming those objects. He argues that clothing choices, for example, are more likely to be made to fit in with an existing lifestyle or sense of identity than to construct one. Silverstone *et al.* (1992) suggest that the consumption of information and communication technology into the home has to be understood in terms of the moral economy of the household. They theorize four processes (appropriation, objectification, incorporation and conversion) by which things such as video recorders and home computers are fitted into the value system of a household. Their argument moves the discussion of consumption on from considering commodities with sign (exchange) value and a functional (use) value to address the context of values and existing practices into which the object has to fit and the consequences that its acquisition and continuing use have for the maintenance or modification of that context.

These approaches attempt to explicate the non-economic features of consumption and avoid reductions to the point of sale and the identity of the individual consumer. They shift focus to the context in which an object is to be located and describe consumption in terms of the use of the thing in that context. Commodities do not have a predefined use-value, and even the sign value of an object is not determined by the discourse of advertising. Its use is variable and negotiable (for example in terms of ostentation, individual identity and leisure practices) and its precise form varies according to specific context. Michel de Certeau (1984: xii) has argued that consumption needs to be seen as a production in that as consumers appropriate goods, information or services there is a 'making' through their particular ways of using or making sense of them. He draws attention to the 'ways of using' objects, representations and rituals which adapt them from the intentions which might have been behind previous productions. He argues that everyday practices such as walking, cooking, dwelling and so on require an individual to construct a particular act from a set of possible actions, much as a speaker constructs an utterance from all the possibilities in a language. His perspective

> assumes that . . . users make (*bricolent*) innumerable and infinitesimal transformations of and within the dominant cultural economy in order to adapt it to their own interests and their own rules.
>
> (de Certeau 1984: xiii–xiv)

For de Certeau, far from being a given set of responses, consumption is an 'antidiscipline', a set of 'procedures and ruses' by which people appropriate culture, including material culture, to fit it into their own lives. While not a key feature of his analysis, Bourdieu (1984: 100) also writes of the 'labour of appropriation' and of the 'labour of identification and decoding' involved in consuming cultural products with an aesthetic dimension such as music, literature or a hairstyle. The work of learning what to consume by which 'the consumer helps to produce the product he consumes' is not for Bourdieu, however, a characteristic of consumption in general, or even especially of material objects.

LIVING WITH THINGS

Theories of consumption put the emphasis on the exchange of goods and the media representations of them rather than on their uses and the ways that material objects are lived with. Consumption is about both goods and services being offered for purchase and then being purchased. The commodity is clean, new, often packaged, ready for use but not in use. It is amenable to discursive construction through advertisements, news items or sales pitch. The process of consumption as buying in late modernity occurs in what Leiss (1978) calls a 'high-intensity market' in which '[c]ommodities are not straightforward "objects" but are rather progressively more unstable, temporary collections of objective and imputed characteristics – that is, highly complex material-symbolic entities' (Leiss 1978: 92).

But living with objects extends much further than this 'high-intensity market' and in many ways continues much as it has done in earlier social forms. Material objects are appropriated into social lives with a variety of non-economic effects; they are used and lived with. Just think of the vast number of items in most of our homes that have considerable use-value to us but have no exchange-value – toothbrushes, fitted carpets, old magazines, crockery, out of fashion clothes, furniture, linen. All of these things have been personalized through use rather than through the discourse of advertisement. The age of these things and the very fact of their having been used may make them unattractive to others but does not mean that for us they are no longer useful. Some of these things are on the way to becoming rubbish when the next clearout comes. Some may have a residual value in an exchange circuit that is not part of the high intensity market – the jumble sale or car boot sale. Other household items that slip from the useful to the useless status will be thrown away, perhaps to be recycled (newspapers, bottles, cans). Some things will be 'recovered' from their status as rubbish to regain value and re-enter the cycle of exchange (Thompson 1979; see Chapter 7).

I have argued that consumption is a restricted way of understanding how material culture shapes and reflects social forms and processes. It has raised a number of interesting themes for the analysis of objects in material culture:

- as signs of status and identity (Veblen, Bourdieu)
- as vehicles of meaning and equivalence within and between different cultures (Appadurai, Sahlins, Douglas and Isherwood, Baudrillard)
- as bearers of aesthetic value (Simmel, Baudrillard, Featherstone)
- as components of ritual (Douglas and Isherwood, McCracken)
- as indicators of lifestyle and identity (Featherstone, Dittmar, Lunt and Livingstone)
- as knowledge and ideas (Appadurai, Campbell)
- as potentially inalienable (Miller)
- objects as the focus of discourse, both institutional and local, about their value (Leiss, McCracken, Jhally, Ewen and Ewen)

In this book I shall argue for an eclectic approach that brings material objects into the foreground of modern social life. One key element of this that will recur in a number of chapters, is the idea that humans interact with objects, sometimes as if they are human, sometimes because through them we can interact with other humans and sometimes because they reflect back something of who we think we are. I shall argue that material culture involves taking on cultural practices in relation to material objects which define the uses and the values of those objects in everyday life. Their importance is not reducible to their political effects or to economic calculations but emerges through grasping the way that objects are fitted into ways of living.

3

FETISHISM AND THE SOCIAL VALUE OF OBJECTS

What else is intended by the concept 'commodity fetishism' if not the notion of false consciousness devoted to the worship of exchange value (or, more recently, the fetishism of gadgets or objects, in which individuals are supposed to worship artificial libidinal or prestige values incorporated in the object)?

(Baudrillard 1981: 89)

What else indeed! Baudrillard neatly draws our attention to the way that the concept of fetishism, the worship of objects, has developed in modernity. As we shall see in this chapter, he draws on both Marx's and Freud's use of the term to develop a concept of fetishism that critically draws attention to the way some objects in the culture of late modernity attract much more attention than either their exchange-value or use-value warrants. I shall explore the way the term 'fetishism' is introduced into cultural critique through the writings of Marx and Freud before moving on to discuss the social value of material objects in terms of how they fit into social lives. For Marx, Freud and Baudrillard, fetishism is a conceptual tool used to critique the overvaluation of goods as against their real value as inert, inanimate objects. I shall argue that the concept of fetishism cannot be based on any simple notion of what constitutes the 'real' but can be used to alert us to how the social value of things may be enhanced through cultural mediations that identify and ascribe properties to them.

For Marx the reality of the commodity is its representation of congealed labour through which it derives its value. In its unreal or fetishized form the commodity appears to have intrinsic value derived from its material character. The fetishized commodity represents a misconception of the origins of value at the base of the system of ideas supporting capitalist production that Marx calls 'commodity fetishism'. For Freud the reality of shoes or undergarments is as clothes, as items worn as part of normal apparel. But the unreal or fetish form of the shoe or undergarment is, for the fetishist, an agent of sexual arousal. The unreal object that arouses the fetishist indicates a perversion whose origins lie in a misconception of the lack in the female genitalia that leads to a substitute for the 'proper' sexual object.

In the work of Marx and Freud the term 'fetishism' is used to identify a misunderstanding of the world in which properties are attributed to objects that can correctly be attributed only to human beings. The use of the term allows them to connect these misunderstandings to a pre-humanistic scheme in which spirits, sometimes residing within material objects, were treated as a significant part of the ontological order of the world. Their use of the terms 'fetish' and 'fetishism' continue a tradition of cultural critique with its origins in commentary on religious practices surrounding objects. To identify a fetish is to expose the inadequate beliefs of those who revere it for what they believe it is capable of, by pointing to the real, material, qualities of the object and identifying its presumed capacities as really residing elsewhere – in the 'true' god; in human labour; in arousal by a person of the opposite sex.

Treating fetishes as 'unreal' overlooks the importance of the object as a mediator of social value. Marx did not explore why some commodities might be more fetishized than others. Freud conjectured on the symbolic origins of sexual fetishes but did not explore their meaning systematically as he did dream contents. What I want to develop in this chapter is a way to use the term fetish analytically, not to critique or debunk a set of ignorant beliefs or deviant perceptions, but to explore how material objects are valued in cultural contexts. It is Baudrillard who begins to treat fetishism as a sign of social value; the fetish object is taken to stand for the owner's social or sexual status. Here the fetish is no longer an unreal object, believed to have properties it does not really have, but is a means of mediating social value through material culture. I suggest that the term fetishism can be extended to look at the way the social value of some objects is 'overdetermined' as against the routine ways in which they are appropriated into culture.

MAKING THE FETISH

Although related to the Latin word *factitius* (made by art), the contemporary English word *fetish* seems to derive from the Portuguese word *feitiço* (a charm, sorcery) a name for talismans in the Middle Ages that were often illegal or heretical (Pietz 1985: 6). The Portuguese word was used to refer to witchcraft and was part of the language of sailors in the fifteenth century travelling from Portugal to the Guinea coast of West Africa (Pietz 1987: 24). The modern meaning of fetish and fetishism is generally agreed to have originated in the work of Charles de Brosses writing in 1760 who used the term to describe the religious practices of worshipping objects (Simpson 1982: 127; Pietz 1993: 134). De Brosses coined the term to refer to the worship of inanimate objects as gods, a practice that had been recorded by travellers to West Africa. It is clear that Marx read de Brosses and it is from his proto-anthropological analysis that Marx derives his 1842 definition of the term as the 'religion of the senses':

> This notion of the fetish worshipper's desire-driven delusion regarding natural objects, his blindness to the unprovidential randomness of physical events was an element in de Brosses's original theorisation of *fétichisme* as the pure condition of un-enlightenment.
> (Pietz 1993: 136)

The connections between the origins of the word 'fetishism', its 'anthropological' meaning and Marx's usage are clear and documented. The connection with its use in psychoanalysis to refer to sexual fixation on an object is not so clear. According to Robert Nye (1993), in a paper of 1882 Charcot and Magnan referred to what we have come to know as classical sexual fetishism (erotic obsessions for aprons, shoes, shoe nails) but did not use this term. In 1887 Alfred Binet, Charcot's student, used the term in a paper discussing these perversions in the context of religious fetishism (Nye 1993: 21; Gamman and Makinen 1994: 17). In 1886 Krafft-Ebing had treated 'fetichism' as a pathological tendency, connected to stealing female linen, handkerchiefs and shoes. While he emphasized the criminological aspect he also connected it to sexuality (Gamman and Makinen 1994: 39). Quite how sexual fetishism is linked with the religious fetishism described by de Brosses remains unclear. However, the term fetishism seems to have taken on its broad cultural meanings by the middle of the nineteenth century so that the *Shorter Oxford English Dictionary* can offer as a figurative definition dating from 1837 'something irrationally reverenced'.

There are then three fields in which the term fetishism is used that we may treat as proto-anthropology, the analysis of the commodity form and the analysis of sexual perversion. The term seems to originate in the first of these fields and is then employed analogously in the latter two. Gamman and Makinen sum up its use in all three fields:

> Fetishism, we would argue, is by definition a displacement of meaning through synecdoche, the displacement of the object of the desire onto something else through processes of disavowal.
>
> (Gamman and Makinen 1994: 45)

It is through the displacement of desire that an object acquires special social value, indicated by the reverence, worship or fascination with which it is treated. That desire may be for religious, economic or erotic value (the three fields in which fetishism has been described) which then accrues in the object. What the Gamman and Makinen definition does is to suspend the realist account of fetishism by treating it as a displacement of meaning rather than a mistake or misunderstanding about the real nature of objects.

A fetish is created through the veneration or worship of an object that is attributed some power or capacity, independently of its manifestation of that capacity. However, through the very process of attribution the object may indeed manifest those powers; the specialness with which the object is treated makes it special. The fetish object will, for example, influence the lives of its human worshippers, determining some of their actions and modifying their beliefs. In this process the object is mediating the powers delegated to it by worshippers. As with all mediation, the fetish is not merely reflecting back the ideas and beliefs of its worshippers, it is transforming them or, in the language of actor-network theory, 'translating' them (Callon 1991). The power of the fetish is not reducible to its material form any more than the meaning of a word can be reduced to its material representation (its sound or graphic shape). The symbolic power of the fetish can be repeated or replicated provided that there is some basis for continuity that is recognizable to the worshipper. The graven image can be copied, the form of the animal is repeated in each example of the species, shoes can be endlessly exchanged as commodities and join countless others in a collection.

The meaning of the specific object is apparent only in a series of objects. The thing to be venerated is distinguished from those to be treated as rubbish or as mere utensils. Such distinctions are embedded within cultural codes that are emergent in sets of practices within the culture. This is precisely why the fetish object cannot be decoded by a realist perspective in any transcultural way; what is 'real' in one cultural code is 'unreal' in another. To use the term 'fetish' in a realist mode is to engage in cultural critique; it is to identify someone else's reality as an illusion, an unreality. I wish to argue that both Marx and Freud use the term fetishism in this realist mode to engage in forms of cultural critique. But there are chinks in the theoretical positions of both which permit a more reflexive position on fetishism to be drawn out.

COMMODITY FETISHISM

In the *Economic and Philosophical Manuscripts* Marx uses the term 'fetish-worshippers' to describe the supporters of the monetary and mercantile system and how they looked upon private property. Following Engels, he compares the fetishism of the mercantilists to that revealed by Luther's critique of the paganism and external religiosity of Catholicism. The objects of private property stand in for real human relations and so appear to have a power that is their own whereas the political economists' critique shows that human labour is the essence of private property. Of course Marx goes on to criticize the political economists for not identifying the contradictory essence of private property as the product of *alienated* labour.

Whereas in proto-anthropology the term 'fetish' referred to the cultural meanings and uses of certain objects, in Marx's account the term is used to criticize more general beliefs about capitalist culture. Nothing more specific than 'private property' in general is identified as the fetish object (although later in the *Manuscripts* Marx does specify metal money as a fetish, referring to the dazzle of its 'sensuous glitter': Marx 1975: 364).

In the later, more famous, account of fetishism in *Capital*, Marx follows a very similar line but here the analysis is of the commodity form rather than private property. The 'real' value of a commodity is analysed as a social relation determined by the amount of labour that has gone into its production; it is nothing to do with the material form of the commodity (Marx 1976: 165). The exchange-value of commodities appears to be something intrinsic to them as objects and their relationship as things. But this form of their value is illusory since the fetishized exchange establishes a fantastic relationship between things that obscure the real relationship between people – workers whose labour produces things of value to others. The cultural forms which incorporate such 'fantasies', mistaking them for reality, are critiqued by Marx in his analysis of commodity fetishism in *Capital*.

Marx distinguishes the use-value of objects (the use they have to the human labourer) from their exchange-value (the fetishized, fantastic form of value they have as commodities). Use-values are to do with the quality of objects and are realized only in use or consumption whereas exchange-values are quantifiable in terms of other commodities (Marx 1976: 126–8). As Baudrillard points out (1981: 130–4), Marx restricts his analysis of commodity fetishism to exchange-value while use-value remains 'an abstraction', a residual category, prior to and outside the economic relations of socially assigned value, of equivalence and of quantity.

The difficulty with Marx's analysis is that it obscures the processes of consumption and the links between use-value and exchange-value. Exchange involves consumption and judgements about the relative quality of similar goods (e.g. their fitness for purpose, their substitutability) which in turn lead to conferring social value on goods which affects the determination of economic value. These judgements are derived from the exchange of signs concerning the relative merits and capacities of goods to meet needs. They are realized as the desire for a particular object which is then expressed in the willingness, given sufficient capacity, to exchange for it. That objects might have some complex form of social value (beauty, functionality, longevity) is overlooked by Marx in order to emphasize the basis of economic value in human labour.

It seems as if Marx, especially in the first chapters of *Capital*, takes needs as biologically given and the natural, qualitative use-value of goods as the same in all societies (Sahlins 1976: 148–61).[1] But Sahlins points out that in the *Grundrisse* Marx showed how consumption was part of the process by which the use-value of objects emerges:

> the object is not an object in general, but a specific object which must be consumed in a specific manner, to be mediated in its turn by production itself. Hunger is hunger, but the hunger gratified by cooked meat eaten with a knife and fork is a different hunger from that which bolts down raw meat with the aid of hand, nail and tooth. Production thus produces not only the object but also the manner of consumption, not only objectively but also subjectively.
>
> (Marx 1973: 92)

Marx is still describing a real basis for the use-value of objects that is a natural given – here the biological need of 'hunger'. But reality is not presented as a fixed, stable state against which fetishized forms can be distinguished. The nature of the object changes and so must its use-value in a dialectical process of production and consumption. Sahlins (1976: 151) suggests that the absence of a theory of meaning is the reason for Marx's failure to deal adequately with the social relations of material objects; it is through their socially construed meaning that they come to have specific use-values that vary with different modes of consumption.

SEXUAL FETISHISM

Freud follows previous usage by Binet (in a paper from 1888) of the term fetishism in discussions of sexual perversion. Fetishistic perversions were regarded as 'the degrading consequences of a weakening of morals in a profoundly vitiated society' (Charcot and Magnan, quoted in Nye 1993:

21) but it was Binet who identified the 'psychic impotence' characteristic of the sexual obsession with a part of the body or inanimate objects that went with a decadent and enfeebled culture. The critique of sexual deviations and perversions by the French writers on deviation was, Robert Nye suggests, tied to a particularly French anxiety about the health and size of the population at the end of the nineteenth century.

Freud treats fetishism as a deviation from the 'normal' sexual aim of copulation leading to the release of sexual tension 'a satisfaction analogous to the sating of hunger' (Freud 1977a: 61). It involves a sexual overvaluation of a substitute object, that while related to the sex object is none the less unsuited to the normal sexual aim. By 'overvaluation' Freud is referring to the tendency for the sexual aim to extend beyond the genitals to the whole body and indeed mind of the desired person; he suggests that it is rare for this deviation *not* to occur (Freud 1977a: 62–3). Fetish objects include parts of the body (the foot, hair) and objects which are connected to the person for whom they substitute (clothing or underclothes). Freud is quite clear that fetishism, along with other deviations in sexual aim, is not in itself indicative of neuroses or mental illness. It is only when it goes to extremes in overcoming the resistance of shame, disgust, horror or pain (he gives the examples of licking excrement or of intercourse with dead bodies) that these sorts of deviations become pathological. What he suggests is that it is normal to make additions or extensions to the normal sexual aim, substituting objects for the 'real' thing (the union of genitals):

> A certain degree of fetishism is thus habitually present in normal love, especially in those stages of it in which the normal sexual aim seems unattainable or its fulfilment prevented.
>
> (Freud 1977a: 66)

There is a problem with fetishism only when the object substitutes completely for the real thing and when the diversity of sexual objects channelling the sex drive towards the real thing is replaced by a single sex object which is 'overvalued'.

The sexual fetish is then a symbolic substitute that has an analogous or metonymical association with the normal sex object (e.g. fur as a fetish is a symbolic substitute for a woman's pubic hair: Freud 1977a: 68). In his paper of 1927 on *Fetishism* Freud suggests that the fetish is a substitute for the penis that the fearful little boy discovers lacking in his mother. The boy child who discovers his mother's lack, and who is later to be a fetishist, fears that if she has been castrated then he might be too. He 'disavows' the discovery which does not amount to a denial because while he retains his belief that women have a penis, he has also given it up (Freud 1977b: 353). This contradiction is resolved by the belief that the woman does have a penis but it is no longer the same; something has been appointed as its substitute – the fetish. Freud says that it is not possible to unravel the associative origins of a particular fetish with any certainty though they are likely to lie in the frozen memory of the moment of discovering the lack. The last thing seen before the realization that the mother is not phallic becomes a symbolic substitute for the phallus that is not there (shoes, fur, velvet, underclothing) (Freud 1977b: 354–5).

It seems as if the fetish is available as a sex object only for men but Jann Matlock (1993) points to the connection between cross-dressing by women and clothing fetishes. Elizabeth Grosz (1993) follows the line, suggested by Freud, that in pampering herself, what the narcissistic woman does is to treat her whole body it as if it were a phallus thereby fetishizing it (a similar point is made by Baudrillard 1993a: 107–10). However, the lesbian lover, suggests Grosz, like the fetishist, disavows women's castration but this is her own castration, not that of her mother. And also like the fetishist, the lesbian takes as a substitute for the phallus, an object outside her own body; the body of her lover. Gamman and Makinen (1994) argue that the traditional psychoanalytic account of fetishism androcentrically focuses the articulation of desire on the penis and its lack. Using an account of sexual fetishism modified through Kleinian theory, they propose a less gendered and genitaled account of fetishism that incorporates oral and other gratifications while retaining the disavowal of the fetishist. This enables them to extend the use of the term fetishism to include pathological and non-pathological relations with clothes and food that express an ambivalence about identity but provide a source of real gratification (Gamman and Makinen 1994: 111). Their gendered but balanced account of different mechanisms of adult perversity explains how sexual fetishism occurs predominantly – but not exclusively – in men, eating obsessions and the obsessive consumption of style are predominantly but not exclusively female fetishes.

Deprived of its phallocentrism the psychoanalytic account of fetishism focuses on the dynamics of human *desire* for objects to substitute or 'stand in' for something human. Freud, and Binet before him, both recognized that desire for objects is a normal part of human existence. Fetishism might be born of a frustration or confusion of normal desire, a sublimation or redirection of sexual needs, but this is almost characteristic of the human condition. It is neither pathological nor in itself destructive of human social being.[2]

SEMIOTIC FETISHISM

It is in the development of his writing about consumption, the system of objects and the form of modern culture, that Baudrillard brings together a critique of Marx's analysis of commodity fetishism and a semiotic analysis of commodities that incorporates Freud's concept of fetishism. He criticizes Marx's analysis of commodity fetishism, arguing that use-value is a fetishized social relation just as much as exchange-value (Baudrillard 1981: 131). The object that is to become a commodity, available for exchange, must be valued according to a code of functionality which orders both human subjects and material objects (1981: 130–4). Use-value is not an inherent property of the object nor functionality reflective of innate human needs or desires. For Baudrillard the 'object', the thing that has a use, is 'nothing but the different types of relations and significations that converge, contradict themselves and twist around it' (1981: 63). The object of consumption does not exist in relation to pure, natural, asocial, human needs but is produced as a sign in a system of relations of difference with other objects. The process of consumption Baudrillard understands not as the reali zation of objective needs or of economic exchange but as the social exchange of signs and values (1981: 75).

Baudrillard describes objects as signs in a code of significatory value that can be manipulated between the two registers of functionality and ostentation (Veblen's conspicuous consumption). Both registers can be part of the same object so the useless gadget combines 'pure gratuitousness under a cover of functionality, pure waste under a cover of practicality' (Baudrillard 1981: 32). Now, it is the extent to which an object demonstrates ostentation, a sign of value that accrues to the possessor of the object, that turns the object into a fetish.

The television set that is broken but retains its prestige value in a culture in which hardly anybody can afford a television is an example of the 'pure fetish' (1981: 55). But in western culture it is the ritual that surrounds the object, the routines and practices of watching the television, that give it its fetish character (1981: 56). The television functions as a machine that mediates communications but it is also an object that is consumed in itself, signifying membership of the community as a 'token of recognition, of integration, of social legitimacy' (1981: 54). The 'worship' of the television set is through 'systematic, non-selective viewing' and the 'apparent passivity of long hours of viewing' that actually hides a 'laborious patience' (1981: 55). The television takes up a place in our homes, requires a reorganization of other objects that inhabit them and demands a certain level of commitment in return for the minimal level of social status it confers. Objects like the television have a sign value that is in excess of their functional capacities. Each object 'finds meaning with other objects, in difference, according to a hierarchical code of significations' (Baudrillard 1981: 64).

It is the system of objects as sign values and their exchange that Baudrillard terms 'consummativity' (1981: 83), a dynamic of capitalist society that he juxtaposes to productivity. Consummativity is the system of needs for objects imposed on individual consumers; it includes their need for choice. Needs cannot be derived from a humanistic notion of the free, unalienated, asocial individual driven by craving or pleasure or even by some essential needs. Consumer needs are mobilized within individuals by the 'strategy of desire' (1981: 85), an ideological effect of the social system achieved through the generalized exchange of signs. It is through the circulation of objects as signs that the quality or use-value of objects is distinguished.

Baudrillard takes Marx to task for using the metaphor of fetishism to avoid an analysis of the ideological labour involved in consumption.[3] Taking up the psychoanalytic use of fetishism as a refusal of sex differences 'a perverse *structure* that perhaps underlies all desire' (1981: 90), Baudrillard points out that the fetish object involves a fetishism of the signifier, a passion for the code. The fetishism of commodities as objects is the fascination and worship of the system of differences, the code of signs that the object or good represents. The system of objects as signs is continually shifting emphasis from one term to another so that, unlike the perverse desire of the sexual fetishist, the perverse desire of the commodity fetishist is constantly being redirected. In describing how the beauty of the body is fetishized, Baudrillard points out that a model of beauty is constructed so that 'It is the sign in this beauty, the mark (makeup, symmetry, or calculated asymmetry, etc.) which fascinates; *it is the artifact that is the object of desire*' (Baudrillard 1981: 94).

The make-up of 'beauty', of the erotic body, is a process of 'marking it' though ornamentation, jewellery, perfume and through using clothing to 'cut it up' into partial objects (feet, hair, breasts, buttocks etc.). This material overlay produces the body as a series of signs, creating it as a subject/object with a significatory value to do with sexual desire.

For Baudrillard the shift from the exchange of symbolic value to the exchange of sign value is characteristic of modernity and 'properly constitutes the ideological process' (1981: 98). The symbolic object had a direct if ambivalent relationship with the person; in the Aztec and Egyptian cultures the sun provided life-giving heat and light but was worshipped because it could also take life away. In modern cultures the object as a sign is exchangeable in a series with other signs (the vacation sun, the sun-lamp, the gym) in an ideological system (the healthy body) through which they can be fetishized. Within this exchange of sign values, fetishism is the 'fascination' felt both by individuals and by the culture as a whole with those signs that have been positively valorized, often associated with sexual desire.

Baudrillard describes how in modern culture, adding material things to the body achieves a merging of subject and object via fetishism because there is a 'symbolic articulation of lack' (1993a: 101). He lists a series of objects that inscribe the surface form of the body including: 'the stripper's G-string, bracelets, necklaces, rings, belts, jewels and chains' (1993a: 101). These objects are theorized, following Lacan, as 'bars' that both divide up the surface of the body and semiologically separate the signifier from the signified. The bar 'erects' the body or body part into a sign of that which is lacking – the phallus. Even material that overlays the surface of the body, lipstick for example,[4] has the effect of inserting the body into the exchange of signs of a phallic (sexual) order.

The significatory adornment of the modern body fetishizes it, creating a seductive sexuality that is no more than a sign or simulacrum transforming the subject body into a fetishized object. This modern form of fetishism articulates the subject in and through the inscription of objects on its bodily surface and then inserts the consequent subject/object into the circulation of signs. Baudrillard distinguishes it from a pre-modern culture of symbolic exchange, of lived and felt relationships with objects, based on ritual, worship and subjugation to the power of objects. It is Baudrillard's obsession with signs and 'the reduction of political economy, sexuality and eventually all material and social reality to sign play' that leads Kellner to brand him a 'sign fetishist' (Kellner 1989: 100, 199).

The account of the body as a fetishized commodity shows how monopoly capitalism not only exploits the productivity of the body as labour power, alienating it through the commodification of labour, but also exploits the 'consummativity' of the body, reifying it through marking its sexuality. However, Baudrillard does not comment on the (at least partially) gendered distinction between the fetishized body as labour power and the fetishized body of made-up beauty. As he turns away from Marx's politico-economic analysis, Baudrillard responds to the anthropological writings of Mauss and Bataille that describe a pre-modern symbolic form of exchange between subject and object. What he seems to disapprove of is the temporary overwriting of the real body and its sexuality by endlessly exchangeable material signs in modernity and his critique harks back to the irreversibility of a material culture based on symbolic exchange.

There are four problems with Baudrillard's analysis of social relations with objects and with fetishes in particular. First, objects seem to have only two social dimensions – function and ostentation. As I shall suggest below there are a number of forms of social relations with objects that could lead to fetishization. Second, Baudrillard treats the consumption of objects simply in terms of the exchange of signs without exploring the relation between sign value and practical use-value. Third, it is not clear in his analysis to what extent all commodities are fetishes and, if they are, whether they have the same fetish quality. After 1972 the only fetish he discusses in any detail is the fetishized female body. Fourth, and this is also characteristic of his work after 1972, the source of sign value is progressively disconnected from social practices until it becomes 'hyperdetermined' (Baudrillard 1990b: 12). At this point he is no longer interested in the fetishization of material objects or in the mundane practices of everyday life.

FETISHISM AND LIVING WITH OBJECTS

As they identify fetish objects, Marx and Freud engage in a modernist form of auto-cultural critique that supersedes the critique of alien cultures and religions. They discover the displacement of real human relations by unreal objects in the secular culture of the nineteenth century by alienation and fetishism. Their critique aims for the liberation of human nature from the bonds of a culture in which some are free but others are either oppressed or repressed, by showing what human life would be like without the inversions of fetishism. For Marx there is a biological 'need' for material objects that underlies the processes of production, consumption and exchange. For Freud the underlying normal sexual aim is a different form of hunger, the biological, sexual 'need' that is manifest as desire which may be redirected towards objects in sexual fetishism. A sublimated erotic desire for objects is then a means by which they attain special social value.

Everyday life in capitalism involves a set of relationships with objects that enable us to do what we do. This is the largely unexplicated use-value of objects, their capacity to fulfil our needs. Commentators on commodity fetishism (Geras 1976; Godelier 1977; Wells 1981; Jhally 1987) recognize that the objects of commodity fetishism have relations with human beings but they do not analyse what they are. In the *Grundrisse* Marx recognized that need and consumption were social products and this is developed by Baudrillard, who incorporates Freud's notion of desire into the relations between individuals and objects. 'Need' is a product of the circulation of signs and objects at the ideological rather than the economic level. This provides a way of understanding how the fetish works as an object in everyday life without leading to neuroses but it does not explore the social practices in which objects are consumed and fetishized.[5]

It is somewhere between the subject and object that the fetish emerges:

> the interesting thing about a fetish . . . is that it is never clear . . . whether it is really an object or whether it is part of the self. A fetish . . . can be thought of as existing in a free space between the subject and the object.
>
> (Levin 1984: 42)

The fetish is an object, a thing that is transformed through the social relations into which it is appropriated – religious, economic or sexual. But what is the nature of the object, the thing, that is so transformed?

Martin Heidegger asks the question *What is a Thing?* (1967) to explore some aspects of the relation between being and other components of the phenomenal world. His aim is not to generate a definition for all purposes but to discover the consequences of answering the question, not only for things but also for those asking such a question. He distinguishes three meanings of 'thing': a material entity, something that is named (such as an event or occurrence), something abstract (such as God). It is the first of these that he follows up in his discussion and he describes it as

> A thing in the sense of being present-at-hand: a rock, a piece of wood, a pair of pliers, a watch, an apple, and a piece of bread. All inanimate and animate things such as a rose, shrub, beech tree, spruce, lizard and wasp.
> (Heidegger 1967: 6)

These are indeed the sorts of 'things' that this book is concerned with (except perhaps living things like lizards and wasps) and the sorts of things which may become fetishized. It is in the description of things as 'being present-at-hand', that his phenomenological account hangs. Such things are what '[w]e take in view, what is most immediate, most capable of being grasped by the hand' (Heidegger 1967: 7). They are objects that are present to the experience of humans as subjects and as such they are singular and distinct, framed but not constituted by their existence in 'timespace' (1967: 31). The thingness of a thing is tied to its being 'this' thing ('The "this" means a thing insofar as it faces us, i.e. it is objective': 1967: 26), that is in relation to a being who recognizes them. This is neither a solipsistic position with no reference to experience in general nor a scientific orientation which might treat the thing as an exemplar of a type. It is a position which is historical in that it changes with time and place but is none the less based on a 'thing' as a bearer of properties:

> It is a nucleus around which many changing properties are grouped, or a bearer upon which the qualities rest; something that possesses something else in itself.
> (Heidegger 1967: 33)

Heidegger is identifying as historically contingent – and we may add, culturally contingent – the properties by which things are identified as things. These properties are not simply material, although they may 'rest' upon the material thing that is present-to-hand in timespace.

Before exploring how things may acquire fetish properties, it is worth going beyond Heidegger to explore some of the routine ways in which humans interact with material objects and respond to their non-fetish properties:

- First, a physical relation that is to do with shape, colour, texture, strength, flexibility and possible movements (think of getting on a bus). It is this that distinguishes material objects from other cultural objects (such as kinship systems, myths). The physical properties of material objects lead to a set of limitations on their capacities (the top speed of the bus, the number of people who can get on) thereby articulating the uses by subjects.
- Second, objects are used within cultural practices that also specify and constrain their use (bus timetables, regulations on numbers of passengers).
- Third, objects are signs in themselves that locate the object within cultural parameters including time and space (as a London bus from the 1960s or 1970s).
- Fourth, the object may provide a surface for linguistic or quasi-linguistic texts to play across (the advertisement on the side of the bus).

It is through these different modes of interaction that subjects explore the properties of material objects. Obviously some objects are experienced more through one mode than another and the orientation of the subject will affect the mode (buses are largely experienced by passengers in a physical mode; car drivers experience them more as signs or surfaces for messages). Interactions with objects work in a number of ways for human beings, some of which were identified at the end of the discussion in Chapter 2 on consumption. These can be set out below as a guide for the sorts of human–object relations we might encounter elsewhere in this book. These properties of objects are of course theoretical constructs that appear to be intrinsic qualities but more correctly 'rest' on things, giving them a role in material culture.

1 **Function** The object extends or enhances the human physical action of its user, e.g. as a tool the car actually transports its user.
2 **Signification** The object signifies the social group membership of its

user, e.g. the distinction of a tiara, the clan identification of a football scarf.

3 **Sexuality** The object arouses its user or others or both, as a sign from a code indicating sexual action, identity and interest, through bodily display, sensuality or substitution, e.g. the wearing of tights or tight-fitting jeans.
4 **Knowledge** The object delivers knowledge to its user by storing simple information or a synthetic understanding of some aspect of the world, e.g. book or any other complex textual object.
5 **Aesthetics** The beauty or form of the object directly moves the emotions of users by representing pure values, e.g. the art work.
6 **Mediation** The object enables or enhances communications between humans, e.g. a telephone, the decorative item that is a talking point, the heirloom that links generations.

Many objects will deliver more than one of these six properties in different degrees – no doubt the list would be refined and extended through empirical study.

Now, the fetish quality of a thing is the reverence or the fascination for it that arises out of its properties but is expressed over and beyond its simple appropriation. This fetish quality is attested through ritualistic practices that celebrate or revere the object, a class of objects, items from a 'known' producer or even the brand name of a range of products. These ritualistic practices will involve expressing desire for the object and fantasizing about its capabilities prior to its acquisition. The object itself becomes a sign for these fantasized and desired properties so that its use or enjoyment can restimulate the play of fantasy and desire. Unlike sexual fetishism where the fantasy is usually personal, the fetishism of appropriation involves the social negotiation and sharing of the value of the object so the ritualistic practices that fetishize objects will involve discursive action related to the object and its properties. Expressing desire for and approval of the object and what it can do, celebrating the object, revering it, setting it apart, displaying it, extolling and exalting its properties, eulogizing it, enthusiastic use of it, are the sorts of practices that fetishize objects. The cumulative effect of these practices amount to an *overdetermination* of the social value of the object in that it is not merely used but in addition, the object or class of objects can be enjoyed at the level of imagination through fantasy and desire.[6]

One way that social value is overdetermined is through the demonstration of excess capability in the object which cannot be used other than as a sign of value. An example would be the car that has an excess of power; the power cannot actually be used on the road but driving the car allows it to act as a sign of that power. The excess in capability of the object is one way of marking the reverence with which it is treated; a photograph of a leader, whether massively blown up or merely given pride of place on the wall, is made into a fetish by the reverence for its value that exceeds its mediative capacity. Excess of capability suggests a latent property of the object to be able to deliver human qualities (love, power, authority, sexuality, security, status, intellect, exoticism). The overdetermination of sign value focuses on these 'human' qualities so that the object can substitute for them in human lives. Provided that others (a group large and coherent enough to secure the meaning of the object as a sign) recognize the extended capabilities of the fetish object, they will also recognize the accrual of these properties as human qualities by those associated with it. So, the powerful car makes its driver powerful, the revered photograph confers authority on the national leader. It is not then a simple property of the object that indicates its fetish character but the significance of its perceived or attributed capabilities. Identifying the fetish is not a matter of judging true or real properties in the object but recognizing the multiple sources of positive valuation that overdetermine its social value. It is the cumulative effect of these multiple sources that attribute excess capability and interpret its significance.

Advertising, critical commentary, discussions of product development, reports of consumer testing, as well as evaluations of objects in interpersonal exchanges not only create a market for commodities but also shape ways of recognizing, responding to and using things. The public use of an object displays its capabilities to others who might then desire to use the same or similar objects. It is through these practices that objects become fascinating, acquire a 'special status', and become revered or worshipped for how they might enhance human capabilities. The process of fetishization is much the same for a work of art as it is for a style of trainer or a motor car. In this largely discursive context objects are not merely sanctified by the claims of producers, commentators and critics, they are subject to a negotiation of their capabilities, of their usefulness to users. It is from the discursive context that desire for objects emerges; to know what one wants, one first has to know what it is and what it can do.

CONCLUSIONS

Baudrillard supplements Marx's commodity fetishism by beginning to analyse the fetishism of use-value and the social impact of consummativity. He incorporates Freud's displacement of erotic value on to objects to understand the desire for objects, expressed in the circulation of signs that makes up the field of consummativity. But Baudrillard's later analysis becomes concerned with the indeterminate causality of the hyperreal. This analysis has the advantage of not reducing to a distinction between the 'real' object and the fetish but it leaves him unable to analyse the complexity of lived human relations with objects and to describe the source of their social value. In continuing Baudrillard's early move towards the social and away from the human, towards the semiotic and away from the real, I have begun to explore the way the enhancement of the use and properties of material things can lead to fascination and reverence.

The term fetishism can refer to the relative quality of desire and fascination for an object that is not intrinsic but is none the less part of it. The reverence shown for its capabilities supplements its material form, showing what it means, how it is valued in its cultural context. A classic example is a perfume with very low production value but a high fetish value that is created by a series of signs attached to the object through advertising, packaging, personal approval and recommendation that are themselves human products that communicate value. The reverence for the object is founded in its properties: its capability to change a person's smell (function), to declare their membership of a particular social group (signification), to express their sexual identity and arouse others' sexual interest (sexuality), to demonstrate their understanding of what aromas are pleasing (knowledge), to explore the beauty of scent (aesthetics) and to communicate through this valuation of capacities with others (mediation). As these properties are identified and extolled, many times over, the perfume becomes progressively fetishized.

The fetish quality of cars, works of art, mobile phones, shirts and Italian food is not an intrinsic or stable quality of the object. It is assigned through cultural mediations, a circulation of signs that includes the objects themselves. It is realized through a worshipful consumption of the objects in which reverence is displayed through desire for and an enthusiastic use of the object's properties. The fetishistic quality of objects varies over time and place and between different groups of people. This is a fetishism of things that does not distinguish their unreality from an essential material, natural or normal reality but recognizes, at both the material and semiotic levels, the fetish as a cultural production, a work of humans that is as real as anything can be.

NOTES

1 See for example, Marx's (1976: 131) account of those things that have not been fetishized, things that have a use-value but no exchange-value.
2 Freud apparently said: 'half of humanity must be classed among the clothes fetishists. All women, that is, are clothes fetishists' (see Rose 1988: 156).
3 Kellner takes Baudrillard to task for his limited reading of Marx (1989: 36–9). He points out that in a number of places Marx does offer a more socio-historical account of needs and their place in consumption.
4 It is clear that much of Baudrillard's interest in the fetishism of commodities and the fetishistic effect of make-up comes from Baudelaire whom he mentions (Baudrillard 1981: 95); he later quotes a large section of Baudelaire's (1995) 'In Praise of Cosmetics' from *The Painter of Modern Life* (Baudrillard 1990a: 93) and then refers to yet again (1990b: 116 fn).
5 As Grosz (1993: 114) remarks, 'the fetishist remains the most satisfied and contented of all perverts (the fetishist rarely if ever seeks analysis for fetishistic behaviour – the fetish never complains!)'.
6 'Overdetermination' means that value is represented many times over (see Freud 1976: 389).

4

BUILDING AND DWELLING

In short, a 'house', wherever it may be, is an enduring thing, and it bears perpetual witness to the slow pace of civilizations, of cultures bent on preserving, maintaining and repeating.

(Braudel 1992 [1979]: 167)

A house contains both people and things, it is both a social location and a physical shelter for loved ones and familiar objects. Dwelling within the building are possessions and people, furniture and family, equipment and emotions. As well as being a material entity in itself, a house is a locus for material culture, a meeting point for people and things, in which social relationships and material relationships are almost indistinguishable because both are bound together in the routine practices of everyday life.

Those of us who share our houses, share talk and experiences just as we share the tables, the crockery and the bathroom. When there is no one else around, it is a social space in the reverse sense of providing a respite from the requirement to interact, of having to maintain a social 'face'. Even if we live alone, we all share our home sometimes as a meeting space, inviting friends and visitors in, keeping not-so-welcome visitors on the threshold. Through mediating devices, especially the radio, telephone and television, we engage in social exchange in the home, even if no one else is present. Between solitary and communal dwelling there are many varities of sharing of space, furniture, facilities, social bonds and domestic work.

We can make a distinction between a 'home' as the emotional space in which people interact with each other and with the familiar things in that space and the 'house' as a physical construction that can contain a home. Paul Oliver (1987) chooses the word 'dwelling' to refer to this dual social and material significance of houses. He points out that they have a continuous useful life that is much longer than other material artefacts such as bowls, boats, ploughs and pitchers. This gives them a central place in material culture since dwellings

> outlast lineages, change hands, are sold, re-occupied, remodelled and adapted, their survival to the present being a record of responsiveness to altering life-styles and societies in change.
>
> (Oliver 1987: 10)

The house is probably the largest, most important and expensive artefact that people will possess, perhaps buy, or (in many parts of the world) build. It will be the place where much of their life passes and where many of the major events, emotions and relationships of their lives will be focused. In this chapter I shall explore some of the material properties of buildings that shape the forms of action of those who live in them, focusing on the types of action that are part of dwelling.

BUILDING AND DWELLING

The way in which human existence is tied into the material world interested Martin Heidegger. In his lecture, 'Building dwelling thinking' (1978), he discusses how 'dwelling' establishes a particular form of relationship between human being and material form that is fixed in space and enduring through time. In exploring the High German origins of the contemporary words *bauen* (building) and *wohen* (dwelling), he uncovers the overlap in their meanings. The history of the words and their interconnections does not reveal 'true' meanings but shows how language encompasses the way human life is lived. 'Dwelling' historically meant to settle a piece of land, work it and build a home on it –

to stay in a place. 'Building' meant much the same thing but with connotations tied to the construction of material form and thereby to the establishing of a form of life. Behind this distinction is the overlapped set of connotations whereby building also means cherishing, caring, protecting, cultivating, preserving and nurturing. These are not the constructing activities of production, of making things that are complete in themselves, but are constructing activities to do with dwelling:

> Building as dwelling, that is, as being on the earth, however, remains for man's everyday experience that which is from the outset 'habitual' – we inhabit it.
>
> (Heidegger 1978: 325–6)

Building involves clearing a space, establishing the place of dwelling, orienting the activities of being human in space and time, staying in a place. The technical procedures of building are to do with letting something appear which was not there before; adding to the things that are already there. But for Heidegger, while this might make sense of making things in general, building has a special quality of not just 'letting appear' but also 'letting dwell'. So a proper building is a dwelling, the other types of buildings (for working, for making other things) follow after; first there must be dwelling.

Heidegger's notion of dwelling describes what home is about for human beings; it is not just any building in which we reside and it is not residing without a building of some sort. The form of the building, whether it is the solid brick built home of the modern era, the wigwam or bender of nomadic peoples or the cardboard and plastic sheet of the homeless, is how home must be constructed for being human. Each material form of home indicates the mode of existence of those who live there. For Heidegger building is not merely a sign, representing a state of being – the nature of dwelling is in the building; it is really how being is: 'Dwelling, however, is the *basic character* of Being in keeping with which mortals exist' (Heidegger 1978: 338).

The way that we build houses reflects our culture, our values, our orientation to the land, whether we move often, whether we work with the land, whether we live in large or small groups. Marshall McLuhan (1994[1964]) suggests that homes in modern societies are rectangular because we are a stable society, a society of stay-at-homes whose homes stay put:

> The square room or house speaks the language of the sedentary specialist, while the round hut or igloo, like the conical wigwam, tells of the integral nomadic ways of food-gathering communities.
>
> (McLuhan 1994: 125)

The nomadic home is, he argues, a structure that follows the lines of force; its form is self-supporting through the round shape (the igloo, dome style tent and yurt) or the triangular shape (the A-framed tent and tepee: see Oliver 1987: 16–31). In contrast the rectangular home (both in plan and elevation) is abstracted from the physical tensions of force; its rectangular shape is more than is needed to keep the structure up. The structure of the nomadic home is entwined with tactile and kinetic space and the building is of the land from which it seems to grow. The development of the rectangular home, sitting upon the land, signals for McLuhan the arrival of a certain specialization of senses and skills. It creates an enclosed visual space with regular, flat, two-dimensional surfaces – the shape of visual representations such as paintings, photographs and screens.

The rectangular form signals a society in which most work, activity and social events happen 'indoors'. Representation and communication through visual text (both graphic and iconic) become important. With the visual environment of the rectangular house come windows that represent the outdoors to the inside through two dimensions. The material of windows, glass, is for Baudrillard 'the ideal modern recipient' because it is colourless, odourless, immune to decay and unlike wood or metal does not change over time; it is 'ranked symbolically at a zero level on the scale of materials' (Baudrillard 1996: 41). Glass has a double effect because its transparency creates a proximity – the surface of the window, the skin of the house – at the same time as a distance – the view through the glass. The presence of glass means that we can see but not touch as the window sets up 'an invisible but material caesura' (Baudrillard 1996: 42) preventing free communication between inside and out. Even if there are no net curtains, social convention, reinforced by the relative lack of light inside, discourages peering in.

McLuhan treats the material things humans create for themselves as an extension of their bodies. Development is historical and social rather than biological but it is evolutionary in that changes in material aspects of life are linked to changes in social aspects. Just as the faces, hands and mouths of human bodies are used for communicating with each other, so are these artefactual additions:

> Clothing and housing, as extensions of skin and heat-control mechanisms, are media of communication, first of all, in the sense that they shape and rearrange the patterns of human association and community.
> (McLuhan 1994: 127)

Amos Rapoport (1969) makes a similar point by arguing that the variety of vernacular styles of building homes cannot be explained merely by reference to the biological needs of humans, the availability of materials and technology and the state of the climate. Given the same material conditions of existence, different cultures will build different types of homes. He argues that climate, construction and materials are secondary modifying factors in determining house form, that limit choices. But the primary determinants of the particular way a culture builds its houses are a series of sociocultural factors to do with ethos; the values and responses to basic needs, family, the position of women, privacy and social intercourse (Rapoport 1969: 61).

Attitudes to privacy and pollution, for example, are reflected in the way the act of defecation is contained within the house. Rapoport tells us that there are different cultural responses to basic needs for living so that 'the Eskimo accepts very high smell concentrations inside the Igloo, and the smell of the toilet is accepted in the traditional Japanese house' (1969: 61). In contrast Shaw (1985: 14) recalls that in the Victorian terraced house of British cities it was considered unhealthy to have a water closet inside the house; it was usually in a separate building in the back yard. Different cultures express social values to do with privacy in the way dwelling is contained within the building. In northern Europe there is a cultural preference for houses that 'look out' with windows and doors visible from the street or over a front garden in contrast to the traditional houses in India, Iran and Latin America where buildings face inwards, towards a courtyard, hidden from the street by a wall (Rapoport 1969: 66). The inward looking style seems to be popular across a variety of climates and religions, although there are links to religious beliefs and customs about the protection of women from view.

A CONTAINER FOR DWELLING

As an extension of human being, the material form of housing reflects the cultural boundaries between different dwelling activities – working, resting, eating, sleeping, bathing, defecating. In this sense the building *contains* the customs and conventions of the particular culture as well as the people who dwell together and their belongings.[1]

Houses made from rectangular structures lend themselves to being fitted together in ways that the round or triangular structures of nomadic people do not. As well as being built as terraces or blocks of apartments, the inside of the dwelling can be easily subdivided – once stairs have been invented. Within each home, subdivisions into rooms may be assigned as living spaces for specific individuals or be demarcated for particular functions (kitchen, bathroom etc.). Charles Gordon (1996) points out that stairs require a mixture of engineering, building knowledge and planning and in making this point quotes John Templar:

> The shape of the stair begins to respond more to the deliberate decisions of the designer and the exigencies of the created structure to be served than to the natural contours of the land.
>
> (Templar 1992 quoted in Gordon 1996: 2)

The complexity of rectangular dwellings that are fitted together into terraces, subdivided into rooms, connected by stairs, depends on a culture with specialist building knowledge and systematic planning.

In perhaps the most famous example of trying to understand the link between culture and material form in the house, Pierre Bourdieu (1973) discusses the Kabyle house. The structure is linked to the divisions of dwelling (space for animals, space for humans) and the distribution of material possessions and activities (tools, clothes, weaving loom). The particular locations for guests, the dead, a bride and other important humans within the house are symbolically linked to the material distribution of activities. Bourdieu is able to 'read' the house as a material expression of symbolic meaning:

> The low and dark part of the house is also opposed to the high part as the feminine to the masculine: besides

> the fact that the division of work between the sexes, which is based upon the same principle of division as the organization of space, entrusts to the woman the responsibility of most objects which belong to the dark part of the house – water-transport, and the carrying of wood and manure, for instance – the opposition between the upper part and the lower part reproduces within the space of the house the opposition set up between the inside and the outside.
>
> (Bourdieu 1973: 100)

Spaces for activities – different types of work, sleeping, sex, giving birth, ceremonial – are distributed around the house according to a symbolic system that includes the direction faced for certain activities, the seasons and the paths in and out of the house. The system of 'homologous oppositions' between people, especially men and women, the material form of the house and the things in it and the cultural values of Berber society seem, to Bourdieu, to render the meanings of the material culture coherent and complete. The material form of the house follows the social distinctions between classes of persons – especially the genders – which is realized in their different activities – most importantly the sexual division of labour.[2]

There is something worryingly neat about Bourdieu's homologies; Gabriele vom Bruck (1997) argues that he does not take sufficient account of the variations and hierarchies within gender groups. Her own study of the use of space within the Yemeni house shows that it is determined by cultural distinctions of which gender is perhaps the most important. But gender alone is insufficient to determine what is culturally acceptable:

> What is read into space depends on what is read into their bodies. For example, Yemeni prepubescent boys are permitted to enter into space occupied by unrelated women because their gaze does not yet indicate carnal desire.
>
> (vom Bruck 1997: 142)

The way that culture is contained in buildings may largely be traditional but it is contingent on historic and social change so that exceptions are made. Vom Bruck (1997: 61) offers as an example the way Yemeni women who become doctors are, within the space and activity of their work role, able to talk to men to whom they are not related and to go without a veil. The same women within the space of their own home would accept more traditional constraints on their relations with the opposite sex.

STYLE AND STANDARDIZATION

Umberto Eco suggests that architecture incorporates a code that is meaningful in relation to other codes within a culture, in particular what he calls the 'anthropological system' (Eco 1986: 80). What he means is that the 'language' of architectural form is related via the function of buildings and their contents to the values of the culture. He is suggesting an even more determinative relationship between building and culture than Bourdieu in the Kabyle house; in Bourdieu's house there was no architect who 'designed' the house to achieve the symbolic homologies he found. Rather than seeing the architect as an artist, free to design according to aesthetic criteria, for Eco the language of architectural form is a translation from the cultural code of the anthropological system. But things are, of course, more complicated than this.

Some buildings last, often for centuries, providing a very powerful cultural imprint on a place, marking it as distinct. Civic buildings, monuments and even the dwelling houses in older quarters outlast their builders and original inhabitants. While many of the material artefacts that such buildings once contained have become mementoes displayed in a museum, such buildings are transformed, renovated, refurbished – often for different uses than they were built for. The architectural code survives in the material of the building, even though the anthropological system changes. For example, the British health service reforms after the Second World War that were putting paid to the legacy of the workhouse, adapted large buildings and mansions dating from the eighteenth century as residential homes for elderly people, physically handicapped people or children in care (Shaw 1985: 217, 242). A cultural and architectural heritage of large but often not particularly beautiful or important buildings was retained for a number of decades longer than might otherwise have been the case. The physical style, at least on the outside, of family homes built for a wealthy elite became the communal home for a variety of not-so-wealthy people, most of whom would have only ever lived as servants in such houses in their heyday.

The development of a professional, expert knowledge to do with building can mean that the anthropological system has to operate within an imposed architectural style. For example, in postwar Britain, a series of manuals, culminating in the report by Sir Parker Morris in 1961, set out minimum standards for the dimensions and facilities for council houses which were made compulsory for local authorities in 1969 (Shaw 1985: 93). One effect was the emergence of very similar house designs that were variations on the most cost-effective way to meet the minimum standards. The architectural code may also cross cultural boundaries. During the 1960s and 1970s local councils in the UK rapidly and cheaply put up many blocks of high-rise flats that used prefabricated sections to replace sub-standard terraced housing. These 'system' built flats were the result of importing designs and techniques developed in other European countries. The flats brought with them the social problems of high-rise living as well as many practical problems (difficult to heat, condensation) but in many respects, especially as functional housing units, replaced inferior buildings. System built flats brought a standardization, not only within the UK, where almost identical blocks of flats replaced tenements in Glasgow and back-to-back housing in the Midlands, but also across northern Europe.

The effects of modernization are apparent in standardization that can begin to erode the distinctions between places. Liz Shove (1995) has shown how changes in building technology have led to changes in the social relations between clients, architects, systems designers and fabricators. Instead of clients drawing on their own cultural context to specify how they would like a building to be, the architect and the systems designer offer a technological solution from within a set of largely pre-specified options. As Shove points out, there are a limited number of contractors in the world capable of developing and installing the cladding for buildings over fifty storeys. Their expertise is in setting up large buildings quickly and cheaply, regardless of where in the world they are or what the terrain or climate are like. The result is buildings that are increasingly uniform, regardless of where they are built. The same 'envelope' of steel structure hung with marble cladding is resistant to rain and sun, the same systems for controlling heat and cold will maintain the same environment inside wherever the building is located.

As containers of people and objects, homes are perhaps becoming more 'rectangularized' in McLuhan's (1994) terms, more a vehicle of visual forms of communication than a vehicle in their own right of social and cultural values. The progress of modernity seems to have introduced greater functionality through greater standardization but at the expense of expressing local material culture in the fabric of buildings. However, building, as understood by Heidegger, is not only to do with the material construction of the container that is the house. Dwelling is also to do with the everyday activities of 'building', of inhabiting that container.

BUILDING AS DWELLING

In modern European cultures, few people build their own homes but there are many activities undertaken by inhabitants to do with the material of the building – cleaning, maintenance, repairs, refurbishment, decoration and gardening. Others are to do with work with material within the home – cooking, washing clothes or making clothes. Somewhere in between are activities like making curtains, choosing furniture or doing craft work. All these activities come within what Heidegger calls 'building as dwelling', undertaken by inhabitants as part of their everyday lives. Some activities are experienced as domestic work, labour on behalf of the residents that is not paid for directly (washing clothes for example), other activities are experienced as leisure, often because the worker chooses to do the activity and finds it intrinsically rewarding (growing things in the garden for example).

Building-as-dwelling is not always what distinguishes a home from simply living somewhere. A home may be based on a distinction between public space, where anyone may go and private space reserved and protected for those whose home it is (Rakoff 1977). David Seamon, the spatial geographer, describes the 'appropriation' of spaces in terms of possession and control of which privacy is a part:

> A place to be alone is part of at-homeness, and the person whose home does not provide such a place feels a degree of upset.
>
> (Seamon 1979: 81)

In interviews with people who were formally homeless, but living in hostels, respondents emphasized control over what they were allowed to do when asked what 'home' meant to them (Dant 1988). They talked about being able to make a cup of coffee or getting something to eat, to come and go as they wanted, to change television channels. But building-as-dwelling involves the inhabitants having control and indeed responsibility for the domestic work which makes the private space distinct from any other space. Dwellers do things, which include interacting with other people but also include interacting with the material stuff contained within their home and sometimes with the material of the container.

The home is a site for material expression by people that is unparalleled elsewhere in their lives. At our place of work we manipulate the material world in routine ways regulated and specified by someone else. The manufacturing worker follows the requirements of a production line but even the craftsperson or artist's work is steered by a commission that comes through their learnt and repeated application of skill. In the home we turn our hands to a variety of tasks, whether we are good at them or not, to produce something that could, in principle, be sold as a commodity in return for wages. But 'domestic work' is directed towards ourselves and those with whom we share a home. It is, as Bourdieu noted in the Kabyle house, often gendered work and linked to the division of space and the use of equipment within the home. In contemporary western culture there is a crude division between the work on the material of the container of the home as 'men's work' (repairs, maintenance, decoration) and the work on the material within it as 'women's work' (cleaning, cooking, washing). As we shall see, things are not so straightforwardly divided in contemporary material culture.

A characteristic of the activities of dwelling is that they are not professional skills; they are not taught in a formal way and are not based on a system of knowledge. They involve a practical level of skill using material that is to hand – in this sense they are *bricolage* following its French meaning of pottering about and doing odd jobs – what the British would call DIY or do-it-yourself (see Miller 1987: 7–8). Claude Lévi-Strauss (1966) famously uses the term to distinguish mythological thought from systematic, scientific thought. He describes the *bricoleur* on the technical plane as one who is 'adept at performing a large number of diverse tasks' who is prepared to 'make do' with whatever tools and materials are to hand (Lévi-Strauss 1966: 17). Now, Lévi-Strauss is interested in how a similar process of *bricolage* works in constructing myths out of ideas and images that already exist in the culture.

The *bricoleur*'s project is not pre-planned according to systematic knowledge, but is worked on with a mixture of planning and adaptation, allowing the project to emerge out of what is available. The connotative meanings of *bricolage* suggest that the result is not altogether satisfactory, either in the sense of a bodge-up (as in a job that is temporary or has been done 'after a fashion') or a fix-up (as in a shady deal). For Lévi-Strauss, the *bricoleur* is working with sign elements that refer to things other than themselves and derive their meaning from their place in a system of signs. The signs available to the *bricoleur* are 'pre-constrained' (Lévi-Strauss 1966: 19) because they already have uses and meanings assigned to them; they are not like materials available to an artist (the paint and canvas, the harmonic series and the instruments of the orchestra) which can be used to create infinite possibilites. The *bricoleur* does none the less create new meanings through the particular way they combine signs, much as an ordinary language user creates new meaning with each new utterance. Lévi-Strauss is careful not to overplay the distinction between *bricoleur* and engineer, mythologist and scientist. All are eventually confronted by the limitations of the resources, material and conceptual, with which they have to work; the distinction is a matter of degree, of orientation towards the pragmatic (*bricolage*) or towards the abstract and systematic (science).

Lévi-Strauss takes the concept of *bricolage* from its largely material context of meaning to refer to the practices of myth makers in pre-literate societies. The activities of dwelling draw on both the material and mythological – *bricolage* in both the everyday sense and Lévi-Strauss's. The dweller takes a set of readily available objects and works on them inside the building the dweller lives in. There is a material practice of putting objects together but there is also a cultural practice of constructing meaning out of the ensemble. As we shall see, the material culture of dwelling involves both an aesthetic of appearance and an orientation to functionality – but neither are learnt as abstract, systematized knowledge.

The term *bricolage* has acquired a particular use within cultural studies. Dick Hebdige follows a reading of Lévi-Strauss provided by Hawkes (1977) to suggest that:

> the mods could be said to be functioning as bricoleurs when they appropriated another range of commodities by placing them in a symbolic ensemble which served to erase or subvert their original straight meanings.
> (Hebdige 1979: 104)

For Hebdige, the appropriation of pills, motor scooters and Union Jacks by the youth subcultural group of 1960s Britain known as the 'mods', was subversive and critical of a dominant or mainstream culture. But this subversive use of cultural goods is more akin to surrealist strategies of achieving a revolution of the object than the pragmatic ends of *bricolage*, both in its everyday use and Lévi-Strauss's. The surrealists had a theory, a set of political, aesthetic and cultural ideas, which guided their art and informed their manifestos – what they did was not *bricolage*. In thinking of the activities of dwelling, I wish to put aside the idea of *bricolage* as subversion and any intentional effect to reflexively produce critical culture.

Instead, I wish to use the term *bricolage* in a way that closely follows that of Michel de Certeau, who has attempted to understand the practices, the 'arts of making' which make up everyday life (1984: xii–xviii). For de Certeau the arts of 'making do' or *bricolage* are combined with ritual practices, habits and routines out of which the shape of everyday life emerges. These actions of people are not reducible to individual choice, but neither are they wholly determined by learned patterns of action. Rituals may be followed knowingly because it suits the purposes at hand but these purposes might lead to a modification of the ritual, of material objects or of skills to meet varying situations or even to bring about variations in action, experience or environment. This is why the practices of everyday life are treated as 'arts'; the agent uses a skill of making, or making do, not to create from nothing, but to creatively adapt both ways of doing things and material things themselves. The activity of *bricolage* involves both, but what it excludes is the application of institutionalized knowledge and skill.

The material cultural activities of dwelling involve transformations of material: raw food is transformed into edible meals, the placing of furniture or redecoration transforms the material environment of dwelling, laundering transforms dirty clothes into clean ones. The introduction of new equipment, say a new kitchen or a new washing machine, will transform not only the environment but also the routine activities of cooking or laundering. The activities of dwelling use the approach of *bricolage* to use what is to hand to bring about these material transformations. Of course professional, knowledge based, paid for labour may be used to achieve these transformations; take-away meals, an interior decorator or a laundry service will turn the inhabitants' domestic work using the practical skills of a *bricoleur* into a systematic and commodified form.

KEEPING

Edgar Allan Poe, writing in 1845, early in the modern period, describes the decisions about the interior of a house or the 'adjustment of a chamber' as 'keeping':

> A want of keeping is observable sometimes in the character of the several pieces of furniture, but generally in their colours or modes of adaptation to use. *Very* often the eye is offended by their inartistic arrangement.
>
> (Poe 1986a: 415)

Poe is reacting to the poor taste of the growing American *parvenu*, the well off, middle class whose interest in interior decoration has as much to do with a desire to display wealth as to live in beauty. In England, he says, taste in internal decoration is 'supreme' and this he connects with the existence of true nobility. Long before Simmel or Veblen discuss the process of fashion as material distinction trickling down through the strata of society, Poe comments on the tendency to imitate the nobles, albeit with a 'diffusion of the proper feeling'. In the USA, however, there were no nobles to imitate and with wealth as the sole determinant of social strata, cost and decorative style became linked. The concern to display wealth rather than develop an aesthetic of line and composition led to what he calls a 'lack of keeping'.

Poe's philosophy is not merely analytic but also prescriptive; he rejects as poor taste those objects (cut glass shades, exaggerated mirrors) that create glare or glitter and describes an ideal room ('The walls are prepared with a glossy paper of a silver gray tint, spotted with small Arabesque devices of a fainter hue of the prevalent crimson.

Many paintings relieve the expanse of the paper': Poe 1986a: 419). The cultural origins of good taste have not changed substantially today. Whereas Poe was writing for *Burton's Gentleman's Magazine* and the *Broadway Journal* (versions of 'The Philosophy of Furniture' appeared in each), today the advice on style would come from a feature in the colour supplement of a Sunday newspaper, an article in *Home and Garden* or a television show with ideas on decoration. What has perhaps changed significantly since Poe's day is that the problem of taste, of how to do the keeping of a house, is not just a problem faced by the nobility or the *nouveaux riches* but one faced by most people who do not live in furnished accommodation.

Dwellers design and shape the interior of the spaces within the home. They choose wallpaper, carpets, furniture, kitchen equipment and so on, putting these items together into an ensemble which is both functional and personal. A key part of this work may be acquiring and installing material objects – furniture, furnishings, kitchen equipment and entertainment equipment. These items are seldom chosen all at once but are progressively added to the ensemble, building up the material contents of the home. Choices are made about design, colour, functionality, cost and where things are put. Each choice involves a complex decision that relates to not only the single item but also how that item will fit into the home and how it will fit in with existing items.

Although furnishing a house involves consuming commodities, it is *bricolage* in the sense of putting together what is available – in the house, in the furniture store, what is given by friends or relatives. The ordinary tasks of 'keeping' a home do not amount to a specialist design problem but they are about creating a particular material environment which gives off what Baudrillard (1996) calls 'atmosphere' (*l'ambience*).[3] He comments on the emergence of 'man the designer', who is

> neither an owner, nor a mere user – rather, he is an active engineer of atmosphere . . . Instead of consuming objects, he dominates, controls and orders them.
>
> (Baudrillard 1996: 26–7)

Adrian Forty (1986) links the emergence of this modern form of 'keeping' to the separation of productive work from the home. As work was removed to the workshop, office and factory, the home became a place for dwelling. The workplace was regulated and organized by the employer, but dwellers were free to imprint their identity on the material fabric of their home. If labour was alienated from its material products, that lack of creative identity between human and artefact could be realized within the home. Forty argues that the dynamic of this relation was to make the home as different from the work environment as possible so that while 'offices were austerely furnished in utilitarian colours with hard surfaces . . . people sought to make their homes colourful, soft and plushy' (1986: 102).

The enforced leisure of the middle class woman kept her indoors and from the 1860s women took a more active part in choosing decorations. Atmosphere in the early modern period was intended to reflect the character of the woman who was choosing, arranging and decorating (Forty 1986: 106). However, during the nineteenth century distinctions were made between the male domain of hall, library, business, billiard and smoking rooms and the female domain of boudoir, music room, morning room and bedroom. These distinctions were reflected in the 'serious, substantial, dignified (but not ostentatious) and dark-toned' male areas and the 'lighter, colourful, refined, delicate and decorative' feminine spaces (Kinchen 1996: 13).

Commentators on contemporary material culture within the home often emphasize possession and identity rather than gendered space. Csikszentmihalyi and Rochberg-Halton (1981) develop a theory that emphasizes the role of material objects in the social and psychological lives of ordinary people:

> The objects of the household represent, at least potentially, the endogenous being of the owner. Although one has little control over the things encountered outside the home, household objects are chosen and could be freely discarded if they produced too much conflict within the self. Thus household objects constitute an ecology of signs that reflects as well as *shapes* the pattern of the owner's self.
>
> (Csikszentmihalyi and Rochberg-Halton 1981: 17)

Their micro-sociological perspective explores the connection between the symbolic meaning of objects and the way individuals represent themselves in social interaction. Gender and age, along with function and use emerge, especially in their quantitative analyses, as dimensions of relations with objects – but often it is more personal. Items of furniture were most often mentioned by respondents as 'special objects'; for younger people tables and chairs were associated with comfort and enjoyment while for older people they stood for 'important memories, relationships and past experiences' (Csikszentmihalyi and Rochberg-Halton 1981: 61). Two of the interviews they quote mention work done on pieces of furniture: one man made his desk from a door, another woman talks of a chest handed down from her parents who painted it different colours before her husband sanded it to the natural wood. Items of furniture do not have an intrinsic meaning but become meaningful through work on them or on the way they were used. Memories of people and past events are associated with current objects in the home; one woman associated two chairs with the memory of having sat in one with her babies while her husband sat in the other.

Harold Riggins's (1994b) study is of just one house, in which memory also plays a key role – his parents' home in which he was brought up. His autoethnographic essay, illustrated with black and white photographs, describes the personal associations of objects (bookcase made by an uncle, snapshot of Riggins with his father) along with the names of manufacturers, colours and descriptions of shape. His descriptions of objects provide a 'key' for memories or supply a context for recollections. Ian Roderick (1999) shows how descriptions in letters locate objects in narrative relations with humans which give the things meaning and value.

What these accounts of the distribution of objects within the home tell us is that they are not simply functional but are entwined with the people who live with them. The way that they 'keep' their homes gives them the chance to express who they are while at the same time reflecting their social location in terms of age, gender, class and so on. The things in the home have no intrinsic meaning but derive it from the activities of dwelling, including keeping, that constitute the social relations with those objects.

TRANSFORMING SPACE

The activities of *bricolage* have become a feature of late modern western consumption culture. Do-it-yourself has become a cultural industry oriented to the affordable and practical rather than luxury and glamour. In the UK the stimulators of taste in magazines and television shows direct us towards the retail warehouses in which we can buy kit furniture and decorating materials from the 'Homebase' so that we can 'Do-It-All'; in France of course we would go to a similar chain called 'M. Bricolage'. The house or flat is, for most of us, not built for any particular person or family. We buy it, lease it or rent it as a container that we shall be able to transform as *bricoleurs* for our use as a dwelling. We may adapt and modify by knocking down walls, rewiring, seeding a lawn, acquiring and placing furniture, putting up some curtains and clearing the yard of debris from whoever was there last. Transforming the shell of the house into a container for our dwelling involves work that gives the house its identity as 'our home'.

Daniel Miller's study of the kitchens of forty tenants on an estate in north London explores how they appropriated and adapted their kitchen space from the local council's original uniform fittings and decor (Miller 1988, 1997). As they replaced lino, purchased cookers, fridges, freezers and placed crockery, kitchen tools and 'knick-knacks', the residents were drawing on culturally distributed ideas of what the kitchen should look like (for example from advertisements for kitchen units) and from the practical consequences of their own lifestyle. Although some tenants had put in expensive fitted kitchens, most changes were not costly but had the effect of transforming the look of the space from its original state.

In reprising this study in 1997 for an Open University course unit (including photographs from the original study), Miller lays much more emphasis on the gendered nature of kitchens as a woman's space that is transformed by men. The women have a sense of what the space should be like: they read the magazines and develop opinions on the aesthetics of kitchens. The men on the other hand apply their skills with tools and materials to achieve the desired transformation:

> In many cases this notion of a gift was quite explicit. A husband or son might offer to 'do up' the kitchen for their wife or mother for a birthday, anniversary or some other gift occasion.
>
> (Miller 1997: 17)

Miller is disparaging about the self-directed efforts of men that resulted in 'a hotchpotch of doors, hinges and contraptions that clearly marked a form of labour unsubjected to an aesthetic concern' (1997: 18). Not surprisingly then, where men lived on their own, they tended to make few if any changes to the original form of the kitchen.

The development of materials (plywood, polyurethane foam) and designs (plain, rectangular) suitable for machine production rather than skilled handcrafting has given the *bricoleur* more scope with furniture. For example, Shea (1965) offers a manual that includes information on design principles as well as sequenced photographs and detailed plans for how to make chairs, tables, stools and bedside consoles. The tools and skills are oriented not to shaping, carving or moulding but to cutting in straight lines and presenting flat surfaces.

Machine produced materials, while originally prepared by one stage of industrial production for another, are amenable to measuring, cutting and shaping by the non-professional, especially using power tools. Fixings are a mixture of slots, plates, blocks, screws, bolts and modern glues. The need to replace craft skill by machine process for mass production has generated an intermediate product (plywood, hardboard, chipboard, medium-density-fibreboard, wood veneer, melamine sheet) that is easily appropriated by the *bricoleur*. These materials have a standard quality with no grain, imperfections, variation in size, shape, density, colour or pattern to be worked with as have natural or hand prepared materials.

Much modern furniture is adaptable and interchangeable. Kit furniture can be bought for kitchens, bedrooms, living rooms and bathrooms and be assembled by the householder who chooses 'units' to fit together. The units may be installed by professional 'fitters', leaving the householder with something machine produced but 'personal' in the sense that it has been designed for *their* kitchen. Design qualities are both built in and chosen; door materials, surfaces and fittings are picked by the householder from 'coordinated' ranges that have been professionally designed. The idea of units machine produced in the factory for later assembly has been extended to furniture that is bought in a 'flat pack' for assembly by the householder. The rectangular form of furniture units means that they can be fitted together in a variety of ways and then put against walls and fitted into corners. Just as modern system building has given an aesthetic continuity to the skin, or envelope of buildings, so the modern materials available to the *bricoleur* produce standardization oriented to function with a measure of adaptability to individual choice.

THE EASY CHAIR

The kitchen is a major site for domestic work and material transformation within the modern home. The easy chair in contrast provides an environment for inactivity and is usually brought into the home ready made and designed. Baudrillard claims that items of furniture have 'a primordial function as vessels, a function that belongs to the register of the imaginary' (1996: 27); as womb-like containers they cradle and protect humans at rest. Galen Cranz (1996), in a sketch of the world social history of the chair, points out how using chairs at all is a western habit and that even when it is the norm, carries connotations of social distinction (the 'chair' or 'seat' on a board or committee signifies status). The chair that reclines and has arms and a broad headrest is reserved for the most prestigious person in an organization; the lowliest person answering telephones is more likely to be on a swivelling stool with perhaps a low back rest. There is a continuum of types of seating that goes from sitting and squatting on the floor through sitting on mats, benches, stools, chairs with low backs, with padding, with arms, with support for the upper back to reclining chairs with support for the head. It might seem that the more wealthy or important we are, the more comfort we can enjoy, but Cranz argues that the social history of the chair is tied up with who was allowed to sit in whose presence. Unlike benches, divans or sitting platforms, chairs are for one person and, unlike stools, chairs have directionality. Chairs with high backs frame the sitter and may carry decoration appropriate to their office. Those that recline allow the sitter to relax while others standing or in less supportive chairs have to remain physically alert, ready to do what is bid.

In the home not all chairs are alike and, traditionally at least, the male head of the household had the largest, most comfortable chair, the children sat on the floor, hard wooden chairs or at best on the shared comfort of the sofa. In the privacy of our homes we can recline, enclosed in a chair that cushions us – the upholstered easy chair. Giedion (1969[1948]) writes of the origins of the *confortable*, the upholstered easy chair, in the workshops of Dervilliers in 1838. The characteristics are still with us today: 'a skeleton entirely cloaked and enveloped in fabric, and voluminous cushions, usually built around spiral springs' (Giedion 1969: 376). The upholstery was originally to cover the iron form used to recreate the *bergère en gondole* (winged chair of bent wood) of an early Rococo period that provided a shell-like cradling of the body. The iron form gave way to glued beech but the enveloping of the chair in upholstery remained. The wings disappeared and the emphasis shifted from the curved surface of wood to the cushioned and mattressed quality of upholstery:

> The seat and the whole chair appear to the naïve eye as a complex of cushions somehow miraculously held together . . . Headrests disappear – the proportions had to be low and squat. Cylindrical cushions on either side walled the sitter in a frontal posture. This is the model found from about 1880 on in almost every home.
>
> (Giedion 1969: 378)

This still describes the form that modern upholstery takes; cushioned surfaces (of springs and horsehair or open celled foam and rubberized webbing) that mould to contours of the body and hide the rigid structure underneath (of beech, plywood or rigid expanded foam). The effect is an atmosphere of neither sitting upright nor lying down, it is rather 'the invitation to informal posture' (Giedion 1969: 386). The easy chair has developed, not just aesthetically by taking on simpler and cleaner lines, but also physically by lowering the body of its user into a recline that increasingly approaches a recumbent posture. Giedion describes the posture of the nineteenth century as based on relaxation – the reclined body.

Forty (1986) describes how in the late nineteenth century the 'art furniture' movement wanted to reduce decoration and reintroduce wooden-framed chairs and settees with loose cushions to replace the heavily upholstered forms of a little earlier (Forty 1986: 111–13). Although such ideals have continued to influence the design of 'modern' furniture, in the twentieth century the easy chair has reverted to its upholstered form in most homes, allowing the dweller to sink into it without the burden of having to follow the rules of employers or art movements. The angle between the back and seat has become more definite, more rectangular and the height of the back has lowered, sometimes to the same level as the arms. The result is an easy chair that allows the sitter to recline but only with cushions to support the spine and the head. The seat of the chair has also become lower, dropping the sitter's eyes into line with the television. Moreover the sofa has become a more 'democratic' seating unit, often replacing individual chairs – even when there are easy chairs, the material distinction between 'his' and 'hers' is more likely to have disappeared.

DWELLING AS WORK

Sociologists, often with a feminist orientation, have studied housework in a number of ways since Ann Oakley's (1976) pioneering study. Recent research has focused on the impact of introducing equipment into the domestic environment. Schwartz Cowan (1989) describes the gradual introduction of the coal burning cooking stove into the home. Her historical analysis of the introduction of technical objects into the home points out that change in the equipment of domestic work is not simply determined by the technical efficacy of the object to fulfill its function. The object has to cross what she calls a 'consumption junction' (Schwartz Cowan 1987) in a network of social actors ranging from the producers of the raw materials, producers of the final object, retailers and distributors, house builders, government agencies and so on. At the centre of her networks is the household inhabited by the user. The history of technology has shifted from focusing on the 'inventor' as the focus of product innovation to recognizing the impact of large companies and the consumer/user. Other studies that have researched the consumption junction include Cockburn and Ormrod's (1993) research on the chain of design, production, marketing and use of microwave ovens and Chabaud-Rychter's (1996) actor-network approach to the development of food processors for use in the home.

The introduction of material objects that affect the everyday domestic work of the home is gendered in its context of production and its context of use. The design and development is largely done by men in an industrial setting but the commodity that they produce is intended to be used largely by women in a domestic setting. The object is produced in a field dominated by work values based on systematic knowledge, to be used in a field dominated by the everyday practical skills of the *bricoleur*. Sometimes the object produced can lead to a transformation of gendered work in the home; the coal burning stove reduced the traditionally male work of gathering, chopping and storing wood but increased the female work of feeding the stove, cleaning it and cooking more complex meals (Schwartz Cowan 1989: 62).

The introduction of the domestic sewing machine however transformed the never ending 'spare' time work of sewing bed-linen and underclothes that traditionally fell to women. Initially it made the work much quicker and less arduous and led, with the development of industrial sewing machines, to the work largely being done outside the home (Hardyment 1988). Both Hardyment and Forty describe the development of domestic sewing machines that, while utilizing technology to change domestic work, were also produced as symbols such as the 1858 machine designed to look like a squirrel 'chosen because of the creature's frugality and providence' (Forty 1986: 98). Such symbolic work was of course part of crossing the consumption junction: industrial machines had no such aesthetic aims.

There has been considerable debate about the impact of technology on domestic work and its connection with waged labour both inside the home and outside (see for example Oakley 1976; Forty 1986). The sewing machine 'illustrates the most successful possible labour saving appliance – one which has completely removed the task from the home' (Hardyment 1988: 52). However, the washing machine has not brought about the same shift of domestic labour outside the home (although Hardyment takes her washing to a launderette with a service wash: 1988: viii). The washing machine has symbolic connotations that are tied up with the cultural specification of gendered work. Washing clothes is a depollution of material intimate to the members of the household – safer kept within the home. Jane Graves (1996: 32) sees the washing machine as reinforcing a double bind for the 'wife-in-a-house'. Cleaning clothes is an essential way in which women are able to show that they care for the members of the household. However, washing clothes is a lowly activity in which it is difficult to display skill.

The washing machine relieves the strenuous and tedious labour of previous systems of domestic laundry (see Hardyment 1988: 55–74) in which women provided the motive energy. While doing washing well might be difficult to spot, failing to do the washing well is all too easy to see with the stain that remains, the paper handkerchief that becomes attached to everything in the wash or the colour that's bled. The washing machine leaves not only responsibility with the housewife but also plenty of work: loading and unloading washing, spinning and drying machines; hanging, folding, sorting, airing and ironing clothes. These tasks still require little human skill or dexterity and machines speed up processes (drying, ironing) rather than relieving drudgery. The washing machine then traps women in the intimate, caring but tedious and unrewarded labour of domesticity. This is achieved by making the machine seem like a toy that has transformed the work into a trivial activity. Graves says with heavy irony that 'with a washing-machine pain is converted into pleasure, back-breaking work into gaity and laughter' (1996: 33).

Although a small study, Gomez's (1994) research found changing gender roles with washing machines. Older men who understood how to use a washing machine still left the washing to their wives, while at least one young man was 'spontaneously throwing in a half-load' when his clothes needed washing 'on an emergency basis' and 'without devoting any special care'. His female partner on the other hand had 'thoughtfully evolved a sorting system for the wash' (Gomez 1994: 143). Gomez points out that the approaches of both men and women to domestic activities sustain a gender distinction between ways of doing tasks and using tools and machines. Even though things are changing it seems that younger men are more willing to 'help' rather than take on an equal share of the work of domestic laundry.

CONCLUSIONS

In this chapter I have tried to show that building, the material form of dwelling, is shaped by culture and, in turn, shapes social action. I have explored a number of types of social relations with the material things of dwelling – the building as a container, the aesthetics of 'keeping', *bricolage* as making and making do, the changing form of furnishings and domestic work as the transformation of materials. The social relations within the home, particularly those surrounding gender and the activities proper for home rather than work, are reflected in the way that dwelling space is organized and used (keeping, transforming, sitting, laundering). At the same time, individual biographies are embedded in objects and furniture through collecting and keeping.

In our homes we confront ourselves and our culture through the material form of things. The shape of the armchair folds our bodies into a particular posture for relaxing. But we have chosen the chair and its position in the living room and leave our impression in the upholstery when we get up. The washing machine is a cultural artefact that signals our modernity and we are glad to bring it into the home to help us remove our residues from the clothes we have worn. Its electric motor may reduce the effort of washing but when it stops we must bend down and reach into it to get the washing out and then dry and iron it if we want clean laundry. The dwelling activities of sitting and laundering – and all the others mentioned in this chapter – are not simply about consuming goods but about living with them, appropriating objects into our everyday lives. As a billboard advertisement declared:

> We shape the things we build, thereafter they shape us.
> (advertisement for Caterpillar clothes, March 1998)

But as we live with things, using them, working with them, altering and adding to them, the work of building is continuous – and so is the process of mutual shaping.

NOTES

1 For a discussion of the patterns of consumption and the influences on choice within the home see Putnam (1990) and other contributors to Putnam and Newton (1990).
2 See Madigan and Munro (1990) who discuss the impact of gender on contemporary western housing.
3 Riggins uses the term 'flavor' to refer to the same overall impression of an inhabited room as he draws on Goffman's ideas to explore the place of domestic objects in micro-social processes (1990: 357–8).

5

WEARING IT OUT: WRITTEN AND MATERIAL CLOTHING

> Our clothes are too much a part of us for most of us ever to be entirely indifferent to their condition: it is as though the fabric were indeed a natural extension of the body, or even of the soul.
>
> (Bell 1992 [1947]: 19)

Of all things, apart perhaps from things that we eat, clothes are the material objects that are most consistently part of our individual and our social lives. As Quentin Bell suggests, they are so close to our bodies for so much of the time they become like an extension of that body, an outer layer or shell with which we confront the social world. Clothes are something we wear on the outside of our bodies, wearing them out into the environment and the social world and wearing out the material of the fabric through use and through washing. In some ways clothes are like rooms and houses – containers in which we are able to live out our lives. But they are less like containers or mini-environments (except perhaps space suits or diving suits – see Chapter 9) as they are like screens or fences. They cover us, affording us protection, but they allow us to look out, over or through the screen. They only partially hide and protect us;

the other side of being able to take in the world through our clothes is that we are also able to present ourselves to the world through them. Clothes are a relatively malleable material form so that the wearer can adjust the screening effect by, for example, taking off an overcoat to enter a building that is warmer than outside and in which a more personal and discerning gaze can fall upon the more complex ensemble previously hidden under the coat.

Clothes are objects that we co-opt as we confront the natural world of sun, wind, rain, heat and cold and the social world of sex, status, power and communication. They have a multitude of properties that we confer and exploit through this co-option. There are three key ways in which clothing has effect as material culture that I shall consider in this chapter. First, as fashion – the link between the shape and look of clothes and a temporal sequence of change in those forms. Much of the attention paid to clothing in social and historical discussions has focused on 'fashion' because of its potential to signify social distinctions of age, gender and status. Second, and deriving from the signifying function of fashion, is the capability of clothing to communicate between members of the culture through forms that may be more or less static over time. The idea that clothes are a form of writing on the body has been inverted by Roland Barthes to treat writing about clothes as an inseparable part of the system of difference between items of clothing. The third key issue I shall raise is the idea that a single garment may be significant because of the relationship between its particular material form and the body that wears it.

FASHION AND MODERNITY

The social distinction of fashion can work without clothes. Journalist Barbara Ellen commented on a 'clothing-optional resort':

> Ironically, the most bizarre sights seem to have sprung from some deep-rooted nudist urge to make a 'fashion statement': the men like to wear tops but no bottoms, leaving their genitals dangling beneath the cloth like giblets escaping from a Thanksgiving turkey; while the women favour the 'shaved crotch' look. However, the

> fact remains that, here [in the clothing-optional resort], it is I who am the freak in my prim little sundresses and 'daringly' sheer tights.
>
> (*Observer Life Magazine*, 30 March 1997)

One of the attractions of nudism is that the absence of clothes could be expected to limit the possibilities for social distinction by fashioned appearance. But here distinctions are being made within the community not only between members (unclothed) and outsiders (clothed) but also among members (more or less unclothed). The male fashion of tops-but-no-bottoms modifies the un-dress code by adding clothes but without disturbing the signal of complete undress – exposed genitals. This fashion does allow some 'management' of the code: sitting down, in a car, with a newspaper on the lap or at a table one could pass for a non-nudist. For women the 'shaved crotch' removes a sign of nudity – the pubic hair – while being consistent with the un-dress code. Its absence suppresses the signal of sexual maturity that is normally covered in even the briefest of conventional bathing costumes.

Simmel's justly famous account of fashion locates two dynamics in fashion which are almost contradictory – imitation and differentiation (1971 [1904]: 296). To follow a fashion is to imitate the norm so that outsiders (such as those wearing sundresses) feel uncomfortable while the insiders enjoy the feeling of inclusion. The code of un-dress is modified by innovations such as tops and shaved crotches, which, when they are imitated, differentiates a new 'in-group' within the resort. The in-group display their familiarity with the un-dress code by their adoption of the two variants which also 'culturalize' the natural differentiation of the sexes.

Simmel suggests that innovation is a result of a 'weakening of nervous energy' (Simmel 1971: 302) that is characteristic of both modernity and the upper classes; simply the widespread adoption of a fashion or clothing style causes its appeal to fade and leads to a desire for the new. He suggests that while simpler cultures resist novelty and strangeness, the complexity of modern society and its vulnerability to foreign influence lead it to be charmed by the new:

> Whatever is exceptional, bizarre, or conspicuous, or whatever departs from the customary norm, exercises a

> peculiar charm upon the man of culture, entirely independent of its material justification.
>
> (Simmel 1971: 300)

The cycle of fashion, of new styles replacing old, has been around since the fourteenth century (Braudel 1981: 317) but the fashion cycle has accelerated since the nineteenth century and even more so since the Second World War (see Davis 1992: 105). The work of individuals became distinctive and known following the introduction of the couture system of designers producing from ateliers which began in the middle of the nineteenth century. Vittoria de Buzzaccarina (1990: 254) precisely dates the emergence of the *haute couture* fashion industry from the trade of dressmaking as beginning in 1858 when Charles Worth opened a *maison* on the Rue de la Paix in Paris. Rather than designing for a specific client, Worth produced designs for wear in different settings which would then be made up to each client's particular measurements and wishes. Although fashion designs had been presented as sketches in magazines, suggesting ideas and ways of using new textiles, Worth introduced *design* as a distinct part of the process of producing high quality clothing. This included presenting the designs as three-dimensional 'models' on living bodies (known then as *sosie*, later as *mannequins* and now simply as 'models').

The introduction of designs and models was still linked to a made-to-measure system of producing individual clothes for specific clients. The development of machine based, mass production techniques was kept in check by the dominance of the ateliers and hand production so that even when industrial production was well established the dressmaking industry was forced to

> adapt hand-sewn garments to machine production, to mimic the very techniques of manufacture it was designed to replace . . . The dominance of couture design, therefore, can be viewed as perpetuating a retrograde orientation in production which trickled down through all layers of dressmaking.
>
> (Fine and Leopold 1993: 112)

On the other hand, the mechanisms for distributing, advertising and retailing the clothes once copied, transformed fashion into a high volume commodity system. The effect seems to have been one of reducing the fashion cycle so that changes are more frequent. The cyclical nature of fashion means that clothes say something about history, locating wearers at a vague point in the passing of social time, cross-connected with the wearer's position in the generational structure. While nothing like as precise as dating a tree by its rings, the width of a man's trousers or tie, whether he wears turn-ups or indeed a tie at all, seem to situate him according to his age and the age he lives in.

Both Simmel (1971[1904]) and Veblen (1953[1899]) are famous for regarding fashion as something that affects only the upper classes and trickles down through the lower classes, maintaining status distinctions through a continuous process of novelty, differentiation and imitation. For Veblen (1953: 121) the clothes of women's fashion such as high heels and skirts were designed to show that their wearer did not work. However, Quentin Bell shows that historically the distinction between breeches and skirts is much more closely linked to occupation than gender (1992: 36) and, what is more, crinolines were worn by domestic servants and even women working in the fields (1992: 109). A more powerful explanation for form in women's clothes fashion, is to do with physical presence; high heels, skirts, bustles, piled hair, hats etc. make the woman appear bigger, strengthening her physical presence in interaction (Bell 1992: 39).

Simmel sees the way that people adopt clothing fashions – ignoring them, embracing them to excess, striving to lead fashion or at least be 'in' fashion, or by standing apart from the whole thing – as reflecting the way in which individuals orient themselves to society. In his account, fashion represents society, something mutable and changing against which the consistency of personality can emerge. So for example, those who accept blind obedience to fashion use it as a 'sort of mask' in order to reserve their personal feeling and their taste:

> It is therefore a feeling of modesty and reserve which causes many a delicate nature to seek refuge in the levelling cloak of fashion: such individuals do not care to resort to a peculiarity in externals for fear of perhaps betraying a peculiarity of their innermost soul.
> (Simmel 1971: 312)

More recent accounts have, like Simmel, emphasized the role of fashion in modernity but also linked it to other changes in society. Campbell (1987: 76) has argued that the tolerance of new social and political ideas, which has its origins in Romanticism, led to the emergence of a new form of hedonism that took pleasure in imagination and emotions. He links the pleasure that can be derived from new ideas and stimuli to the modern desire for novelty including new fashions in clothes. Elizabeth Wilson (1985) sees wearing fashionable clothes as a reaction to enlightenment thought that became possible due to the relative cheapness of machine based production techniques. The continuous expression of the new

> does suggest what is *common* to much of modern art: its oppositionalism and iconoclasm, its questioning of reality and perception, its attempt to come to grips with the nature of human experience in a mechanized 'unnatural' world.
>
> (Wilson 1985: 63)

For Herbert Blumer fashion is not driven by class distinction but by a 'collective groping for the proximate future' (1969: 281) and he suggests that the individual's engagement with fashion is not so much the desire to explore new ideas or to express opposition but more prosaically the '*wish to be in fashion, to be abreast of what has good standing, to express new tastes which are emerging in a changing world*' (Blumer 1969: 282 – emphasis in the original). But how, Blumer's study wanted to find out, can this collective response operate through the *haute couture* fashion system? Of the hundreds of designs presented to buyers, whose professional skill was in guessing how new fashions would be received by their customers, only about 10 per cent were ordered. The buyers, however, apparently acting independently, made very similar decisions, even though they were only able to explain their choice of an item as its being 'stunning' (Blumer 1969: 279). The designers and buyers were of course steeped in a fashion culture that was concerned with the recent development of clothing forms and styles, as well as developments in other cultural forms. For Blumer, fashion is a dynamic of modernity, a system of change and innovation that always understands the past, particularly the recent past and distinguishes itself as new in contrast to that past. Collective taste, which is expressed in fashion, is a product of social interactions and experiences.

The particular role of fashion in the lives of some women is nicely summed up by Sarah Mower, Fashion Features director of *Harper's Bazaar*, originally writing in the *Evening Standard*:

> Fashion is our play. It's our dialogue with ourselves. It's our backchat to other women and underneath that, our coded competition with one another. Fashion is what we do instead of cricket or duffing each other up on a Saturday night.
>
> (*The Guardian* 2, 19 September 1996: 6)

This sort of view might be held by only some women and perhaps a few men but it does show how fashion is a social engagement within culture. Much of the *haute couture*, catwalk fashions are designed to be seen rather than worn but there is a 'spin-off' effect as certain designs or features are picked up by other designers and, more importantly, appear in mass produced garments. Fashion is also incorporated into individual clothing styles by altering clothes and recycling old fashions through second hand markets and hand-me-downs.

FASHION AND CULTURAL IDENTITY

Angela McRobbie (1989) describes the mixture of market stall holders who recognized some value in second hand clothes and the imaginative customers who found ways to integrate them into their own wardrobe. To begin with, these markets were outside the circuit of fashionability defined by couture houses, fashion magazines and fashion editors in newspapers. In the 1960s a generation of young people were attracted by the natural fabrics and craftmanship of clothes that had survived to be recycled. The old styles were recovered, not through nostalgia, but for an enthusiasm for putting together new and old ideas of what would look good. For example, the colour and decoration of military dress uniforms was taken at face value, not as an insignia of rank or membership of a particular unit, and were worn by the hippies unbuttoned, with jeans and long hair. McRobbie's short history shows that between the 1960s and the end of the 1980s a series of recyclings of clothes were connected with the development of punk, the new romantics, glamour and cross-dressing styles. All of these were street 'fashions', created on the margins of commodity capitalism which in time began to feed back into the fashion industry which either reproduced the originals or mimicked the modifications achieved by street fashion.

The idea of fashion as part of youth culture has become a theme in British cultural studies (Willis 1975; Hebdige 1979) and disturbed the traditional ideas of fashion as something associated with the upper classes and 'trickling down' through the class structure or with *haute couture* and dispersal through the high street. Instead, fashion, or the wearing of clothes to distinguish social groups, has become associated with the idea of style 'bubbling up' from the street to influence high fashion. The plethora of styles that remain in fashion in the 1990s has led Ted Polhemus (1994: 130–4) to write of a 'supermarket of style' available for the young or would-be-young to choose from. The emergence of a 'fashion pluralism' has been noted before of course (Bell 1992; Davis 1992). What the account of second hand and 'alternative' or 'subcultural' styles tells us is that the material culture of clothes is not simply determined by a single hegemonic cultural process, although commodity capitalism and the ideological fashion system is never far behind.

If the idea of fashion becomes disconnected from the macro-social changes of modernity and linked to the later emergence of subcultural styles, the relationship between fashion and individual identity becomes more important. Joanne Finkelstein (1991) argues that a particular sensibility linking appearance and image to a subject's personality and character emerged at the beginning of the modern period, and has led to strategies oriented to 'fashioning the self' in late modernity. This fascinating argument explores responses to human deformity, literature about changed bodies, and medical interventions to create 'beauty' as well as the role of clothes. Finkelstein argues that the features of clothing such as the necktie, a garment that is useless for keeping the body warm and protected, function to support the personal and social identity of the wearer:

> The tie must be worn as if it were a natural appendage: from its pivot at the throat, the tie should hang along the body as if it belonged. Thus, the status generated by the tie is paralleled by its unobtrusiveness.
>
> (Finkelstein 1991: 126)

The tie is a small part of a dress code that seems very simple; it is associated with masculinity,[1] a white collar job and a claim to power and status. It is also the site within the sombre uniform of the business suit in which adornment and colour in male attire can be expressive of allegiance (old school tie) or personality (exuberant patterns and shades). The material of the tie can express luxury and status not only through the richness of its material (silk, crêpe de chine) but also through the difficulty of cutting and working such materials. Finkelstein points out that the tie is 'a sign of conspicuous immobility' (1991: 120) worn to best effect when the wearer is inactive or idle. She makes a powerful argument that a series of clothing indicators such as the necktie, the business suit, lipstick, dresses, skirts, stockings and heeled shoes carry straightforward messages of gender and status. The fact that such clothing features may be used as masks to hide behind or subverted through people 'dressing up' or 'cross-dressing' does not alter the power of these messages to communicate about human character (see Ash 1996). The argument presents the modern person as one who controls her or his own distinct 'self' not through rumination or reflection but through external objects, often commodities (Finkelstein 1991: 172). For Finkelstein, the delusion of late modernity is the excessive concern with image, surface and appearance rather than personality (Finkelstein 1991: 119).

Jean Baudrillard (1993a [1976]) is much more ambivalent about the role of fashion in modernity and steers a fluid line between any essential notions of self or society. As he compares pre-modern cultures with modern, he reveals the quality of symbolic exchange and shows how the signification of clothing and the signifieds of fashion become unthreaded in late modernity. He suggests that fashion itself is indicative of life in late modernity; indeterminate, stripped of reason and liquefying of values and meaning. Compared to moral, linguistic or political codes, clothing codes are a relatively trivial part of people's lives but for the sociologist the play of the codes provides an indicator of the state of culture. For example, Baudrillard notes the way that fashion plays promiscuously with the past, reviving styles and cuts, colours and features, and as it does so, recalling but not readopting the values and meanings associated with them. Fashion acts as a living museum that stockpiles signs, extracting them from the flow and change of culture. Whereas the historical time of production and technology is linear, the time of fashion is cyclical.

For Baudrillard fashion is not reducible to anthropologically interpreted rituals and dress codes, it has to be grasped aesthetically and in relation to modes of thought. Fashion signs are 'afloat' in their indeterminacy, no longer connected to class, gender, occupation. The forms of fashion have no model; they are not derivable from another system so, as Baudrillard puts it, they are 'never produced, but always *reproduced*. The model itself has become the only system of reference' (Baudrillard 1993a: 92).

This field of signs, floating, influenced by previous signs but undetermined by the practicalities of experience, cannot be reduced to the operation of individual will or consciousness. Those entering the field of fashion (not only fashion as clothing of course) might feel that they are playing freely, letting their creative energy and imagination guide them to choose one sign rather than another. But for Baudrillard the fashion strategies of recycling, mix and match, subverting established dress codes, founding new ones, all demonstrate the *pulsion* (the drive) of late modernity to desire the code itself rather than to communicate messages of substance. The same happens with poetry which intentionally explores the possibilities of the linguistic code, or other art forms where an 'avant-garde' plays with conventions and traditions.

So far the idea of wearing clothes as fashion has tended to suggest that it is to do with the relationship of the individual to the society in which they live. The cycle of fashion, its speed of change, the sources of new ideas, all seem to be linked to the historical changes that occur in modernity. But perhaps this link between fashion and culture has run its course: the 'supermarket of style' indicates a breakdown in what was once a system of cultural communication that used the material form of clothes to carry messages about status, gender, wealth and the integration of the individual. Even if this link between fashion and the form of society is breaking down, fashion as distinction in the dress codes of work and domestic life, of street and party clothes, sustain meaning for wearers and their viewers while catwalk fashion suffers from the 'the subversion of all order' and the 'hell of the relativity of all signs' (Baudrillard 1993a: 98). It is in the routine of everyday life that such simple clothing codes as dressed/un-dressed, tops-but-no-bottoms/shaved crotches become established.

CLOTHES AS WRITING

The idea of wearing clothes as a way of communicating meanings that are more or less independent of fashion has always been popular. In

1957 Barthes distinguished the *langue* and *parole* of the clothing system as *costume* (the social institution of style, the store of possible styles) as opposed to *habillement* (the individual choice from the possible choices, the clothes actually worn) (Barthes 1957: 435). The system of relations between these two structures, one social and held in the awareness of the community of users, the other personal and manifest in material culture, makes up the *langage* or clothing system. The whole clothing system changes over time, not in a mechanical or wholesale way but by tendencies in a flexible system. As with a language, the whole system cannot change simultaneously or the individual capacity to make clothing choices (*habillement*) would collapse but changes to the clothing system can be far more rapid than those in a language. To illustrate his argument, Barthes uses the example of funeral clothing which used to be white but now is black (see also Hollander 1993: 373). The actual colour is not in any natural way tied to the social act of mourning but what is important is the social recognition of *a* colour for mourning clothes in a culture (*costume*) and then individuals recognizing that colour in their choice of clothes when grieving (*habillement*). Barnard (1996) draws out the logic of a structuralist approach to clothing as meaningful communication; his example of the arbitrary link of signifier to signified is pink and blue booties to indicate the sex of a baby.

Barthes's structuralist approach to treating clothing as a language system is not widely referred to although the general idea has become commonplace. Rubenstein (1995) for example borrows Goffman's (1959, 1963) dramaturgical metaphor to describe how clothes create particular images of power, authority, gender and seduction. People dress for 'front stage' when they wish to impress with their seriousness and worthy intentions. In the 'outside region' clothes wearers relax, taking off their ties and changing into 'casual clothes'. Rubenstein calls the clothing cues that identify wearers as a member of a social subgroup 'clothing tie-signs' (1995: 191). She gives the examples of Hare Krishnas, the Amish and Rastafarians but we could include the un-dress codes of the clothing optional resort. Tie-signs often link groups who are somewhat marginal in society, especially groups who dissent with society-wide cultural values. 'Clothing tie-symbols' on the other hand are expressions of support for an idea or a cause such as lapel ribbons or badges: they express values that the individual has consciously chosen rather than acquired through adopting a style (Rubenstein 1995: 206). Rubenstein is drawing on an interactionist approach which owes much to Stone's (1962) work exploring how people responded to each other's dress.

Allison Lurie (1981) has used the metaphor of clothes as a language to enable her to interpret the tone of what clothes are saying:

> Casual dress, like casual speech, tends to be loose, relaxed and colourful. It often contains what might be called 'slang words': blue jeans, sneakers, baseball caps, aprons, flowered cotton housedresses and the like. These items could not be worn on a formal occasion without causing disapproval, but in ordinary circumstances they pass without remark.
>
> (Lurie 1981: 8)

This simple level of meaning in clothes can however become very confused. Cullum-Swan and Manning (1994) look at the simple T-shirt as a casual clothing item that becomes the bearer of ever more complex codes as it is drawn into mass production and the fashion system, until finally it becomes a surface on which language itself in the form of text, slogans and image can be presented. The meaning of the words, let alone the garment, becomes confused by irony ('This is a T-shirt') and cultural references (Bart Simpson screaming 'Cool your jets man') when clothing and language are combined.

Whether it is the writing on the clothes or clothes as writing, there are problems about the capability of these material objects to communicate meanings specifically and flexibly. Fred Davis (1992) points out that ordinary language is a communication system in which complex messages impart abstract information in an interactive process and in comparison clothing is 'undercoded' in that the link between signifier and signified is unreliable:

> *meaningful* differences among clothing signifiers are not nearly as sharply drawn and standardized as are the spoken sounds employed in a speech community.
>
> (Davis 1992: 13)

A further problem with analysing the meaning of clothing as a language is that it is unable to take account of 'fashion'; the system of signifieds is on the one hand fixed in contextual styles (such as uniforms or subgroup codes) and on the other changing so rapidly that 'meaning' is in constant flux. Campbell (1996) also argues that we cannot conflate meaning with the clothing object itself. A fur coat might have symbolic meanings associated with class, glamour and animals but there are also instrumental reasons for using the object (warmth, comfort) and perhaps personal meanings (it belonged to a beloved grandparent). Clothing items cannot be treated as signifiers in a system of meaning constituted by the material of all other possible items of clothing. Interpreting the meanings of clothing objects requires looking at them in the context of a lifestyle along with other clothing choices, objects and activities. So, for example, failure to follow a clothing code would disturb the flow of interaction – 'forgetting' to wear a tie to a business meeting may unsettle the other participants. The habitual wearing of a style of clothing, say, a woman wearing fitting trousers and a bare midriff, may be construed as a lifestyle choice to fit with the flow of action and interaction at her evening dancing in a club. In these instances the clothes have meanings which are not properties of garments but of the garments-in-a-situation.

WRITTEN CLOTHING

Barthes (1990 [1967]) recognized this problem with clothes – that they don't speak for themselves – when he came to apply his semiological approach to the fashion system. This work was not a great success (Moriarty 1991; Calvet 1994) in applying the tools of semiological analysis to clothing and has largely been ignored or referred to obliquely in the literature on clothing. This is because the book is about what Barthes calls the 'fashion system', a cultural system that includes language, images and clothes, but he chooses to study only the linguistic component of this system by analysing the statements made in a series of fashion magazines. From these statements he derives a 'vestimentary code', more or less equivalent to the signifiers out of which clothing fashion is constructed. This analysis is detailed and painstaking and so rather tedious. It seems to lack the flow and imagination of Barthes's earlier analyses of cultural forms in *Mythologies* (1973; 1979) which link the distinction of form to cultural and ideological importance. In *The Fashion System* (Barthes 1990[1967]) the discussion of meanings, of the possible signifieds, is dealt with separately in an analysis of the 'rhetorical system' in the second half of the book. The failure of the work is perhaps in terms of these two subsystems not adding up to make a coherent and graspable 'fashion system'. This 'failure' of semiology came to be a strength of Barthes's later works, especially *S/Z* (1975 [1970]) and led to the post-structuralist realization that there is no fixed or determined relationship between signifier and signified in mythic systems. Meaning is more fluid than can be captured by a single code; different codes within the same system do different ideological work.

The remarkable thing about *The Fashion System* is that the vestimentary code is a linguistic system that has almost a direct equivalence to the material stuff of clothes. It provides the means for describing the *substance* of clothing as items ('objects' organized as 'species', 'classes', 'genera') that have components ('supports') which vary ('variants') and exist in relations with each other – and to the human body. For example the variants of connection are to do with how two garments in an ensemble are connected together: '*a blouse floating over a skirt; a toque matching the coat; a twin set brightened up with a silk scarf*' (Barthes 1990: 151 – I have added underlining to indicate the variants). The limitations of this system are material; the properties of different garment-making materials and the usual form of the human body which those garments will cover. The combination of materials and body limit the range of possible garments, though not the precise form of the garments for which there is, potentially, infinite variation. But Barthes is deriving the system from examples of language used routinely to describe changes in clothing and not from a phenomenology of the material world or an analysis of wardrobes. What he is doing, via his analysis of the statements in fashion magazines, is to set out what I shall call a 'material discourse' of clothing. This is both the *language* that must be used if clothing is to be described in sufficient detail for the changes in fashion to be apparent and at the same time the *material* system of clothing items and features by which fashion, in the form of material clothes, is realized. The vestimentary code is not the language of a dress-maker or a specialist in making cloth, but it is the language of the fashion watcher, both the writer of the fashion magazine and its reader.

The language of the vestimentary code is what makes the clothes part of the fashion system; Barthes is pointing out that fashion does not exist in the form of clothes themselves but must be modified through discourse if the values of 'in fashion' or 'out of fashion' are to be distributed through the culture:

> In the vestimentary code, inertia is the original state of those objects which signification will seize upon: a skirt

> exists without signifying, prior to signifying; the meaning it receives is at once dazzling and evanescent: the 'speech' (of the magazine) seizes upon insignificant objects, and, *without modifying their substance*, strikes them with meaning, gives them the life of a sign.
>
> (Barthes 1990: 64–5)

There are potentially many sources and types of utterances that give significance to items of clothing (ordinary talk between clothes wearers for example) but Barthes has found in fashion magazines an accessible set of statements available to be analysed. Prior to some sort of discourse, clothing has no meaning; Barthes's analysis shows how clothing objects are appropriated by a culture through discourse such as that of fashion magazines.

The rhetorical code is that which gives meaning to the formulations in the vestimentary code. In its simplest form the rhetorical system of fashion is the utterance which tells you what is, or will be, the fashion:

> *Women will shorten skirts to the knee, adopt pastel checks, and wear two-toned pumps.*
>
> (Barthes 1990: 37)

This statement has a structural form:

> short skirts • pastel checks • two-toned pumps ≡ Fashion clothing ≡ Fashion

The fashion statements in magazines also describe the clothes in relation to the world, suggesting the sorts of places or activities that particular garments or ensembles will go with.

> *This blazer is for the girl who's something of an Anglophile, perhaps smitten with Proust, who spends her vacations at the shore.*
>
> (Barthes 1990: 247)

The structure of this statement is more complicated:

blazer • Anglophile • Proust • seaside ≡ Fashion
clothing ≡ world ≡ Fashion

The wearer of the blazer is inserted into a set of worldly relations which give value to the blazer (Anglophile, Proust, seaside) but they are in turn given the value of being fashionable.

The rhetorical system is the way that fashion becomes linked to the flow of the modern world. It is not the real world of action and interaction or even of material clothes, it is the world of fantasies and ideas, of images and significances, in short the world of ideology. The rhetorical system has three registers according to Barthes – the poetic (alliteration, rhymes), the world of fashion (association, place, activities, types of people) and the reason for fashion (function of the item or ensemble). The problem with the rhetorical system is that the link between written clothing and ideology is vague and, compared to the systematicity of the vestimentary code, analysis of the rhetorical code is also forced to be less formal and precise. As Barthes accepts, the realm of the rhetorical signified is usually 'nebulous' and 'this is where the system, touching the entire world, comes undone' (Barthes 1990: 232).

The fashion statements that Barthes analyses are from the sorts of magazines that are characterized by photographs of the clothes mentioned and the settings they are worn in.[2] They will be worn by models who give the clothes a certain shape and pose that is also part of the fashion system, but Barthes has hardly anything to say about this despite his interest in the photographic message (Barthes 1977a; 1977b). He does point out that in image-clothing the whole ensemble, or at least what is visible, absorbs the whole being of the garment in what he terms a 'configuration (*form, fit, movement*)' (Barthes 1990: 119). Written clothing focuses on specific features giving them value and making them signify through the force of the abstraction from real to written. For example the complex feel of a garment can be represented by a single word such as 'clinging'. What written clothing does is to attach meaning to what is a small, finite element which in the real or image-form is part of a complex structure. This is precisely why the written system is ideal for analysing the fashion system, which is one of change.

But the 'look' of clothes is part of the way that they are appropriated as material objects. Anne Hollander puts it like this:

> The way clothes look depends not on how they are designed or made but on how they are perceived . . . People dress and observe other dressed people with a set of pictures in mind – pictures in a particular style. The style is what combines the clothes and the body into the accepted contemporary look not of chic, not of ideal perfection, but of natural reality.
>
> (Hollander 1993: 311)

There is a 'scopic regime' (the term is Christian Metz's: see Jay 1992) of clothing as well as a written fashion system. Ways of seeing are an important aspect of distinguishing between clothes as material objects. The detail as articulated in the vestimentary code may signify the specifics of fashion, but the look of the ensemble, including the setting, is a key aspect of fashion that is irreducible to words. Hollander argues that our perception of what we see when we look at clothes on someone else or on ourselves in a mirror has already been acculturated by our visual learning. It is through paintings, photographs and cinema that we learn what things should look like; what is beautiful and pleasing, what is natural, what is shocking. Hollander looks at the relation between clothing and the body and figurative representation. She shows how what is taken to be acceptable in fashion, what is 'normal' whether in body shape or costume, is established through a visual culture of the image. She argues for example that the way female social and sexual freedom is expressed through dress is not through a particular form of dress but through a reaction to the accepted norms. A new sense of freedom can be conveyed through trousers, short skirts or long skirts but it is what went before that determines which specific form carries the new message (Hollander 1993: 312–13). She dismisses the emergence of women's trousers as a dominant fashion in the middle of the twentieth century as being more 'comfortable' – the actual reason she claims was 'visual indigestion' with the variations on the skirt (Hollander 1993: 349).

Visual culture makes values such as beauty appear natural and timeless; the ideological effects of the visual codes are at least as difficult to unpack as the linguistic codes of fashion but Hollander's analysis points to the historical contingency of ways of seeing clothes.

MATERIAL SURFACES

The discussions of clothes and fashion considered so far have been macrosocial in that ideas of what is appropriate to wear derive from values that are sustained through cultural dissemination, through cultural groups, through the accepted meanings of clothes and through the fashion system including images. Peter Corrigan (1994) has looked at a more intimate economy of clothing – people's wardrobes. He found that between a quarter and a third of items were 'gifts' – some bought, others cast-offs, some had been borrowed without permission. This very small study reminds us that clothes are often acquired, chosen and worn through a variety of social processes that are on the margins of anything approaching a fashion system. Corrigan writes of a 'familial-sartorial world-view' (1994: 443) that refers to the non-cash, non-public, informal economy that determines what many of us actually wear. Within the family, in peer groups and among friends, ideas about what is appropriate clothing are passed on, criticized, refused and revised. These ideas moderate the influence of culture-wide forms of mediation – magazines, newspapers, television, film – and of style leaders – actors, singers, models, designers and so on. This informal approach to wearing clothes is not anti-fashion (as Baudrillard points out, 'fashion makes the refusal of fashion into a fashion feature – blue-jeans are an historical example of this': 1993a: 98) and will take place within some established codes of appropriateness of different clothes for gender, occasion and activities. The everyday response to the clothes is oriented to what they look like rather than what they look like in a photograph, how they feel rather than how they are described, how others respond to them not as abstract indicators but as particular clothes on a particular person's body and how the garment ages. In other words, how clothes are when they are being worn out.

Blue jeans are something of a conundrum because while they clearly are part of fashion in that they constitute a recognizable style of clothing, at the same time they express an ambivalence to fashion. They have remained a style of clothing that makes a fashion statement for 50 years but have never the less remained available for many different meanings to be attributed to them – as well as being regularly re-introduced as a 'classic' form of clothing. These features of jeans as fashion have often been commented on (Fiske 1989: 1–21; Davis 1992: 108; Fine and Leopold 1993: 140; R.R. Wilson 1993: 98) and some commentators have given direct attention to jeans as a fashion classic with a remarkable design history (Sudjic 1985; Cuomo 1989; Rica-Lévy 1989; Scheuring 1989; Finlayson 1990). But I wish to argue that there is something in the nature of the material form of the garment that makes jeans available for this particular fashion history and ambivalence of meaning.

Denim jeans threatened to break with the tranquil order of modern life when they moved from rural work clothes to become an emblem of urban youth reacting to authority.[3] These meanings became attached to the garment, according to the commentators, as they girded the loins of James Dean and Marlon Brando in films of the 1950s (Scheuring 1989: 227). Jeans went against the grain of the dominant clothes culture of western modernity and reversed many established clothing signifiers. They were made of cotton (vegetable) instead of wool (animal); fixed in shape instead of tailored; had visible seams but no pressed creases; revealed the form of the body rather than covering it. This can be summed up as a set of reversals of the material features of the tailored lounge suit (see Wright 1996). The tailored suit presents fineness of material, cloth which is smooth, consistent and restrained in colour but hangs from the body, seams which are invisibly stitched, buttons which blend in colour even when they are decorative. In contrast with the formality of the tailored suit, jeans are 'casual' or 'leisure' wear. But they are also 'workwear' in so far as that was how they originated – so the oft-repeated story of origins goes – and continue to be workwear for many people, both in paid work and private domestic work. Jeans are made from hardwearing cloth that is resistant to ripping when stressed through bending and stretching, many seams are double stitched and there are 'strengthening' rivets at key points. These are material indicators of the appropriateness of jeans for activities that will put the clothing under stress – using the body for lifting, pulling, carrying heavy objects, dealing with dirty or potentially damaging materials. They are of course no more appropriate for these tasks than overalls, work trousers and dungarees, all of which have become 'fashion' garments for periods of time. The difference is that jeans are made from denim and are cut in a distinctive way.

As leisure wear for men, jeans have replaced a range of trouser styles that retained a much closer affinity with the dark lounge suit:

- slacks – lighter in colour and material than the lounge suit but retaining the crease and the fineness of material and cut

- tweeds – a rougher, aristocratic form of the worsted suit, appropriate for the countryside, shooting, fishing, walking
- flannels – the soft light woollen version of suit trousers, used for sports like cricket and golf
- twills – the diagonal wool weave that tolerated the knee bending of horse riding.

The tweed 'sports' jacket or blue blazer together with slacks or flannels provided the ideal leisure wear for the white, western classes who could afford clothes purchased for leisure. Poorer classes traditionally wore third best clothes, originally bought to fit into a cycle of best, everyday work clothes and weekend clothes. In postwar USA the khaki cotton twill chinos, white T-shirts and leather 'bomber' jackets of ex-service personnel provided the model for leisure wear.

Perhaps the most powerful cultural feature of jeans as clothing objects is that they are worn by both sexes. The wearing of jeans by women signals their release from the gendered clothing of formal dress. Trousers became acceptable for women first of all in sporting and leisure situations (there is a long tradition of women wearing trousers or breeches for riding). Although designed for men (work trousers, front fly), jeans became an acceptable substitute for slacks and other leisure trousers (capri pants, pedal pushers) that women wore in the USA in the 1950s. These cotton, close fitting trousers often coded the gender of the appropriate wearer with a zip located at the side or the back with a minimal placket or overlap. Although masculinizing with their front flies, jeans became an acceptable substitute for other leisure trousers for women and they were possibly the first unisex garment. Jeans came from the same pattern, the same pile, in the same shop,[4] whereas suit jackets and riding breeches were structurally the same but tailored to distinguish the sex of the wearer. In the 1950s and early 1960s, jeans on women would have been regarded as a possible sign of lesbianism, along with short hair and no make-up.

In wearing jeans for leisure there is a parodic form of conspicuous consumption. For the office worker, wearing jeans to the cinema, the coffee bar, the pub or just for lounging, there is a display that the wearer is not working. There is a display of 'pecuniary strength', as Veblen (1953[1899]) puts it, in being able to purchase jeans just for leisure, but it is parodic of the display by the wealthy of their continuous leisure with the elite hallmarks of tailoring and quality cloth because jeans are workwear. Jeans are democratic rather than elite. Each pair is mass produced and cut the same, regardless of the shape of the body they cover, and all are made from the same, basic quality cloth in exactly the same colour – blue, the colour of the blue collared industrial worker, working with metals and machines.

Of course the fashion system has produced designer jeans with labels that signify degrees of pecuniary strength and the form of jeans has varied with fashion (flares, bell bottoms, hipsters, baggies etc.) as has the colour (black, white, stonewash etc.). But the 'authentic' or 'original' form and colour has remained dominant with its visible material features: dark blue colour; brass rivets; orange stitching; double seams on inside leg, back pockets, flies placket, crotch and back seam; through-stitched hem; belt loops; ticket pocket and the 'yoke seam' that gives the characteristic shape between hips and waist. This classic form also includes brand name indicators visible on the outside: stitching on the back pocket; 'leather' label on the outside of the waistband; tags inserted into seams. Jeans have always asserted their commodified, mass manufactured form by being self-advertising.

Distinctive and visible seams have been a constant features of jeans in all variants. With the exception of the outside leg seam, the interlocked joins of the main structural seams (inside leg, back, yoke) are strong but bulky, emphasized by the orange thread of double, parallel stitches. The visual effect of the seams is to dissect the form of the body, revealing it as made up of parts (legs) that are joined at the top (crotch, flies, back seam) and merge into a unity (the waistband). This material feature of jeans presents the body as a fetishized object, chopped up ready for consumption like the images of women in soft porn when clothing is used to divide parts of bodies – belt and garters, bra straps, shoe straps, stocking tops, half removed clothing. The cutting of the body by the seams of the jeans even presents the sexual parts. The buttocks are separated by the back seam, their cleavage is reflected in the yoke seam (and the Levi's pocket logo). The patch pockets, like a brassière, mark and emphasize the presence of buttock shapes. The flies, in true pornographic style, both hide and represent the sexual parts with a single seam on the opening edge and double seam parallel on the trouser front, both picked out with surface stitching in orange to create a six-inch long tube, running vertically from crotch towards the navel, which is both a flap and a gap in the material.

If the seams emphasize the form of the body underneath,

this form is re-emphasized by the material of the denim. The cotton twill material does not 'hang' as woollen fabrics or thinner cotton weaves do. Unlike close fitting garments like tights, hose or stockings that fit with the form underneath, the cut and material of the jeans means they are stretched against the skin, moving against it, as the body moves.[5] The material takes up some of the shapes of the particular body that is wearing it. Knees, buttocks, testicles, labia, hips, thighs, all stretch the material, moulding it in a way that doesn't fall out when the pressure is released. The stiffness of the material gathers in creases which also become impressed in the material – beside and behind the knees, at the crotch, radiating from the top of the legs, under the buttocks. The twill weave, involving three directions (up, down and diagonal) retains distortions impressed upon it and even 'remembers' them after washing and ironing.

The regular process of washing actually reinforces this reflection of the body underneath on the surface of the denim. Denim is usually a mixture of white and blue dyed cotton yarns and when new, the outer surface is mainly dark blue, the inner surface white, but the colour is not smooth and continuous. As the jeans are worn and washed, their colour fades. The effect is variegated according to the thickness of the material and the creasing. Where the body pushes at the surface, knees and buttocks especially, it fades most. The bottoms of creases remain bluer and the tops fade most so that those features of the jeans that they take up as shape are re-emphasized as colour. The effect of fading is to re-emphasize the impact of the form of the body on the surface of the jeans like shading on a pencil drawing; the colour is darkest on those points furthest away from a viewer and bodily shape is picked out in a 'relief' effect in which the closer surface is lighter in colour. As the material wears out, the body may begin to represent itself, exposed through tears and damage to the fabric. As a unisex garment, jeans reflect the body and sex of the wearer while at the same time neutralizing gender distinction through form, material, colour or decoration.

The ambivalence of blue jeans is that they are all, more or less, the same cut and colour, but each pair becomes different when they are used. They take on their identity through being worn and washed and worn; it is the identity of the wearer, not of the designer or even the manufacturer. The form of the garment has very little to say for itself, which is precisely why manufacturers have such an aggressive branding and advertising strategy.[6] The form of jeans does not carry strong connotations of class, sex or even nationality.

CONCLUSIONS

Wearing clothes is social in that what people wear is treated by those around them as being some sort of indicator of who they are. The cultural system by which the values of clothing and people are connected is generally agreed to be 'fashion'. This is a system of relationships between ideas and values, material things (clothes) and people – who wear clothes out into society. The fashion system is in constant flux in modernity and it cannot be pinned down to one system; there are competing influences and ideas that have an influence but are not precisely represented in fashion. The fashion system does not represent in any direct way social relationships of status, gender, occupation or allegiance, but it does allow for these relationships to be reflected through the changing orientation to clothes. There are also competing fashion systems within the cultural field of clothing; second hand clothes, street styles, family and peer groups, that cut across the production/consumption system of mass manufactured clothing.

Following Barthes we found that the fashion system is not accessible as a linguistic code or as a material system but only through a combination of both. Material discourse is the term I have used to point to the connection between language, material and cultural values. Hollander (1993) is also persuasive (as are many books on clothing and fashion by their example) that images are as important as words and ideas in contributing to the material discourse of fashion.

What the discussion of fashion often avoids are the characteristics of clothes as they are worn. By discussing how the materiality of blue jeans works, I have tried to show how their status as clothes is not determined simply by the fashion system or any language of clothes but emerges from the interaction between the wearer and the garment. Wearing clothes is a material experience; they are available to be looked at on other people and to be worn by ourselves. Clothes are given meaning in the fashion system by the aesthetics of design, the mechanics of production and the inducements of consumption. But the engagement of the wearer with the garment such that they become part of each other, also gives clothes meaning. Jeans more than many garments have a rigid form as fashion but become a vehicle for individual identity through their material malleability.

NOTES

1

> The conventional long tie runs from the prominent male larynx, along the torso and terminates as a signal to the male sex organ, particularly when the man is seated. In this capacity the tie links together the physical symbols of virility, and as such, can be used as a psychoanalytic proboscis that demarcates a line from manhood to manliness.
>
> (Finkelstein 1991: 121–2)

2 Barthes says very little about his method of working, which was based on a corpus of statements gathered from four magazines (*Elle, Le Jardin des Modes,* plus *Vogue* and *L'Echo de la Mode*) between June 1958 and June 1959. He does not tell us how many magazines he studied or how he chose certain statements for quotation, nor does he identify the sources of the statements he quotes.

3 The name 'jeans' derives from the material, 'jean fustian', the tough twill weave, cotton fabric used for workwear. Jean seems to be a transformation of Gene, for Genoa, indicating the original location of the material or its manufacture. Fustian is a hard wearing fabric in which cotton is mixed with flax or wool. The plural form, 'jeans', refers to the garment, which like the word 'trousers' is pluralized presumably to indicate its two legs. The word denim also derives from a place, 'serge de Nîmes'. Serge is a woollen fabric of twill weave; denim is a cotton variant.

4 Manufacturers have in recent years diversified the form of jeans so that different body shapes, including women's, can look similar when wearing jeans.

5 Umberto Eco writes entertainingly of the sensations of wearing jeans, of having 'a sheath around the lower half of my body' so that from waist to ankles his body was 'organically identified with the clothing' (Eco 1987: 192). The encasement within the clothing affects the way he moves; walking, turning, sitting, hurrying are all changed. In turn this affects his demeanour and the constraint on his body led to constraint in his behaviour. But the transformation did not stop there: 'A garment that squeezes the testicles makes a man think differently' (Eco 1987: 193).

6 In doing so, the sellers of jeans will reassert distinctions of taste, gender and sexuality. Stuart and Elizabeth Ewen are repulsed by a 1980s advertisement on a bus for Gloria Vanderbilt jeans that shows

> an assembly line of female backsides, pressed emphatically into their designer jeans. . . . These buttocks greet us from a

rakish angle, a posture widely cultivated in women from time to time, in place to place. What was termed in nineteenth century America the *Grecian bend*. The bustle. Foot-bound women of China. Corsets. High heels. Hobble skirts. Here it is, women hobbled in the finery of freedom.

(Ewen and Ewen 1992: 75)

6

PLAYING WITH THINGS: INTERACTING WITH A WINDSURFER ■

In Ventre's view, the World-Thing, to which he sometimes refers impartially as the Thing-World, opposes man's partial *stealing*, as it were of consciousness – of his dividing it into the separate 'minds' with which human history has made increasingly fatal attempts to create a separate world of men. Man's increase in this illusory domination over Things has been matched, *pari passu*, by the increasing hostility (and greater force) of the Things arrayed against him.

(Jennings 1960: 395)

Anyone who has tried to windsurf will have experienced the hostility of 'things' and will recognize the frustration with material objects that Paul Jennings (1960) turned into an account of 'resistentialism', a spoof philosophy attributed to the fictitious 'Ventre'. The top-heaviness of standing on the board, together with the articulation between rig and board which seem to give them separate minds of their own, make getting on the windsurf board difficult enough but getting started apparently impossible. Other people have managed so it must be possible; either the people have dominated the things or they, in some subtle way, have been dominated *by* the things! Jennings describes a form of theatre inspired by *resistentialisme* in which the principal characters are things and the human beings are reduced to mere *poussés* (which he translates as 'pusharounds'). The play concerns the resistance of a medicine cabinet to be fixed to a wall, a piano to be mastered and a sticky mess to be cleared up. Aspiring windsurf sailors feel that *they* are being pushed around by the board and the sail; ironically, getting the thing to sail requires balancing the rig against the resistance of the wind and the board against the resistance of the water and letting them push you along. Part of the attraction of playing with things is to overcome their resistance and to make them malleable to interaction with human beings. In this chapter I want to explore the idea of playing with things, using the example of windsurfing.

The sociological literature on leisure activities and recreational sports treats objects and things as marginal to what is an essentially human activity (Roberts 1970; Kelly 1982; Parker 1983; Rojek 1985; Horne *et al.* 1987; Olszewska and Roberts 1989; Critcher *et al.* 1995). There are of course exceptions such as Bourdieu's recognition of the significance of equipment in the leisure activity of photography (Bourdieu 1990). The potential for developments in equipment to change leisure experience is sometimes noted (e.g. Rojek 1985: 19; Heywood 1994: 186). But what is missing is any consideration of the ways in which play, which involves objects, brings about the experience of leisure. I shall discuss the idea of 'playing' and then look at how objects and humans interact and form 'actor-networks'. This will raise the question of their agency; do objects like windsurfers have any capability to be 'hostile' and resist human efforts?

THE WINDSURFER

I shall use the windsurfer as an example of a class of object that is used for leisure.[1] The windsurfer is a thing, first introduced into the UK in 1975 (S. Turner 1983), which seems of little use other than for playing.[2] It is one among a group of similar types of objects that offer extended motility to a human being and that provide a leisure experience either through being transported or through competition; skis, water-skis, hang-gliders, bicycles, roller skates, ice skates, surfboards, snow-boards and so on.

The windsurfer, like all of these objects, encourages fantasies about what it can do for someone who plays with it. It can enable a human being to skim over the water, blown by the wind, in a manner at once natural and yet so alien to the body. The usual limitations of the human body keep it immersed in water, vulnerable to being buffeted by the wind wherever it is exposed. But the object of the windsurfer enables its sailor to transcend these constraints, raising the person onto the surface of the water and harnessing the propulsion of the wind. The resulting experience of speed, with a certain acrobatic grace, liberates the body from its humdrum uses and experiences. As a sign the windsurfer connotes freedom, escape and excitement. As part of an activity it can deliver such things.

To windsurf a person needs money to buy (or even hire) the equipment (board, sail, mast, boom, harness, wetsuit) as well as the time and ability to indulge in this form of play. This means that unemployed people and those with low incomes are effectively precluded, as are many whose incomes are less available for leisure, perhaps through family commitments. People with insufficient physical coordination, balance or strength will be limited in ability to take part. There is also a requirement for commitment on the part of the person who wishes to windsurf; there are sacrifices in other aspects of life that have to be made if the aspiring sailor is to make any progress (see Wheaton 1999).

It is arguable that windsurfing is a distinctly masculine form of play; it involves technology, functioning objects, individual activity, excitement through action, movement in space. Of course this type of activity is not in any essential way gendered although it is likely that it appeals to more men than women in contemporary culture (in Wheaton's ethnography between 10 and 20 per cent of the participants were women: 1997: 83). Women take part at all levels, in all aspects of windsurfing, but they are likely to be effectively excluded from participating, partly through their more limited access to resources and partly through the effects of gender ideology on how women should behave – or even move. Val Woodward (1996) discusses the different orientation of women to windsurfing, drawing on interview data and the literature on women in sport. She cites Iris Young's work on the different ways women and men have learnt to use their bodies and the constraints this places on women in sports whose 'learnt feminine body movement starkly contrasts with body movements needed for a relaxed and efficient windsurfing style' (Woodward 1996: 7).

There is then a leisure class, not in terms of the traditional 'productivist' economics on which Veblen's (1953[1899]) analysis of conspicuous consumption was based, but in terms of those people who are in a position to windsurf as a leisure activity.

PLAYING WITH THE WINDSURFER

To show how an object like a windsurfer is incorporated into social action I want to explore ways of thinking about play derived from Caillois (1961[1958]), Mead (1962) and Elias and Dunning (1986). They describe the social forms that are constitutive of play and leisure; I shall insert the object (the windsurfer) into their accounts.

For George Mead (1962: 149–54) engaging in play is a characteristically social activity. It involves active negotiation with an 'other' who understands the meanings exchanged in the play and is one of the ways that human beings learn and confirm the social values of the group of which they are a part. It is a context in which individual identity – the self – is discovered and expressed and shared with others. Mead describes a form of play, which he calls 'play at something', which is directed to taking on roles, discovering the self through getting outside it and trying to be another self, or as Mead (1962: 151) puts it 'being another to one's self'. As well as talking about the play of children, he also uses the example of playing a game of baseball in a team to explain his concept of the 'generalized other' (1962: 154). In a ball game the ball itself is central in bringing about the activity; it focuses the attention of team members (and of course those of any opposing team) on the pattern of relationships between the players and becomes for them a part of the generalized other just as much as do other players (see Mead 1962: 154 fn 7). Their social organization, their construal of the team as a generalized other, is mediated by the ball and the sorts of actions it requires of them (kicking, bouncing, passing, shooting, stopping, catching) in the context of the particular game of which that ball is a part (football, baseball, netball etc. – each ball is specific to its game and calls forth the rules and conventions of that game).

In a similar way the sailor interacts with the windsurfer to generate 'play'. The activity is specified by what can be done with the board, mast, sail and boom (what I shall call 'the kit' – the collection of material things needed to windsurf). By using the kit in the appropriate way the windsurfer can develop action that will involve getting going, sailing in straight lines, turning and returning to the point of departure. There is a sense in which sailors are playing by getting outside themselves, taking on a role that they do not follow in non-leisure time. Looked at in this way the sea, the wind and windsurfing kit are in the place of other players in a game without rules (although the constraints of the material and elements have effects somewhat like rules). The role that the sailor takes on is of one who engages with these elemental forces. But this is rather different from Mead's account, which is more to do with play as socialization, in which social beings take on the roles of other social beings to learn about them and how to respond to them in social life – as when the child plays at being a teacher. Mead's analysis of play does not have much to say about play with objects; I shall return to consider what he has to say about human interaction with objects below.

More in line with Mead's view of play, windsurfing involves interactions with other people. Although only one person is on each board at any one time, windsurf-sailors will shout, wave and grin to each other on the water to share their experience. Body movements are exaggerated to express feeling and whoops of spontaneous joy communicate to those in earshot. Off the water, or at its margins, more articulate and subtle communications about the activity focus initially on the wind and water conditions. There need be no names, no reference to personal identity or alliances; it is enough to be, demonstrably, a fellow windsurf-sailor. However, the experience of shared values, experiences and emotions can bring windsurfers together (see Wheaton 1997 for a detailed ethnographic account of such a 'subcultural' group among windsurfers).

One line of conversation, which sooner or later becomes of great importance, is discussion of the kit which is in turn linked to the skill of the sailor. Talk about the kit can be extended by a speaker because there is always more kit, somewhere else, in the car or at home or in the shop waiting to be bought. Another line of conversation refers to personal skill which adds history and fine tunes the place of the sailor-and-kit in a social order of windsurf-sailors in which skill is a prime determinant (Wheaton calls 'prowess and skill' the subcultural capital of the windsurf-sailor: 1997: 86). These two lines are often connected;

using 'better' kit requires more skill and so signifies it. On the other hand if only one had even better kit, more skill could be demonstrated; competence is shared between sailor and kit. Windsurfing has a discursive culture through which much of the pleasure of sociable participation is realized. This does not avoid the appearance on the beach of people whose kit exceeds their skill and who may be referred to as 'equipment junkies' or 'fashion victims' and provide a new line of conversation for others (see Wheaton 1997: 89). Where, when and how to play and what to play with are topics that feature not only in the informal talk of sailors but also in the formal discourse of windsurfing schools, the Royal Yachting Association scheme, instruction manuals, magazines and sales brochures.

Roger Caillois (1961[1958]) provides a rather broader and more detailed account than Mead of the place of play in social life as existing in a tension between 'paidia', the realm of fantasy and improvisation, and 'ludens', the realm of effort, patience and ingenuity. He defines play as activity which is essentially *free* of obligations beyond those entailed in the activity and *separate* in time and space from other activities, some of which may entail obligations (Caillois 1961: 10). It is a form of activity in which the outcome is *uncertain* in the sense that ends are not prescribed or planned and *unproductive* because the activity is an end in itself. The form of play is governed by *rules* and *make believe* but to engage in play is to act in a realm in which at least some aspects of ordinary social life are suspended:

> play is a parallel independent activity, opposed to the acts and decisions of ordinary life by special characteristics appropriate to play.
>
> (Caillois 1961: 63)

There are four sorts of activities in Caillois's typology that count as play: competition, chance, mimicry and vertiginous play. The first category, competition (which Caillois calls 'agôn': 1961: 14–17), emphasizes a particularly social dimension when applied to windsurfing. It is the dimension in which the competence relationship between sailor and kit is tested most forcefully and results in a hierarchical differentiation of sailors and kit; as an Olympic sport, on the 'World Tour' professional circuit and at local club events. Competence is demonstrated through a mixture of speed and manoeuvrability in a number of disciplines – course racing, slalom racing, wave sailing, freestyle (performing gymnastic manoeuvres on the board while sailing), speed sailing and long distance sailing. In each there is a constantly changing relationship between sailor and the kit through which success over other competitors is achieved. The more casual 'play-form' of the beach or lake sailor seeking fun aspires to emulate the play between sailor and kit achieved in formal competition and often involves informal contests of skill or speed.

While there is little of Caillois's second type of play (chance or 'alea' – the pleasure of gambling or gaming) in windsurfing, there is something of the third type, 'mimicry' (1961: 19–23). The dressing up in wetsuits, the attempt to complete manoeuvres which demonstrate physical skill, the apparently risky activity of braving the elements, the rules and rituals of competition, all involve the windsurf-sailor taking on a role that is other to what she or he does normally. Benjamin (1985[1933]) comments on the decline of the mimetic faculty in modern humans, perhaps he is too ready to associate play, which he regards as training of the mimetic faculty, as the preserve of children (1985: 160). But Elias and Dunning (1986) discuss the link between mimesis and play in adults by distinguishing the class of non-work, 'mimetic or play activities' directed to sociability that give pleasure to participants and spectators (Elias and Dunning 1986: 69). They argue that in contemporary society the human need to experience spontaneous, elementary excitement is channelled through activities that we recognize as sport or leisure. These 'mimetic' activities imitate the passion and emotion aroused in previous societies when everyday life was more violent and risky. For Elias and Dunning (1986: 288), much of the excitement in competitive sport is related to the contest of battle but with the risk of death or serious injury of uncontrolled violence largely removed. Leisure that offers pleasurable 'play-excitement' (Elias and Dunning 1986: 72), such as windsurfing, complements the realm of formal, impersonal, task-directed, purposeful and rational activity that is more closely associated with work-time and the routine of domestic life.

It is the fourth category of vertiginous play, which Caillois (1961: 23–6) calls 'ilinx', that is most relevant to windsurfing and is the basis of its pleasurable 'play-excitement' even when there is no competition. He takes the term 'ilinx' from the Greek word for whirlpool, from which the word vertigo is derived. Play in the ilinx category is directed towards the pursuit of vertigo and the attempt to:

> momentarily destroy the stability of perception and inflict a kind of voluptuous panic upon an otherwise lucid mind. In all cases, it is a question of surrendering to a kind of spasm, seizure or shock which destroys reality with a sovereign brusqueness.
>
> (Caillois 1961: 23)

He mentions a number of examples of ilinx type play (whirling dervishes; Mexican *voladores*; tobogganing; racing downhill; horse riding; skiing; motor cycling; driving sports cars; funfair rides: Caillois 1961: 23–6) which humans (and other animals) seek out to give themselves pleasure. The vertiginous pleasure of windsurfing is derived from the sensations of moving off, accelerating, sailing at speed and making turns, especially while moving fast; there is also a vertiginous pleasure in the disorientation of falling off! Balance is a key motor skill for sailors who not only must keep their own body upright as on a bicycle but also have to counteract the lateral force on the sail which varies with wind speed. Wind and water surface are continually changing and balance is a continuous process of responding to forces in two planes.[3] Mead's account of play focuses on social interaction and the formation of the social self in relation to society or the 'generalized other'. Caillois's account of ilinx play lays much more emphasis on the sort of physical sensations which are tied up with an activity like windsurfing. However, he relates it to a tendency towards social interaction that leads towards competitive play. As he says: 'Possessors of the same toys congregate in an accustomed or convenient place where they test their skill' (Caillois 1961: 38).

Windsurfing is a social form of play in that sailors take on a role, engage in competitive struggle and seek physical excitement difficult to find in ordinary life. I am arguing that the object itself is a key part of the pattern of activity in windsurfing which involves competition, mimesis and 'ilinx'. In leisure activities such as windsurfing and skiing, the kit or material equipment must first of all be made tractable. It is then available to interact with the sailor in overcoming the environment and only then, perhaps, in entering into competition with other windsurfers-and-sailors. The effect is a particular orientation of self to the social group and the play pleasure that results from engaging with the kit as well as from competition and mimesis.

OBJECTS AS MYTHS AND SIGNS

The role that the windsurf-sailor adopts is mimetic of the experience and excitement of a form of mobility in space that would normally be the preserve of birds or mythical beings – skimming over or walking on the water. In Barthes's account of the Eiffel Tower as a mythical object whose principal function is oneiric, the symbolic power of the object lies in the way humans are attracted to it while it remains fundamentally useless and beyond reason (Barthes 1979: 3–17). The mythical capacity of the windsurfer also lies in its uselessness which is tied up with its irrationality; it is a plaything that promises to transport the sailor nowhere other than to the realm of excitement and pleasure. As the Eiffel Tower rewards those who ascend it with a bird's-eye panorama of Paris, so the windsurfer thrills the sailor with a sea-bird's view, inches above the sea surface. In their rubber garb, harnessed to the rig and with feet linked to the board through toe-straps, sailors are transfomed like mythical characters from their ordinary state of being.

As Barthes (1973: 109) tells us, myth is a message, a mode of signification, a type of speech. Whatever its content, whether true or false, myth is always laden with cultural valuation. The mythic capacity of windsurfing gives it a cultural significance beyond the immediate activity of play. While not many people actually *do* windsurfing, many people can engage with the idea of it, allowing their imaginations to be stimulated by representations of the activity. The windsurfer shares with skis, hang-gliders and hot-air balloons the capacity to transcend the constraints of the human body through its enhancement in a relationship with a thing. This is why these objects provide potent images for advertisements; they signify desirable possibilities which sellers wish to associate with their product.

There is an exchange of signs between windsurfers and the kit which is part of what we have seen in Chapter 3, Baudrillard (1981: 82) calls 'consummativity' – the material discourse of producing value in things. The windsurfing kit itself is an assembly of signs in a code to do with the competence of the sailor, and the specific properties of the kit. Price, brand, age, size, weight, materials, colours and decoration together with shape are all distinguishing features of a range of boards and other kit. Different components can be fitted together in different combinations for different uses and sailors often own more than one board and a number of sails.[4] Choices about what to buy or what to use are influenced by the sailor's size, strength and skill, by the sailing conditions, by what is available and by how much he or she can spend. Interestingly, the diversity of equipment means that a windsurfer is not a unitary 'thing' for its owner or user. Unlike yacht and dinghy sailors, windsurf sailors do not give their boards names or paint them in a colour of their choice to personalize them.

Boards, sails and other kit are rapidly superseded in design and construction and the new kit is introduced into the material discourse each year through advertisements and by magazines who test and report on it. Fashion in the windsurfing world, as with many other commodities (cars, hi-fi systems, computers, TVs etc.), is played out under the sign of functionality (the 'function-sign' as Barthes calls it: 1990: 264). Newness is not an end in itself (for a discussion of the desire for the 'new', see Campbell 1992) but promises to be better (lighter, faster, easier to turn) in terms of the function of the object.[5] Design innovations are presented as having been proven in high-level competition then made available to consumers of ordinary production boards. For example, in the early 1990s custom built boards with long tapered noses were successful in professional competition and subsequently the 'no-nose' design became a standard production style. The development of windsurfing designs and performance has been linked with the development and application of new materials (polyethylene, polyurethane, polystyrene, epoxy resins, glass, carbon and kevlar fibres) and production techniques that give a high strength to weight ratio. While dinghy sailors still keenly race designs dating from the 1950s in classes that date back to the 1920s, few windsurf-sailors who have got beyond the beginner stage would sail on a board designed more than a few years ago. As Way (1991: 13) puts it, 'Equipment and development have come a long way since 1968; boards are now a lot lighter and easier to manage in and out of the water'.

The objects of the windsurfing kit have a seductive effect on the subject of the sailor – the seduction of play-excitement and of mimesis coupled with that of fashionability. Although by the time of writing *Fatal Strategies* (1983) Baudrillard had left behind his earlier interest in relations with material objects, signs and consumption, he describes existence in the modern world in terms of the play between subject and object:

> What makes you exist is not the force of your desire . . . but the play of the world and seduction; it is the

> passion of playing and being played, it is the passion of illusion and appearance, it is that which comes from elsewhere . . . the surprise of what exists before you, outside of you, *without you* – the marvellous exteriority of the pure object, of the pure event, of what happens without your having anything to do with it.
>
> (Baudrillard 1990b: 139)

The promise that play with a windsurfer can turn sailors from their humdrum selves into mythical, mimetic beings, is the promise of play with a pure object that is encouraged by the material discourse of text, images and discussion about the objects and their functions. This is truly seductive in that while there is no final moment, no point at which the individual is merged with the object to become a different being, the possibility keeps attracting the sailor to enter into play. Paul Rosen (1995) discusses the merging of racing cyclists such as Chris Boardman with their bikes such that they become 'hybrids' or 'cyborgs'; it is not clear whether it is the rider or the machine that wins the race (Rosen 1995: ch. 3). As in any sport, there are sailors who are so good that the fluidity of their play with the kit appears to transcend the distinction of subject and object – but even they have to stop playing sometimes.

INTERACTING WITH THE OBJECT

To windsurf there has to be an interactive relationship between sailor and kit that is constitutive of the play. The kit offers a set of possible lines of action and limitations on action and just sailing requires continuous coordination of sailor and kit within the material context of wind and water. Learning how to sail requires learning what 'messages' the equipment is giving about how it is functioning rather as if it were an extension of the body. The information is not simply about the kit but about how the board is interacting with the water surface and the rig with the wind. The interaction is completed by giving 'instructions' to the kit through movements or muscle tensions of the body. This interaction between sailor and kit is not easily learnt and while it can be reduced to a theoretical form and presented in a manual (e.g. B. Oakley 1987; Way 1991) it still has to be learnt through practice in which the messages from the objects are progressively understood and the messages to the kit are increasingly effective. Mead (1962[1934]) describes the importance of human relationships with physical things – though not in the context of play. I wish to argue that playing with things, especially complex things like windsurfing kit, involves something like 'interaction'.

We do not normally think of the relationship between human beings and objects as 'interaction' because human beings have intentions and construe meaning while things do not. For Mead of course it is the capacities of mind and thought that make human (symbolic) interaction what it is and distinguish it from animal interaction. Human interaction is not just communication

> but also an arousal in the individual himself of the response which he is calling out in the other individual, a taking of the rôle of the other, a tendency to act as the other person acts.
>
> (Mead 1962: 73)

We cannot communicate with the objects of our everyday world in the same way that we communicate with each other. It might be a fantasy of science fiction and software writers that computers will in the future achieve this capacity but at the moment we are some way from *symbolic interaction* with objects in Mead's sense. However, even though there is no sense of 'taking the role of the other' it does not mean that our relations with objects cannot be understood as *interaction*.

Mead (1962: 77–8) describes how we have an organic (physical/chemical) relation to objects but that they are 'constituted' through a social process of experience and behaviour involving symbolic communication and the mutual adjustment of meanings. It is this process of social interaction, which for Mead is prior to any mental functioning, that abstracts features from the mass of information available as 'relevant for everyday social behaviour' (1962: 80). Objects are noticed, are given attention, are drawn into relevance and constituted as meaningful through social interaction. What I have called the material discourse of windsurfing – the texts and images in magazines, the discussions between windsurfers, the kit itself – draws the objects of windsurfing into relevance.

The realm of objects constitutes a landscape in which social beings interact. Each item of the furniture of a room, for example, has value, is recognized and is part of any action within that space. Mead even suggests that the individual 'takes the attitude' of an object as when a chair 'invites us to sit down' (1962: 280) although he makes it clear that the assumption that physical things think and act as we do is 'magic' (1962: 186). What is important is that the objects in the landscape are not undifferentiated but 'call out' various responses that the 'me' of the social self responds to. Most of these invitations to act are ignored:

> The chair, the windows, tables, exist as such because of the uses to which he normally puts these objects. The value that the chair has in his perception is the value which belongs to his response; so he moves by a chair and past a table and away from a window.
>
> (Mead 1962: 278)

The objects of windsurfing form a field or a landscape of objects that 'call out' particular human interactive responses – the board to be climbed on, the harness to be put around the body, the boom to be held in the hands and so on. This 'calling out' is a very limited form of communication between the object and the human, in that the response to the invitation cannot be responded to (as a footnote in Mead's text puts it, 'The objects with which we cannot carry on social intercourse are the physical objects of the world': 1962: 184 fn 15). The flow of symbolic meaning is all one way, from the kit to the human.

The basis of Mead's own analysis of human–object relations is in the 'manipulatory area'; the human being's field of touch (Mead 1980: 119–39; see also McCarthy 1984). Here objects are constituted by their physical presence to the senses of sight and touch, to hand and eye. We experience the inside of objects as a 'pushiness' – Mead (1980: 121) borrows the term from Whitehead (1920: 43) – a resistance to the touch. The object is experienced through a transference of the experience of bodily surfaces pushing against each other:

> To take hold of a hard object is to stimulate oneself to exert that inner effort. One arouses in himself an action which comes also from inside the thing.
>
> (Mead 1980: 122)

The windsurf-sailor works within a 'manipulatory area' of the kit and has to learn the particular 'pushiness' of the board which gives resistance to movement on it according to the water state, the properties of the body and the position of the sailor. An equivalent 'pulliness' of the rig, once it is filled with wind, also has to be managed and resisted by the sailor's bodily movements.

It is the awareness of the inside of the object that enables us to have a social relationship with an object, to, as it were, put ourselves in its position:

> This resistance is the occasion for one to grasp the personal action of holding or pushing a thing from the standpoint of the object.
>
> (McCarthy 1984: 108)

It is through experiencing the inside of a thing, through sensing and responding to its 'pushiness', that we are able to collaborate with material objects, recognizing from their inside something about the rest of the world, including ourselves as physical objects. It is through this process of experiencing objects as having an inside that we identify with them and they become meaningful. Once we know something of their inside we can anticipate their response in the present or in the future, in my actions now or the possible actions I can perceive in the distance. This is what is involved in the process of learning to play with an object such as a windsurfer; its responses under a variety of conditions have to be learnt and incorporated into current action if play-excitement is to be realized.

Prior to objects entering the 'manipulatory area' in which they become available to touch, there is a perceptual area in which we deal with objects through senses of distance – sound, smell or sight. A distant object 'invites' us to action, and as McCarthy (1984: 110) puts it 'perception implicitly contains the forward-looking contact experience of the distant object'. The field of perception is one of anticipating, of dealing in advance in the mind with objects of which one has some experience. Here the meaning of the object in terms of its resistance, weight, manipulability and its use is available to the mind even though the object is not yet available to be interacted with. The presence of other objects in the windsurf-sailor's field of perception also have to be anticipated and responded to – other windsurfers, boats, buoys, the shore, waves and so on.

AN ACTOR-NETWORK

One of the difficulties that McCarthy points out with Mead's account of interaction with objects is that it seems that '*the individual constitutes its life-world*' (McCarthy 1984: 111) while at the same time the minded organism or self is a product of social interaction. This leaves little room for the complexity of *creating* objects, of designing them, of endowing them with meaning or purpose. Mead provides a way of understanding how we interact with objects that are already there and which have an orientation to action but he does not provide any help with understanding how we collaborate with objects in bringing about action. Perhaps most importantly, he does not provide a way of treating the object as a product of human actions that were intentional and invested the object with meanings. Meanings, in the communicative interaction or aesthetic sense, are carried on the surfaces of objects just as much as the meanings in the physical interactive or 'pushiness' sense are carried on the inside. Both types of meaning are built in by prior human action which is both aesthetic and physical.

In the jargon of Latour and his colleagues and collaborators, the windsurfer can be thought of as an 'intermediary' in the sense of being '*something passing between actors which defines the relationship between them*' (Callon 1991: 134). Rather than thinking of the windsurfer as a single object that exists simply in relation to its rider, this is to see the windsurfer as an object (a 'non-human') which has been designed and made by other human actors and enables the sailor to relate not only to the physical landscape but also to the other humans that inhabit it.

The connections between actors and intermediaries are what is treated as an 'actor-network' within Latourian social studies of technology. Unlike science, which discovers things that were 'always already there', technology constructs things first as projects, a system of signs, that sometimes then become objects, a system of things with which people can interact. In these studies the 'things' (doorclosers, cars, batteries, keys, personal rapid transport systems and so on) are part of the actor-network of relationships which develop technological understanding. The objects of the material world interact with human agents in a network of actors and intermediaries who are trying to bring an aspect of the material world under human control. I want to extend this actor-network approach to describe how things are incorporated into social action which is not primarily addressed to changing or controlling the material world.

Thinking of the windsurfer as an 'intermediary' in actor-networks ascribes a measure of agency to the object in bringing about social action – in the case of the windsurfer, play-pleasure. There are of course a series of problems in attributing agency to non-human objects (see Ashmore *et al.* 1994; Edwards *et al.* 1995) but the concept of an 'intermediary' seems to neatly sidestep most of these by leaving intention and motivation clearly in the power of human agents. The status of an intermediary is conferred through 'delegation' (Latour 1988: 300–4; Akrich 1992: 216; Latour 1992: 229–34) and the thing takes up its position in the actor-network through 'translation' (Callon 1986; Latour 1986: 267–9; Callon 1991: 143). The windsurf board is delegated as the source of buoyancy and the intermediary between windsurf-sailor and the water surface; it is hard and flat underneath to generate lift when driven forward over the water. The sail is delegated as the means for harnessing wind power and the intermediary between the windsurfer and the air; it is flexible enough to take up a foil shape for the wind to flow over and be utilized as a force that will drive the board. Clearly the wind and the sea are also part of the network, providing buoyancy or lift and energy. But unlike wind and sea, the windsurfer is not already constituted as part of the environment, it has to be enlisted or delegated by a series of humans for a specific use. The windsurfer is both produced in terms of the labour that makes the object and produced as a text which signifies the specificity and purpose of the object by a network that includes designers, makers, marketers and distributors (Akrich 1992: 208; Akrich and Latour 1992). Rosen (1995: 126) suggests that to think of bicycles simply as objects is limiting; they are better understood as constructs in the double sense of being physically constructed and socially constructed through negotiations between groups. The same idea could be applied to windsurfers.

There are at least two actor-networks that we can identify in windsurfing, both linked to each other. First, a sailor will form an actor-network with the windsurf kit through the way the sailor interacts with it. The board and rig (boom/mast/sail) provides continuous information and must be interacted with if sailing is to be possible. The weight of the sailor is supported partly by the board and partly by the rig and the sailor must continually adjust the balance necessary to keep sailing. The sail needs continual trimming by the hands (and hips if the sailor is also attached to the boom with a harness) to maximize speed and keep control. Steering requires both the manipulation of the rig and the adjustment of the sailor's weight on the board. At speed, steering is via manipulation of the lateral trim of the board through the toes. It is the pushiness and pulliness of the rig (via the boom to the hands, the harness to the hips) and the board (via the top surface and footstraps to the feet) that generates constantly changing information about what is happening to the combination of windsurfer and sailor. The sailor 'interacts' with the windsurfer by responding to this information with pushiness from hands and feet as well as by inclining the body in relation to the kit. What makes windsurfing unusual and gives it its particular form of play-pleasure is the multiple articulation between rig and board, sailor and kit that must be continually 'attuned'. All the controls are involved in all manipulations of speed and direction and even going in a straight line requires continual fine adjustment.

In the actor-network of board, rig and sailor, the human actor has a distinct status as an agent; it is only through her or his intention and capacity that 'windsurfing' can take place and only the actor experiences pleasure and excitement. If the sailor lacks sufficient skill or strength then the sail and board will not be sufficiently competent 'actants' (Akrich 1992: 206) to transport the human; without an adequate human the windsurfer is useless.[6] On the other hand, while its agency is limited, the material equipment constrains as well as enables the actor-network. The board may, for example, be relatively heavy and slow to plane, leaving the sailor envious of others who are getting more excitement for their investment of skill and effort.

A second actor-network extends to other actors and other equipment that participate in the material discourse of windsurfing. There will be other sailors who will see it coming and avoid it, some of whom will be impressed by its beautiful lines, others who will be dismissive of its cost or design features. The specific properties of a board or sail have been delegated through an extended network of other sailors, designers, manufacturers, marketers and so on. Properties are inscribed in the material form of the kit and translated through the descriptors (e.g. 'a raceboard', 'a dedicated slalom board', 'a wave board'), model names and measurements (of length, volume and weight) which become part of the material discourse. The sailor is likely to enlist the advice of dealers, journalists who test equipment, manufacturers' advertisements, brochures and the talk of other sailors in choosing kit.

This network would include previous sailors, designers and builders, whose experience, translated through speech, writing, photographs, kit and demonstration, also contributes to the material discourse of windsurfing. This extended network produces both new windsurf equipment and new windsurf sailors. Without these prior experiences, mediated through texts that include the object of the windsurfer itself, each designer would have to invent the whole thing and the new sailor would have to 'discover' the potential for play-excitement from nothing. The extended network of windsurfing constructs not only the object's 'availability-for-use' but also its 'use-for'. The material of the windsurf kit mediates the use that has been delegated by the network, unlike the discarded cardboard box which is used as a toboggan by imaginative children. The cardboard box may not declare itself as a toboggan (it declares as a box for carrying things in) but the windsurfer readily fits the image of that sort of intermediary which is needed to engage in the play-excitement of windsurfing.

I have extended the idea of the actor-network derived from the work of Latour, Callon and Akrich, to include things such as windsurfers, emphasizing the process of interaction between human actors and material intermediaries or actants. Interaction is not between agents of equivalent power or capacity to orient the line of action because it is only human actors who exert choice in the series of actions entailed in 'use' of the thing. None the less, the windsurfing equipment as a specific series of intermediaries makes some lines of action possible while closing off other lines. It is the interaction between the components in the actor-network that gives the action a particular form as it mediates the interactions of wind, sea and sailor – a form that may lead to play-excitement for the sailor.

CONCLUSIONS

In describing how windsurfers are used I have tried to suggest that the boundary between the 'thing' and the human is not as simple as it might at first seem. To be sure, the human is recognizably alive in ways that the windsurfer is not; the human can make decisions about which way to go, choose which windsurfer to buy and whether or not to windsurf at all. But these decisions cannot be reduced to individual human actors – although that is how it may feel to individual participants at the time

– since they occur in the context of the material discourse of the actor network.

I have tried to argue that the activity of windsurfing is made meaningful by the sort of society in which it takes place; the possibility of vertiginous play-excitement that it offers is mimetic of, a substitute for, other types of activities that would deliver similar levels of excitement, perhaps not always playfully. The activity is 'framed' (Goffman 1986[1974]) and experienced through a variety of representative or imaginary contexts in which the windsurf-sailor necessarily becomes involved. I have also argued that the windsurfer as a thing is an active part of the networks through which leisure is realized; it contributes to the experience so that when windsurfing is successful it is unclear to what extent the human is responsible and to what extent the windsurfing equipment is. There is a state of tension-balance between human and windsurfer which is constantly being adjusted in an interactive way. It is clearly the human that experiences pleasure and excitement and is finally determinative of the process because of the need for its will and physical energy to get things going. However, it is the set of properties of the windsurfing equipment that offers a systematic set of possibilities and constraints which will shape any developing line of action.

I hope to have suggested that the things that we play with cannot be treated as mere things – as inanimate, inert, incapable. True, what life they have is given to them by humans through design, production, discursive articulation and use (a series of delegations and translations), but once inserted into a network with human actors, the things we play with contribute to the action in specific and special ways to realize leisure. Even things that seem resistant and hostile at first can be fun to play with.

NOTES

1 The term 'windsurfer' is ambiguous in that it might refer to the thing, or the human sailor or to a combination of the two. Although this ambiguity neatly encapsulates the network of user and thing I shall argue for later, I shall refer to the human part as the 'sailor' or 'windsurf-sailor' and to the non-human part as the 'windsurfer' to reduce confusion.

2 Windsurfers were used by a few people as a means of getting from Cuba to Florida during a period in August 1994 when Castro tolerated people leaving

without permission. Compared to makeshift rafts they were a poor means of transport; they carried only one person, who had to be skilled in their use, there was no room for luggage of any sort, they offered no shelter and no opportunity for the sailor to rest. The risk of being washed overboard was great but at least the experienced windsurfer is used to getting back aboard and continuing sailing.

3 The pleasure of windsurfing might also be described in terms of the 'flow experience' (Csikszentmihalyi 1975) it provides for the sailor which results from the merging of action and experience; the actor loses ego, cannot reflect on the action or consider results but remains in control of his or her actions and the environment: 'The purpose of the flow is to keep on flowing, not looking for a peak or utopia but staying in the flow' (quoted in Csikszentmihalyi 1975: 47).

4 In 1994 there were 10 major international manufacturers each offering between 6 and 17 different boards – a total of around 120 different shapes and sizes, from 3.80 metres length and 260 litres volume down to 2.5 metres and 80 litres (*Boards*, December 1994: 9). The 16 major manufacturers produce nearly a 100 different sail designs between them, each offered in a range of 4 or 5 sizes usually between 4 and 7 square metres but occasionally down to 3, and up to 10 square metres (*Boards*, December 1994: 53). Masts, booms, fins, harnesses and so on are also sold in a wide range of ever-changing versions, each apparently designed for a specific function.

5 Rosen (1993) argues that design development within the mountain bike industry cannot be understood by simple reference to production techniques and enhanced performance. Reference to the development of the culture and economy in general and to the response of marketing and business strategies, is needed to understand the diversity and distinction of ever new products. The same could be said for the windsurfer industry, which is also post-Fordist and operating under similar postmodern cultural conditions to those he describes.

6 Advertisement for second hand sail: 'Neil Pryde 5.5 World Cup Wave Cam. Used 3 times. Very good condition. Useless Windsurfer! £130 Tel. . .' (*Boards*, January–February 1995: 96). Here of course the advertiser is not denigrating the equipment – the 'windsurfer' refers to what I have referred to as the 'sailor', highlighting again the ambiguity between thing and human. None the less, the sail is useless unless the sailor can put it to use, which is why he has put it up for sale.

7

OBJECTS IN TIME: MODERNITY AND BIOGRAPHY

> The object I've chosen is a Strathmore glass paperweight. It's attractive to me inasmuch as it's terribly tactile. I love the smoothness of the glass and the smallness of the way it sits in my palm. The other thing I really like about it is the colours inside and the way in which the light plays in this tiny little world upon the colours. I love the way it's made up of pieces of millefiori glass that, kind of, um, has the resonances of the Anglo-Saxon period for me and the colours are so deep and striking. These wonderful greens and blues and they remind me of holidays in Scotland, the quality of the sea with the sun playing on it . . . the beauty of the little rock pools. These are all kind of, encompassed up so that the millefiori glass comes to appear like little tiny sea anemones and this wonderful clean world is all enclosable within my hands. It was given to me by a close friend as a birthday present.
>
> (S.H. speaking on a video, *More Than Things*)[1]

This woman is talking about an object which is a special possession for her on a video that was part of a 1997 exhibition called *Objects of Our Time*. She explains how the object is a 'memory capsule' in that it reminds her of periods of her life – childhood holidays, the occasion she opened the present, her historical research work around churches. As an object of her time, it stays with her, is pleasant to hold and engaging to look at. All the while as she spoke, she turned and held the object in her hands; small enough to be enclosed within one hand, substantial enough to be held with all the fingers of two. This object, probably made through a mixture of hand and machine processes, was apparently inexpensive and almost certainly one of a series of very similar objects, all slightly different due to the way the materials had been worked rather than a designed intention of the producer.

The personalized, biographical account of objects in the video contrasted with the objects on display in the exhibition, which according to the catalogue were made between 1994 and 1996 – the time was reasonably 'ours'. The pieces had not, apparently, been used or owned but their designers were named, they had 'titles' and dates. These objects were all singular, unique models only to be looked at, not picked up, touched or sat on. Some objects were sculptural, in wood, metal or clay, either directly representing figures or with figures shown on the surface of a domestically proportioned vessel. Other objects were more familiarly 'useful' – cutlery, cups and saucers, chairs and stools, dressing gowns and shawls. Some objects transformed traditional functions through the use of materials or design – lamps attached to small tables that were neither flat nor square, a radio filling the exhibition hall with Radio 4 despite its shrivelled plastic shell. All were distinctively 'designed' so that their appearance was striking and stood out from the more familiar types of such objects that might be found on sale in department stores a few streets away. They had been chosen to say something about cultural rather than personal time.

Social relations with objects change in time in two ways. First, our response to the object changes with time. In a personal possession like the paperweight, the object's biography reflects our own, but other objects change hands and their biography reflects changing human responses and valuations of them. The object itself may visually age and this may be associated with it becoming rubbish or a collector's item. There is a tension between personal possession and the place of the object within the system of objects that varies over time. Second, the form and the meaning of objects change as society changes; this was raised in relation to fashion in Chapter 5. In modernity, industrialization has changed the form of society in ways traditionally studied in sociology but industrialization has also had an impact on design and aesthetics, on the way objects are incorporated into daily lives and on the material world we move through. These are some of the themes that will be raised in the first half of this chapter. In the second half I shall look at the theme of the biography of the object as it survives in time.

INDUSTRY AND AESTHETICS

Much of the modern history of technology and industry celebrates the developments in science and technology which transformed the production of material objects but some commentators such as Lewis Mumford and Herbert Read have considered how industrialization has impacted on material culture.

Mumford (1934) describes the development of human technical ingenuity in exploiting the material world, focusing on the dramatic increase in the capacity of that exploitation brought about by the machine age. As he charts the technological developments in mining, the machinery of war and the field of engineering, he argues that social values and forms of life emerged which did not all celebrate the advantages of the new:

> Genuine value lies in the power to sustain or enrich life: a glass bead may be more valuable than a diamond, a deal table more valuable esthetically than the most tortuously carved one, and the juice of a lemon may be more valuable on a long voyage than a hundred pounds of meat without it. The value lies directly in the life-function: not in its origin, its rarity, or in the work done by human agents.
>
> (Mumford 1934: 76)

This is not an economist's account of value as arising from scarcity or the investment of labour power but focuses on how particular objects fit into the life-function of particular people at particular times. As well as describing the 'push' of developing technology on material culture that was directed to practical function, Mumford also borrowed from Veblen and Sombart a 'pull' theory of the desire for goods. Desire, he recognized, is linked to aesthetics, ostentation and the consumption of luxury to express status.

The machine is characterized by the separation of the source of energy from its application and control; it is this which transformed material culture in the modern era. The speed and endurance of machines, including the loom and the lathe which had been around for some time, was increased by making them independent of the motor power of a human or animal source. Inventions that refined the operations of machines like the flying shuttle and the rotary press also increased output for a given input of effort. Mumford recognized that the introduction of technology in production was linked to the cultural acceptance of a new way of thinking which tolerated the 'impersonality of the new instruments and machines, particularly the automata' (1934: 132–3) and brought about a shift of values towards function. Technologies which affected ordinary lives were more significant than the most dramatic and technologically innovative devices. Mumford describes, for example, how the clock and the printing press brought about in modernity the 'space–time compression' rediscovered 50 years later by postmodern cultural theory (see e.g. Harvey 1989: 201–323). The clock regularized human activities, coordinating them even when they were not co-present. The printing press enabled complex communication over large distances to many people at once, bringing ideas and inventions to people without them having to discover them or see them or even meet people who used them.

Mumford's account in *Technics and Civilization* (1934) of the relationship between industrialization and material culture was history with a purpose. He wanted to encourage a reaction to technological progress towards a 'dynamic equilibrium' in which the excessive enthusiasm of the nineteenth century for the machine would be tempered by a move towards the social, spiritual and artistic needs of culture. This included a call for the 'equilibrium of the environment' – conservation and redistribution of land use, natural resources and machine technology.

At about the same time as Mumford's polemic about keeping control of technology, Herbert Read (1956 [1934]) was writing about the impact of machines on the aesthetics of objects in everyday life. He describes the human response to beauty in the artefact as originating in design for function with the symmetrical Stone Age axe. The aesthetic later developed as the symbolic properties of objects, such as elaborate Bronze Age axes, were incorporated into culture through ritual (Read 1966). The design of objects involves a tension between function and aesthetics, which includes its symbolic and communicative features. Prior to machine production, an object revealed something of the intentions of its makers; the experience and values of their society were embedded in the design of the object. But machine production separates the intentions and values of the designer from the production of the object and threatens to disconnect them from their culture of origin. The object will have a function but it will not have the *singularity* of a handmade product; it will not embody the intentions of its creator. Each object will be one of a series, each more and more the same as techniques of standardization and precision are built into machine reproduction (for an excellent historical account of mechanization and its connection with standardization, see Forty 1990).

The tension between the functionality of machine production and the loss of intentionality in creation was often counteracted by decoration or ornamentation to show that the object had an aesthetic. A recurring theme of such decoration was the mimesis of natural forms such as waves, curls, leaves and flowers on objects that did not need these shapes for efficiently achieving their function. The modern object embodies this tension; all that is needed is for the object to efficiently function, why should it matter what it looks like? Read (1956) follows the history of this tension through the public debate about form and function, the establishment of committees, galleries, schools and educational exhibitions such as the Great Exhibition of 1851 at Crystal Palace. The objects to be produced needed to be not only useful but also appealing to people who would buy, use and accept them into their lives (see also Forty 1986: 42–61; Naylor 1990).

Forceful commentators on design in the nineteenth century such as John Ruskin, William Morris, Henry Cole and Richard Redgrave (see Forty 1986: 42; Marcus 1995: 9, 33–46) had articulated an aesthetic which rejected ornamentation to cover up the effects of machine production and applauded the work of human handicraft. Rather than return to handicraft, Read wanted to establish an aesthetic appropriate to the machine age based on classical principles of form. In *Art and Industry* (1956 [1934]) Read offers many photographs of buildings, engineering tools and everyday objects such as cutlery and ceramics that despite being produced by machines under a principle of function and efficiency, none the less displayed a beauty of form. For Read the solution was to assert the role of the artist within the context of the machine age. He argued that the power of the artist

> must be absolute in all matters of design and, within the limits of functional efficiency, the factory must adapt itself to the artist not the artist to the factory.
> (Read 1956: 61)

The interaction between art and design continued throughout the development of machine manufactured objects for use. Early in the twentieth century, art began to recycle design when the dadaists renamed objects of industrial production by signing and displaying them as 'readymade' art. The surrealists intervened in design by modifying ordinary objects to make them useless and thereby comment on the nature of materiality (for example Meret Oppenheim's 1936 *Objet: Le Déjeuner en fourrure* – a fur-covered cup, saucer and spoon). At the same time designers such as Le Corbusier, Marcel Breuer and Ludwig Mies van der Rohe produced useful objects (buildings, furniture, domestic equipment) that were regarded as worthy of celebration as works of art. While following the Morris tradition of designing a coherent lived environment, they developed an aesthetic, which we might call 'functionalism' (Marcus 1995) that embraced machine art, revelling in new materials such as concrete for buildings and steel tubes for furniture as well as the use of machines and technological skill to produce the finished item. What they retained was concern with line and form along with a high quality of production that ensured not only usefulness but also robustness and solidity. Function was not hidden beneath form, rather the form of function was revealed and treated as the aesthetic; most obviously in the tubular steel and leather chairs and loungers – Le Corbusier's *Grand Confort Sofa*, Breuer's *Wassily* chair, Mies's *Barcelona* chair (see Marcus 1995, but each is a design classic reproduced in many books on modern design and even in local furniture stores).

In the industrial age machine production had threatened to alienate material culture from social values other than those to do with practical use. But the realignment of art, design and industry recovered the practical values of function as a new aesthetic, 'functionalism', that represented the artefact as a user's object rather than an alienated producer's object. This modern form of material culture, which Simmel calls 'objective culture' and Baudrillard calls the 'system of objects', is one in which things appear in relationship to each other and are appropriated as a system prior to being acquired for use.

THE DISTANCE OF THE MODERN OBJECT

Georg Simmel, as a sociologist describing the emergence of modern society, is remarkable in recognizing the change in the style of life characteristic of modernity as linked to the shift in the appropriation of material culture. Simmel (1990[1907]) describes the cultural object as having a 'claim or demand' on the modern social subject:

> This demand exists, as an event, only within ourselves as subjects; but in accepting it we sense that we are not merely satisfying a claim imposed by ourselves upon ourselves, or merely acknowledging a quality of the object.
>
> (Simmel 1990: 68)

In simpler cultures, objects were absorbed into the practice of everyday life with little distinction between subject and object. But in modernity there is an increased 'distance' between the subject and the object which is for Simmel measured in terms of desire. This distance is at once a postponement of the possibility of obtaining the object that will deliver satisfaction and the abstract, cognitive appraisal of the object before it is obtained. Modernity brings a greater proliferation of objects that might meet needs (see the discussion in Miller 1987: 76–8) which requires that individuals make even subtler distinctions between them to identify which they desire. This is at once both a psychological process and a social one; the social subject's perspective is not simply pragmatic but incorporates 'the whole world viewed from a particular vantage point' (Simmel 1990: 60).

The increasingly complex relationship between people and material culture leads to the assimilation of objects through consciousness. Instead of human relations with objects being a practical matter of meeting needs, the awareness of material objects and their potential properties and uses precedes their appropriation. This is no longer a matter of internal awareness but becomes projected into the realm of the social through discourse; 'the inner process is, as it were, projected by the word into the external world' (Simmel 1990: 70). Representations, such as pictures and displays of the object, increase the distance between the subject and the material of the object.

Simmel is interested in how the world of the modern subject is made available as a series of impressions, of fragments, which stimulate a cool and distant blasé sensibility as opposed to the passion of engagement directly with life (Simmel 1950). This development of objectification emphasizes the aesthetic value of objects over their usefulness (Simmel 1990: 74), the place of the object in relation to other comparable objects rather than to the functional demands of everyday life.

The division of labour breaks the connection between the meaning of an object and its producer's intentions, shifting it to the network of relations with other objects:

> The significance of the product is thus to be sought neither in the reflection of a subjectivity nor in the reflex of a creative spirit, but is to be found only in the objective achievement that leads away from the subject.
> (Simmel 1990: 454)

The specialization of production, and the growth of what Simmel calls 'objective culture', led to a decline in subjective culture which at its most pure is characterized by the work of art expressing the spirituality of its single producer. In contrast 'objective culture' expresses the individual subjectivity of neither producers nor consumers:

> The more objective and impersonal an object is, the better it is suited to more people. Such consumable material, in order to be acceptable and enjoyable to a very large number of individuals, cannot be designed for subjective differentiation of taste, while on the other hand only the most extreme differentiation of production is able to produce the objects cheaply and abundantly enough in order to satisfy the demand for them.
> (Simmel 1990: 455)

Material culture in modernity is shaped by industrialization: factory-based, machine production with wage labourers taking different roles in producing each object in a series of similar objects. Simmel, however, describes how this change in the form of production alters the way objects are assimilated into the culture; they are produced in exchange for money rather than directly for use. Exchange itself becomes a form of social life which is characteristic of modern, metropolitan culture. Money becomes an 'intermediate link between man and thing', enabling people to have 'as it were, an abstract existence, a freedom from direct concern with things and from a direct relationship to them' (Simmel 1990: 469). Exchange for money requires a quantitative rationality that weighs and measures, keeps accounts and distances people from a more personal style of life.

The very range of objects available in industrialized cultures to meet an ever expanding list of identified needs is in itself a source of alienation between human subjects and material objects (Simmel 1990: 460). The increasing independence and autonomy of objects (he is thinking of domestic machines) threaten individual freedom because they are unassimilable by the ego. But perhaps the most fundamental threat lies in their capacity to keep on coming like zombies in a B-movie:

> What is distressing is that we are basically indifferent to those numerous objects that swarm around us, and this is for reasons specific to a money economy: their impersonal origin and easy replaceability.
>
> (Simmel 1990: 460)

In the *Philosophy of Money* Simmel does not offer many examples of material culture in modernity but one that does illustrate the changes he describes is the typewriter. Both a product of mechanized labour and a tool of mechanized production, the typewriter symbolizes the transformation of what was once a personalized, individual form – handwriting – into an impersonal 'mechanical uniformity' (Simmel 1990: 469). The content of what is written becomes more dissociated from the producer and treated in its own terms or in relation to other similar looking texts, rather than as the particular product of an individual.

THE MODERN WORLD OF THINGS

Changes in the means of production also affected the way objects were assimilated in terms of fitness for purpose and as aesthetically appealing in themselves. Manufactured objects increasingly constituted the material environment of the social world, and took up much of people's energy in looking at them, using them and becoming familiar, even attached to them. There are signs of a shift in the way objects were treated as they became more plentiful, more distinct from their original form and substance as raw materials, and more separate from the human work of their production.

Edmond de Goncourt, a great collector of eighteenth century art writing in 1880, called the psychology of accumulation that was emerging at the end of the nineteenth century 'bricabracomania' (Saisselin1985: xiv). The collection of items for the sake of collecting, for obsessively acquiring objects that had some aesthetic quality, became a possibility for the bourgeoisie. Saisselin charts the conditions for this manic extension of the consumption of objects linking it to the changes taking place in the great cities; the introduction of arcades as a new form of commercial gallery and department stores as palaces opened to the middle classes:

> It was in these new spaces that the nineteenth century aesthetic observer discovered the most powerful aesthetic activity and experience of the modern man and, even more important, the modern woman: the attraction of commodity and luxury items and the pleasure of purchasing same; in short, the aesthetics of buying and selling.
>
> (Saisselin 1985: 19)

While the great exhibitions had displayed the possibilities of new forms of production, the arcades and department stores displayed the possibilities of new forms of consumption. This was a change in bourgeois culture, not mass culture. Objects that were appreciated for how they looked were available to the newly enriched members of the owning and professional classes obsessed with the gathering of fineries around themselves – '*bibelots*', curios, *objets d'art*, souvenirs. The appreciation of objects involved acquiring them and displaying them in the home as part of the decor. Possession is a key element in this late nineteenth century bourgeois mania[2] – soon to become a mass mania in the twentieth century. To meet the demand, many of these objects were mass produced forms and images utilizing modern casting and moulding techniques rather than handworked traditional materials. They were often copies of classically crafted works but the importance of appearance meant that a plaster copy or an ormolu moulding were acceptable for many. The goods on display were not unique but were produced acording to an aesthetic standard that presumed customers would be tolerant that others owned similar pieces.

While only those with money could buy, just about anyone could look at these objects. Displayed in shop windows, on department store counters, behind the glass of the arcades, the modern abundance of objects provided a visual landscape that could be enjoyed by anyone. The articles, shown as advertisements of themselves, advertised again in images and descriptions, became the detail, the flora and fauna of the modern urban world, engaging the gaze and the imagination of the passer-by.

One of the inspirations for Saisselin's exploration of bourgeois consumption was Benjamin's reaction to Baudelaire's fascination with the urban wanderer who was both hidden within the crowd and gazing out from it, the *flâneur* for whom the city had become both 'landscape' and 'room'. The department store was 'the *flâneur's* final coup' (Benjamin 1997: 170) and the arcades 'both house and stars' in which the commodity appears as a fetish, 'a dialectical image', the object that is both commodity and advertisement, 'seller and commodity in one' (Benjamin 1997: 171). The *flâneur* does not own, possess or buy the material world of the arcade, he strolls through it, taking it in, inspecting it and commenting on it. Simmel had described a cultural shift from using the sense of hearing and direct communication to that of seeing, of passive absorption of the visual. For Benjamin the city, especially the Paris of boulevards and arcades, provided a 'phantasmagoria' of visual delights; the objects in the arcade window or the exhibition hall revealed themselves and their qualities without their having to be purchased and used.

Simmel (1991[1896]) provides a brief account of the display of objects in the Berlin Trade Exhibition of 1861 in which he remarks on the 'shop-window quality of things', that is, the need things have to show a 'tempting exterior as well as utility' (Simmel 1991: 122). Part of this is the aesthetic importance of showing things together, of presenting them in a set of relations with each other. What strikes Simmel is the similarity between this process and the sociological one of distinguishing the individual within society. Items on display, like people in society, are judged against each other: this one is good enough, but that one is better; these are all much the same. Distinction of worth is not intrinsic to the particular item but judged, on appearance, in relation to those around it.

The era of modernity is marked by the proliferation of made objects, their display in public, the reverence with which they are treated, both by those who can afford to collect and those who can afford only to view. The scopic regime involves not only the presentation of the objects as examples of themselves, but also the form they take on as images. Simmel comments that the marking of distinction between objects is not only a feature of exhibitions but also occurs in the relationship between advertising and poster art. Benjamin also remarks on the link between the exhibitions and the emergence of an advertising that represents 'dead objects' by proclaiming their '*specialité*' and designating their luxury quality (Benjamin 1997: 165). He describes the dying days of the Paris arcades, declining with the introduction of electric light, the ruins of the era dominated by bourgeois consumption of the bibelot. But this is no reason to ignore these objects of early modern life:

> For Benjamin, the truth content of a thing is released only when the context in which it originally existed has disappeared, when the surfaces of the object have crumbled away and it lingers precariously on the brink of extinction.
>
> (Gilloch 1996: 14)

Benjamin is interested in what the afterlife of objects has to say to us; when they are no longer current, of the moment, when they are cast aside, falling into decay, then there is the possibility that they will give up a 'dialectical image'. This is the moment in which the forgotten is remembered 'an image is that in which the Then and the Now come into a constellation like a flash of lightning. In other words: image is dialectics at a standstill' (quoted in Gilloch 1996: 113). As Graeme Gilloch explains, Benjamin's 'Arcades Project' was an attempt to create a montage, describing the nineteenth century in a series of images whose juxtaposition would bring dialectics to a standstill. For him, each historical artefact had the potential to illuminate the whole of history, each image the capacity as a moment of remembrance to redeem humanity. In the task of montage, of juxtaposition, Benjamin took his cue not from the displays in the shop windows or the exhibitions but from the work of the surrealists.

Louis Aragon, whose surrealistic text *The Paris Peasant*

(1987 [1924]) was an inspiration for Benjamin's arcades project, describes the shops, bars, barbers and brothels in the *passage de l'opera* in Paris. As he details the material forms in the arcade he situates them in a broader social context through a string of surrealistic metaphors. As Barthes was to do 30 odd years later (1973[1957]; 1979[1957]), Aragon treats these objects which inhabit the city street as constituting a mythological environment for modernity. By viewing them as dialectical images, rather than seeing them in the routine manner of the shopper, Aragon explores the meaning these objects have for their time. Petrol pumps have changed in shape and in the way they appear on the street as part of its furniture in the seven decades since he wrote of them as 'modern idols':

> Painted brightly with English or invented names, possessing just one long, supple arm, a luminous faceless head, a single foot and a numbered wheel in the belly, the petrol pumps sometimes take on the appearance of the divinities of Egypt or of those cannibal tribes which worship war and war alone. O Texaco motor oil, Esso, Shell, great inscriptions of human potentiality, soon we shall cross ourselves before your fountains, and the youngest among us will perish from having contemplated their nymphs in naptha.
>
> (Aragon 1987: 132)

The form of the petrol pump may have changed but his vision of it as the fountain of the spirit which fuels modernity's battle with the environment still rings true. The object as symbol, tied to brand names in a conjunction of meaning and function, remains the key to the objects of our time. They deliver the 'goods', signalling their properties, while simultaneously telling us who we are and in what cultural time we live.

THE BIOGRAPHY OF AN OBJECT

At the beginning of the chapter I introduced an account of a special object by someone whose personal biography was symbolized by the object. Igor Kopytoff has proposed the cultural biography of things but he has something different in mind. He is suggesting accounts that would tell us about the life of the object itself, especially the incorporation of alien objects into a culture:

> The biography of a car in Africa would reveal a wealth of cultural data: the way it was acquired, how and from whom the money was assembled to pay for it, the relationship of the seller to the buyer, the uses to which the car is regularly put, the identity of its most frequent passengers and of those who borrow it, the frequency of borrowing, the garages to which it is taken and the owner's relation to the mechanics, the movement of the car from hand to hand over the years, and in the end, when the car collapses, the final disposition of its remains.
>
> (Kopytoff 1986: 67)

Objects cannot tell their own biographies – although logbooks, black-boxes and memory chips carry useful biographical data – it has to be put together for them. Telling the story of objects has become a sub-genre within modern literature which tends to favour particular objects and television documentaries which favour types of objects.[3] Kopytoff takes the perspective of an anthropologist and his biographies are concerned with exchange. He draws a distinction between the commodity which is saleable and exchangeable and is therefore 'common' from those objects that escape reduction to this commodity status and are therefore 'singular' (Kopytoff 1986: 69). Most things are somewhere on a continuum between these ideal forms although the cairn, discussed in Chapter 1, would be 'singular' while the mini-strip would be 'common'. In modern, industrialized societies commoditization makes most goods in principle exchangeable within the same market. The move towards singularization keeps the value of certain goods above the process of exchange so that their cultural biography 'becomes the story of the various singularizations of it, of classifications and reclassifications in an uncertain world of categories whose importance shifts with every minor change in context' (Kopytoff 1986: 90). Kopytoff's notion of the biography of an object is linked to 'singularity' as a cultural status that is conferred by evaluation within a particular cultural context of exchange, within a particular historical time frame.

The process of the re-evaluation of objects has also been discussed by Michael Thompson (1979). He describes, among other things, the biography of a group of objects called 'Stevengraphs'; he remembers one that played a part in his own biography. These were pictures woven on a Jacquard loom, originally at the York Exhibition of 1879 by Thomas Stevens. They had a novelty appeal when they were first produced that derived from the scenes and portraits and from being woven by a machine. A Stevengraph cost one shilling in 1879, became worthless by 1950 and yet by 1973 could fetch £75 at auction (Thompson 1979: 14). The Stevengraphs fascinated Thompson because they had no particular cultural value when they were originally produced: they were not works of art or even the first products of a new machine technique. But in the early 1960s an American dealer bought some examples, which led to requests for more to be sent across the Atlantic. The value of Stevengraphs was dramatically stimulated by an exhibition at a London Gallery in 1963; from then on during the 1960s their prices rose, individual items were sold at a London auction house and a book on them was published in 1971. When their value began to rise and they were in effect retrieved from the rubbish heap, they had acquired a collector value; they had, in Kopytoff's terms, become more 'singular'. The increasing singularity of the Stevengraphs was helped by the cessation of production but to become more singular over time the physical object must survive intact, in sufficiently good condition to be repaired and renovated to be as 'good as new'. Durable value is precisely about the distance of time between the culture into which the object was produced and the contemporary culture in which it is revalued. The Stevengraphs, with their quaint historical scenes (Dick Turpin robbing the London to York stage coach) reproduced in silk by machine, represent a distinctly Victorian mixture of values; they became singular objects precisely when they were no longer objects of their time.

POSSESSION AND THE SYSTEM OF OBJECTS

There is a limbo between the production of an object being completed and the object being taken into possession. The thing waits in a warehouse, is in transit, sitting on a shelf, being displayed in a window; waiting to be possessed it has no claim to singularity.

Possession can be expressed in terms of the legal rights

of ownership but this is only a formalizing of the social recognition of the individual's connection with an object. There is a link between the person and the object which is physical and spatial which signals the beginning of possession. The object is usually picked up and carried, taken into the personal space of the possessor's body which usually means it is taken into the home. This physicality of possession works with gifts, purchases and thefts; any form of acquisition of a material object involves its appropriation and assimilation into the space of the possessor. The physical relationship of touch and sight is accompanied by the object coming into the care of its possessor; given space, not abused, used with respect, protected from weather and damage by animals and other people. Material objects might not accurately be described as having 'a life of their own' but once possessed, they share the life of their owner.

It is through being recognized as having a value, despite their lack of function and even aesthetic appeal, that objects like Stevengraphs are desired, and are taken into possession. This is a thoroughly modern relationship with objects in Simmel's terms and in Benjamin's it is a fetishization of the object that becomes singular through its survival into an 'afterlife'. The modern desire for the singular object is often merely to possess it. In *The System of Objects* (1996[1968]) Baudrillard argues that objects have two functions 'to be put to use and to be possessed' (1996: 86). Possession involves bringing the object into a relation with the subject which gives it a form of singularity, much like the paperweight at the beginning of the chapter. The clock, as Mumford recognized, unlike a Stevengraph, does have a function and symbolizes much of the relation between the modern object and the material culture into which it is inserted. A watch becomes a singular, personal version of the clock, always with us, available to tell the time while also chopping time itself into manageable and measurable segments. It becomes an ordinary possession situating its possessor in the time of late modernity:

> Beyond just knowing the time, 'possessing' the time in and through an object that is one's own, having the time continuously recorded before one's eyes, has become a crutch, a necessary reassurance, for civilized man.
>
> (Baudrillard 1996: 94)

The object means that its possessor is no longer dependent on someone else's clock and can fine tune the way their routine fits into that of society. The watch can of course be a fashion or status symbol, a means of displaying, even transporting wealth or it may have gained a singular value through personal possession (e.g. my grandfather's watch). But its functional capacity, its ability to keep accurate time reliably, situates individuals both in the time of their daily routine and in the time of their historical period.

Baudrillard does not relate the singularity of objects that become possessions to their place in the commodity market. He describes the 'system of objects' (1996: 137–55) as a set of relations of difference and similarity, models and series. The system is not stable over time, which is precisely why the cultural valuation of objects like Stevengraphs varies. No object is isolated, unconnected with any other object; there must always be a set of relationships of similarity and difference by which we can 'think' the object, grasp its meaning in relation to other objects about it and before it (Baudrillard 1996: 93). The modern proliferation of machine produced objects that were essentially the same, Baudrillard argues, led to the dissemination of an increasing range of material values through the culture because each model could be replicated in a series of virtually identical things. The model need not be unique because it is an ideal object held in the imagination as much as a real object. As Baudrillard points out, there is not only a well established circulation of objects but also a discursive circulation through the 'mass information and communications systems which promote models' so that 'the model is internalized by those who are involved with serial objects' (Baudrillard 1996: 138–9).

The serial object is one which is regarded as just another one, the same as the one next to it, with no claim to cultural distinctiveness. The model is in contrast an object that claims a value of distinctiveness and singularity even though it might be manufactured on a production line. Baudrillard offers as an example the Facel-Vega as a model object and a Citroën 2CV as a serial object. The limited production line and hand finishing of the former contrasts with the mass produced 2CV of which early models all shared the same colour. Of course the problem with this classification of objects is that designers and producers are keen to 'modelize' their commodities to make them more attractive to purchasers. Adrian Forty points out that the Model T Ford did change considerably over its 18 years of production, despite the company's myth of standardization and uniformity, to keep prices down (Forty 1990: 60). The policy of 'any colour so long as it's black' introduced in 1914 was abandoned in 1926 at a time when the motor industry was accepting that production lines needed to vary annually. With smaller products, variations can be introduced much more quickly. Nigel Whitelely (1993) describes how shortened product development times have impacted on design in the 1990s so that, for example, Sony were offering 50 new Walkman variants a year (Whiteley 1993: 35).

As Baudrillard recognizes, a superficial modelization happens when a thing is personalized through the body colour, distinctive hubcaps, optional extras and so on. Modelization is a form of fashion, of differentiation that simply leads to more series:

> Ultimately, therefore, every object is a model, yet at the same time there are no more models. What we are left with in the end are successive limited series, a disjointed transition to ever more restricted series based on ever more minute and ever more specific differences.
> (Baudrillard 1996: 142)

The interplay between model and series driving the system of objects in industrialized culture does not, Baudrillard argues, offer any prospect of a democratization with everyone equal before the object. The object system is one in which the tension between model and series is constantly changing but without any resolution of that tension; the more objects we have, the more we need to obtain the singular object or possess the series.

COLLECTIONS

Most people have only one watch (some do have different watches for different costumes and occasions) but this does not usually represent a passionate relationship with the object. When possession becomes a passion, the need for the object can be satisfied only by the possession of a succession of objects – the collection. Veli Granö, who collects images of collectors, photographed one of his subjects, Kaarlo Salovaara, who collects wristwatches (as well as miniature elephants and ballpoint pens) and says:

> It's so exciting. My hands start shaking when I see something interesting, I have to get it before someone else notices it.
>
> (quoted in Granö 1997: 92)

If the passion of the connoisseur is for the unique and exquisite object, the collector's passion is expressed through the possibility of possessing the series, each item singular but still linked through similarity with every other:

> In both cases gratification flows from the fact that possession depends, on the one hand, on the absolute singularity of each item, a singularity which puts that item on a par with an animate being – indeed, fundamentally on a par with the subject himself – and, on the other hand, on the possibility of a series, and hence of an infinite play of substitutions.
>
> (Baudrillard 1996: 88)

The collector's objects accumulate, gathering about their possessing subject, who organizes, classifies and locates them. They in turn reflect back a desired image to their possessor, more faithful than a dog, less honest than a mirror. It is the collector who is most sensitive to the biography of objects, both stimulating and responding to shifts in the cultural valuation of objects that are often linked to their survival beyond 'their time'. Some objects appear to cheat time, their biographies recording their survival into a world that its makers neither saw nor imagined. Such objects can provide a 'dialectical image', as Benjamin (1989: 67 – see Gilloch 1996: 113–16) calls it, through which the past can be seen; their biography and their place in the collector's series documenting the revaluations of the object – and of its type.

Collecting is a passionate rather than a functional form of possession:

> collecting is the process of actively, selectively, and passionately acquiring and possessing things removed from ordinary use and perceived as part of a set of non-identical objects or experiences.
>
> (Belk 1995: 67)

Collected objects are not acquired for use; old stamps that are no longer useful for mailing letters actually have a higher value for the collector. There is a special relationship with the objects in a collection; they are each brought into possession as if they are a part of a whole, as if at some point the collection will be complete and there would be no point in further acquisition. The collector works with the objects, orienting and identifying each item in relation to every other, arranging and even cataloguing.

The collection is a form of what we could call 'seriation' (Hayles 1996: 13); objects acquired in a serial way are then placed into other series according to some system of classification (time of production, place of origin, functional differentiation, size, monetary value, beauty etc.). As we have seen, modernity with its machine produced mass of identical objects raises a tension between the model item and the series. The modern collector – often willing to collect the ephemeral (miniature elephants), even waste (old ball-point pens) – takes a stand by recovering what might be serial in production as a model within the collection. Seriation within the collection is a form of classification and arrangement but each item is treated as individual, as distinct in some respect from all others. The motive for collection is to increase the range of difference within the class 'wristwatches' or 'ball-point pens'.

Not all collections of objects are so benign. Patricia Turner (1994) describes a series of objects that she refers to as 'contemptible collectibles':

> Peeping from amid a cookie jar dealer's collection of colorful, plump, ceramic animals or brightly glazed quaint structures will be a toothsome, overweight mammy or a neatly uniformed pappy cookie jar. Yellowed pages of once-popular rags such as 'Old Nigger Joe' or 'My Dark Virginny Gal' are crammed into countless carboard boxes of sheet music. Golliwogs, pickaninnies and the occasional ebony-toned bisque doll-baby are posed on the shelves of the doll collectors.
>
> (Turner 1994: 4)

These material objects freeze attitudes and values about race and skin colour. The stereotypical view of black people as being subordinate, poor, poorly clothed and limited in imagination was widely accepted in the culture at the time when they were originally produced. Some of these objects survived being thrown away as rubbish, having lost any decorative or entertainment value, or perhaps because of disquiet among owners of the values incorporated in such objects. At a remove in time, when these same objects have become collector's items again, the racist implications become painfully apparent. For example, Turner describes the Jolly Darkie Target Game, produced originally in 1890 for white consumers. The 'game', which involved contestants trying to score bull's-eyes by throwing a ball into the gaping mouth in a cardboard image of a black figure, has now become a collector's item. Presumably the collectors are aware of the racist implications of these objects and are unlikely to want to score bull's-eyes. Their interest in the collectibles as artefacts of a previous time seems to override the offence they may have given then and now. As Turner (1994) points out, demand is so healthy there is a roaring trade in reproduction and fake contemptible collectibles.

CONCLUSIONS

In this chapter I have argued that objects are 'of their time' in a number of ways, as products of an era, as artefacts that age and as objects whose value changes.

First, objects are a product of the technology that shapes them. In the modern era, characterized by industrialization and machine production, this has led to an increasing capacity to produce material things. More objects can be manufactured, more quickly, by fewer people using machines, which has made a wider range of objects more available to more people. The variety of objects increases as new ones are designed and some become much more complex in themselves. On the other hand, objects intended to be the same become more exactly similar to each other. The cultural impact of machine production has resulted in a shift in aesthetic standards away from the demonstration of human skill and imagination towards the demonstration of purpose – function. The alienation of objects, their increasing distance from both producers and users, has resulted in an increased respect for technology and machine culture and for the visible presence of artefacts. In the modern era, objects are as much a product of the changing sensibilities of the material culture into which they have been appropriated and assimilated as of the techniques of production.

Second, objects are of their own time in that they age according to the particular material and form that they have. They may acquire a 'patina' which becomes part of their aesthetic appeal and may contribute to their singularity.[4] As objects age they sometimes lose their functionality, perhaps because they are broken, perhaps because they have been superseded, as warming pans were by hot-water bottles. Like humans, objects are products of their time, bearing the style of their production and the aesthetic of their design under the patina of age much as humans bear the style of their education and their formative experiences under ageing skin. As the object ages it reflects features of its own cultural past. The biography of the object may be tied to that of its possessor – as with the Strathmore paperweight – but it may reflect the values of a culture, like the 'contemptible collectibles'.

Third, the object is of the time in which it is being appropriated and evaluated, through being exchanged or added to a collection. As it is taken into possession it is revalued, often contrasting with the previous cultural value it has had. This is Kopytoff's sense of the biography of things, the economic history of its previous valuations which are often at odds with its current value.

These three senses of the 'time' of an object (the history of production and reception, the ageing of the object, the revaluation of the object) show that material objects emerge into a system of objects. Over time the system changes, both because of changes in production and changes in assimilation and appropriation. Over time the object itself changes in its material form, parallelling human ageing. And over time the value of the object, its attractiveness and capability to seduce varies. The object is always singular in so far as it is produced, exchanged, possessed and used as a thing. But it always exists in relation to series of other objects, more or less similar, more or less different, that give that thing its meaning, its degree of singularity and its place in material culture. Over time that set of relations changes and with it the meaning and value of the object in the culture.

NOTES

1 The video was made by Mary Griffiths, Jeff Horsely and Liz Paul to accompany 'Objects of Our Time', a Crafts Council Exhibition at Manchester City Art Galleries, 1997.

2

> Even if a bourgeois is unable to give his earthly being permanence, it seems to be a matter of honour with him to preserve the traces of his articles and requisites of daily use in perpetuity. The bourgeisie cheerfully takes the impression of a host of objects. For slippers and pocket watches, thermometers and egg-cups, cutlery and umbrellas it tries to get covers and cases. It prefers velvet and plush covers which preserve the impression of every touch.
>
> (Benjamin 1997: 46)

3 During the 1990s this has become a popular theme of television documentary makers. The classic example is Nicholas Barker's 1994 BBC series *From A to B: Tales of Modern Motoring*, which includes people talking about their cars. Interestingly their talk is often as much of the type of car they drive as of the particular car they drive. It has also become a device for novelists so that telling the life of an object to tell the story of people around it is used by E. Annie Proulx in *Accordion Crimes* (1996) and Tibor Fisher in *The Collector Collector* (1997).

4 A 'patina' represents 'the small signs of age that accumulate on the surface of objects' (McCracken 1990:32).

8

TURN IT ON: OBJECTS THAT MEDIATE

'the medium is the message' because it is the medium that shapes and controls the scale and form of human association and action.

(McLuhan 1994 [1964]: 9)

In an important sense all objects are media. A mediating object is one that carries communications between people – information, emotions, ideas and impressions that could have been communicated by speech, gesture, touch or expression – if the people had been with each other. The mediating object carries messages across space or time (or both) between people who are not co-present. All artefacts are treated by human beings as having meaning; we recognize them, understand what their properties are, and treat them as having particular cultural significance. In everyday life we take their meaning for granted when we know what the objects are but we do come across objects that we do not recognize. These are the things that we cannot name, could not use and cannot make sense of; very new things, very old things or things that come from other cultures. These strange things are usually put on display in demonstrations, museums or exhibitions where they are treated as mediators of past, future or distant cultures and their meanings are 'translated', their messages decoded, by historians, archaeologists, anthropologists and technologists, often through the medium of accompanying texts.

A certain type of object mediates messages that are not directly recognized or translated; complex messages come out of them whenever they are 'turned on' and given attention. These turn-on-able, mediating objects are familiar parts of material culture: books; art works; telephones; record, CD and tape players; televisions; video players and computers. Usually these objects are treated as mere vehicles for media – what is regarded as interesting is the content of the messages. But what I want to do is to attend to the material *form* of mediating objects because it is the form of the objects that affects the way that we interact with them. This was precisely what McLuhan was getting at with his famous slogan 'the medium is the message'; the form of the mediating object, the functional possibilities it incorporates, the way that it commands our *attention* are what determines how it fits into material culture and competes with the messages from other objects and other humans.

Objects that mediate are not generating their own messages, they are mediating messages from other humans removed from the receiver in space and time. All objects mediate, carrying messages about the culture they originate in, but only some carry messages that were *intended* as messages. A cooking pot tells us about the culture it comes from – the technology, the mineral resources, the aesthetics, something of the style of cooking and the size of the group who eat together. None of these messages is intentional in the same way that the communication of a work of art or what is broadcast on television are.

In this chapter I shall discuss art works, ordinary objects and written texts to explore the effects of different material forms of mediating objects on the way that we interact with them and assimilate them into material culture. I shall also look at the form of telephones, televisions and computers – all modern electronic mediating objects that have transformed culture in the way that McLuhan was describing.

ART WORKS

Mediating objects have to command our attention to communicate with us, much as other humans do in face-to-face interaction. When someone speaks it commands our attention through the auditory channel: we have to hear and to listen if we are to understand the messages. Gesture and expression command attention through the visual channel: we have to watch and notice to be able to make sense of them. The sort of art works I wish to discuss here command attention through the visual channel – paintings, sculpture, installations. They are static and if we are to interact with them we have to look at them; to give them that sort of attention is to 'turn-them-on'. The amount of intensity of attention can be varied from hardly noticing as one walks past the piece, to intense attention that blots out other goings-on in the room.

The art work communicates a sense of humanity or human experience. Any representation – photograph, drawing, sculpture as well as a painting – can give the viewer a sense of displacement, of being there where the person was who made the image, either in a real place or an emotional place or a mixture of both. When it works we say we are 'moved' by what we see; usually this refers to a stirring of our emotions, but there is also the sense of having moved to the perspective of the creator of the art work, of having seen and felt what they saw and felt. There is a sense of co-presence between creator and viewer that gives the viewer the sensation of being both here, now, looking at the image and there, then, looking at what the image represents or evokes. There are clearly a number of codes that operate in this mediating process but with static art works the codes operate on two key levels. One is to do with the representation of the form of the visual world, the other is to do with emotion and the evocation of human presence.

In a short story by Edgar Allan Poe, 'The Oval Portrait' (1986b[1845]), a wounded man becomes spellbound by the 'absolute *life-likeness* of expression' (1986b: 251) in a painting of a woman; he thinks at first that he is looking at a real woman. He later discovers that the woman died at the moment that the artist completed the picture, as if her human essence had been transferred from her living body to the object of the painting. The exchange of life between the image and the real person is a recurrent theme in stories with mythical power.[1] Part of the work of the artist is to mediate through an object form something of life, especially the life lived by humans, such that others looking at the work will recognize it as if they were there.

James Gibson (1979: 272) says that a 'picture' is not a representation of reality but a record in two dimensions of 'invariants of structure', the forms and shapes present to vision. Thought of in this way, the picture does not have to conform to any convention of representation such as perspective to be able to evoke the reality which it records. The 'invariants of structure' refer to the way surfaces interconnect in the object when it is viewed; surfaces are noticed as more or less distinct, continuous and in relationships to each other. But by treating the picture, whether it is a photograph or a cubist painting, as a record of information that was selected by the artist:

> It enables the invariants that have been extracted by an observer – at least, some of them – to be stored, saved, put away and retrieved, or exchanged. Pictures are like writing inasmuch as they can be looked at again and again by the same observer and looked at by many observers.
>
> (Gibson 1979: 274)

Pictures, including art works, store up the investment of human observation and emotion which is then released when the work is viewed. In static works of art the mediation does not alter with the passage of time; when you return to the same painting, it is still available to be viewed in the same way. The object may age, may acquire a patina, but can be restorable such that it can be viewed centuries after it was produced. The cultural context of viewing may change but the material form of the object remains the same. Because the static art object has no other purpose than being viewed, which does not wear its physical form or put it at risk of accident, the chance of the pure art work surviving intact is good. This is very different from the craft work such as the chair which is sat on and so worn, and the glass, pottery and china ware which are vulnerable to damage during use. The message of art works may attract the sort of attention that leads individuals to attack the object, as Marcus Harvey's *Myra* (1995) was during its exhibition at the Royal Academy in London in 1997. In general, the art object is protected from wear and abuse by being put in a gallery, screened with glass, protected with ropes, attendants and 'do not touch' notices. The only form of interaction with it that is allowed is looking at it.

Baudrillard (1981[1972]: 102) identifies two features needed for an object to be offered for sale in modern society as an art object – the signature of the artist and a series of works bearing the same signature, the *œuvre*. The signature is the sign of the creator's claim that this is to be recognized as an art object and that it is his or her particular intentionality behind whatever the object mediates. But for Baudrillard the signature is characteristic of modern culture and the relations between objects within a modern system: traditional cultures organized around symbolic rather than sign exchange showed much less interest in the 'authorship' of symbolic or mediative objects. In the modern system of art objects, the signature is a key sign of authenticity and provenance. As art objects are valued, both in monetary terms but also in status within collections and exhibitions, the provenance is often more significant than the mediated content.

The signature locates modern art objects in a system that is juxtaposed to the system of everyday objects. Baudrillard points out that modern art playfully elevates everyday objects into art objects by simply signing and exhibiting them (for example, Duschamp's 1914 ready-made *Bottle Rack*: Baudrillard 1997b: 21). Duschamp went further three years later not only by challenging the convention of exhibition as a sign of art, but also by exhibiting a urinal he had signed 'R. Mutt' (*Fountain* 1917); Baudrillard does not refer to the piece but it predates his comments on the role of the artist's signature by some 50 years.

The aura and authenticity of the modern art work does not lie, as it had traditionally for Benjamin (1973[1936]: 215) and Adorno and Horkheimer (1979[1944]: 19), in the singularity of the original image/object, prior to mechanical reproduction. Baudrillard points out that there can be 'an authentic form of simulation' (1997a: 11), that copying has itself been incorporated into modern art; he refers to Warhol as a 'machine' (Baudrillard 1997a: 15) and describes the exact reproduction that Rauschenberg makes of an apparently daubed and hurried canvas (Baudrillard 1981: 106). The capability of the art object to mediate depends on the illusion that it is the product of the intentionality of a particular individual creator. The object's provenance enables it to enter a world of exchange where there is no set pricing and where the value of the object is unpredictable. This distinctive form of exchange, exemplified by the auction, contributes to a fetishization of the object and its value which has nothing to do with its mediative properties (Baudrillard 1981: 118). Mechanical reproduction does not itself damage the status of the art object as a singular mediating object, but there is an 'aesthetic disillusionment' which comes with the failure of the two-dimensional, still picture – the painting or drawing – to continue to evoke the illusion of reality (Baudrillard 1997a: 7–18). In contemporary art the loss of the power of illusion leads to an 'irruption of *objective irony*' in the world of objects (Baudrillard 1997a: 13).

An example of how the art object uses reality not as a representational mode but as a device for irony is a small piece by

Cornelia Parker, *Pornographic Drawings* (1996), that consists of three sheets of paper which have been folded in half onto a small quantity of ink to produce a blot which is mirrored on each half of the paper. Each blot is different, but each evokes images including those of bodies and genitals. The work is dependent for its ironic power on the legend that explains that the ink was made from pornographic film confiscated by Her Majesty's Customs and Excise; without the legend the images would be mere Rorschach test blobs. The illusion of representation has gone, the work of creating the record of the picture has been transformed from the technique of drawing to one used to some effect by nursery school children. As always the art work depends for its status on its place in the gallery and, more than ever on the *textual* work which accompanies it on the wall and in the catalogue.

ART WORKS AND ORDINARY OBJECTS

The context of an art work distinguishes it from other objects; it is precisely because it is exhibited, displayed, framed, protected, catalogued, titled and signed that it becomes a singular object that mediates a certain type of message in the visual channel. But the context of the art work may become confused with that of ordinary objects.

Outside and slightly around the corner from the exhibition *Objects of Desire: The Modern Still Life* at the Hayward Gallery in London in 1997, there was a BMW Z3 Sports car on a show stand in a glass case – BMW (GB) were sponsors of the exhibition. The car was not part of the exhibition which contained paintings and other art objects signed by or attributed to Picasso, Duschamp, Warhol, Oldenburg and many others. In the foyer were two 'Art Cars', models of BMWs painted by Andy Warhol and Roy Lichtenstein. These were clearly making a claim to being art works in that the one-sixth size models were effectively canvases that famous artists had been invited to paint over; they were not working models and though the shape of a BMW was recognizable, these were not vehicles that could be driven away.

The Z3 in the glass case outside was 'real'; not a model or a representation of a car. It was an object that was practical – its design was quite clearly as a car, a form of transport – and yet it made a claim to being an aesthetic object too. Its sleek shape, mint green metallic paintwork and gleaming brightwork were set on a pedestal, like a sculpture. This was a production model but it had been put in a glass case to be looked at and admired as an exhibit prominently displayed near a major exhibition of 'the still life', a set of unique and singular objects.

Randall Dippert (1993) distinguishes practical objects from art works. What he calls 'ordinary artefacts' are

> primarily objects to fulfil our 'practical' goals and purposes: to turn screws, transport us, and so on. The goals concern our 'outer', physical being. Ordinary, practical artifacts have as their highest, well-conceptualized goal the alteration of the physical world.
>
> (Dippert 1993: 107)

Cars which fulfil our outer, physical goals by transporting us are practical objects. Car-like objects such as the BMW Art Cars are sometimes exhibited for display only; they cannot be construed as ordinary objects. But the BMW Z3 was clearly not what Dippert would call an 'art work'. His definition of an 'art work' is expressed in a beautifully impacted negative form which makes us respect the work of philosophers:

> An art work is an artifact that is not conceived to have been made with an unsubordinated intention other than one that is such that its recognition implies its fulfilment.
>
> (Dippert 1993: 112)

Art works are those that are created with the intention that they will be recognized as art works: he abbreviates the definition to 'recognition-implies-fulfilment'. The point of Dippert's negative form of definition is that while it specifies both the necessary and sufficient condition for an art work, it allows that some will fulfil a higher intention to communicate. His definition also recognizes that sometimes art works get used as firewood but that they were never intended to have such a practical use. Inside the Hayward exhibition were objects such as Warhol's brilliant but empty *Brillo Boxes* (1964) and Claes Oldenburg's piece of giant but inedible *Floor Cake* (1962). These objects were art works because of the intentions which oriented both maker and viewer to the object. Despite the form of its exhibition, the BMW Z3 was clearly a car, a practical object and its claim as an art work was parodic; to claim recognition of its aesthetic qualities and so advertise the car.

Objects that are not art works can give rise to an aesthetic pleasure or experience in the human who appreciates it – a sunset, a graceful animal or a sports car. There is an 'aesthetic attitude' in which the form, line, colour and so on of an object are appreciated and enjoyed without ignoring the capacity of the object as 'ordinary' and its lack of claim to being an art work (Dippert 1993: 112; see also the discussion in Wolff 1983: 73–4). The aesthetic attitude locates the object in a cultural tradition since some valuation is made as to the quality of this object in relation to other objects; this is more beautiful than that. While this works equally well for sunsets, animals and sports cars it is only the sports car that, like the art work, has been designed by human intention to elicit this response. The aesthetic object, both the art work and the car, is produced within an 'aesthetic dialectic' (Hauser 1982: 390) in which what has gone before is preserved within the very newest form; this new model of sports car is related to the form of previous sports cars. The aesthetic appeal of an object like a sports car can be in how it mediates the ways in which it might be used, such as how good it would be at accelerating and cornering. The aesthetics are partly what we might call 'pure' – the interaction of lines, shape, mass, colours – and partly functional – the relation of mass to wheelbase and track width, the location of the driving position to wheels and engine.[2]

We can engage with the properties of an object before we use it. Baudrillard (1996: 65) describes the car as an object that epitomizes the mediation of 'atmosphere'. The aerodynamic shape of the vehicle is not a sign of real speed, but of a sublime speed, the speed of dreams and fantasies, the form signifying the *idea* of function, rather than the actual function. The fascination, the pleasure in looking, evokes the myth of humankind's technical power over the natural world and becomes a signal of social status (Baudrillard 1996: 65). The design cues of speed – streamlined wings, tail-lights, chrome grills etc. – create a distinctive aesthetic. In trying to grasp the status of the sublime in modernity, Dick Hebdige (1987) describes the place of a maroon Ford Thunderbird in an English neighbourhood car culture of Cortinas and Range Rover replicants (Japanese imitations): 'the sublime functions as that-which-is-aesthetic-but-not-beautiful' (Hebdige 1987: 65).

Ordinary objects like cars have a practical function that

art works do not but the ordinary object can have an aesthetic appeal that is not simply to do with beauty; it may lie in its mediation of functional properties or it may lie in a singular quality that transcends form and function – the sublime.

TELEPHONY

Telephones are ordinary, practical objects that do nothing else but mediate by allowing humans to communicate through the auditory channel by talking. They are familiar and although they vary in design, telephones have a form recognizable and usable by anyone who has ever used any telephone.[3]

The telephone is a little over 100 years old. Invented by Bell in 1876, it became a usable communications device with exchanges and a sufficient number of subscribers within a decade in the USA. By the 1980s 90 per cent of US households had telephones and the rest of the world was fast catching up. In the UK 54.7 per cent of households had telephones in 1976–7 but by 1996–7 this figure had reached 93.1 per cent (Department of Employment (DoE) 1977; Office for National Statistics (ONS) 1997). In that 20-year period there has been a 'telecommunications revolution' (Dyson and Humphreys 1990: 2; see also Humphreys and Simpson 1996) driven by technological developments, particularly computerization of switching and terminals, and an explosion in demand from corporate users. Telephony has come to mean much more than the household or office telephone connected to a network of other telephone users. Fax, computer connections, videophones, ansafones, voice-mail and a host of telephone services have changed the traditional meaning of the telephone as a system.

Perhaps the most important change has been the rapid introduction of the mobile telephone, which links the individual, rather than the home or workplace, to the network. By 1996–7, 24 per cent of households in the 30–49 age group had a mobile telephone (ONS 1997: 148), although it no longer becomes meaningful to talk in terms of 'households' who have such an individualized item. Some analysts project that there will be over 10 million mobile subscribers in the UK by the millennium, nearly 60 million in the US and 350 million world-wide (*Financial Times* 'International Telecoms Survey', 2 October 1995). The materials, shape and the functionality of a particular telephone will locate it within the material culture of a particular time and place but not usually limit those who can use it. Out of date telephones or those from other countries look different but work in recognizably similar ways. The most recent mobile telephones have switches and screens that require new skills but this has not held back the rapid adoption of the 'mobile' throughout the world.[4]

The telephone mediates between people separate in place but not time; unlike both the ordinary and the art object, the telephone provides a continuous flow of messages once it is 'turned on'. Most telephones are 'turned on' by simply picking up the receiver; in the early days a handle had to be wound, on mobiles a switch is pressed. When the object is turned off it has a 'standing reserve' (Heidegger 1977: 17): the object is not there to be looked at; it is there so that it can be interacted with when it calls for attention by ringing. Like other modern, electronic mediating devices it is small and easily transportable. But unlike televisions, radios or players of recordings, it can be used to communicate either in two directions or in one direction only (in Budapest in 1893 the telephone was used to broadcast daily programmes: Briggs 1990[1988]: 384), it can allow one to one communication or one to multiple communication (recorded messages, conference calls). Leon Kreitzman comments on the effect of the mobile phone in making users available for public communication even when they are in spaces that have until now afforded a certain privacy, especially when in a car, train or aeroplane (Kreitzman 1999: 37). With the mobile switched on, its user is available for private conversation however public the setting, however far from the office desk of business calls or the domestic space of personal calls.

In mediating objects, switching turns on and off its capability as a medium and is part of interaction with objects such as the telephone. The modern telephone has affordances or functions that enable the user to control the mediation – transfer calls, put a call on hold, link instruments for a conference call. Don Norman (1988) comments on the difficulties that arise when switching systems for these functions use a combination or sequence of keys. The problems for the user occur with switching systems that are not 'mapped' (i.e. linked in some direct and physical way to what they do) and do not utilize 'feedback' to keep the user informed about how the system is proceeding. In other words, the affordances of the object are not visible to the user and are not part of an interactive flow with the object. The result is that many users of the telephone system in an organization, cannot remember the sequence of keys to put a caller on hold while they are transferred, let alone those for more complex functions.

Of central importance to the material impact of the telephone is the *immediacy* of the medium; it requires little or no skill or technical knowledge to use and its mediation is simultaneous. The telephone is, as McLuhan would have it, 'an extension of man':

> With the telephone, there occurs the extension of the ear and voice that is a kind of extra sensory perception.
> (McLuhan 1994: 265)

Human speech normally communicates through co-presence in the same auditory space and time. That co-presence extends to the visual channel so that speech is supplemented by gestures, facial reactions and so on. Telephonic communication removes the limits of being in hearing range but also removes the visual channel which intensifies the attention to communication.[5] People doodle but do not effectively visualize during telephone conversations as they do when reading or listening to music or a radio play. Unlike the radio, telephone communication can rarely become background noise.

As well as the visual channel, the ambient noise which is part of physical co-presence is also lost; telephone sound quality is limited, both for tonal range and volume range, so that sound information is restricted to speech and loud background noises. Based on a series of comparative empirical studies, Rutter (1987) sums up the impact of telephone communication as 'cuelessness': it is the loss of visual cues or those from background sounds (such as someone moving in their seat) which makes telephone communication 'depersonalized' in content, 'less spontaneous in style' and favour the 'stronger case' in negotiations (Rutter 1987: 74).

Telephones are relatively simple objects that fit with human beings in a fairly consistent way; their form 'affords' certain types of engagement and not others. The ecological psychologist James Gibson (1979) coins the term 'affordances' to refer to the way that the material of the world fits with human beings:

> The *affordances* of the environment are what it *offers* the animal, what it *provides* or *furnishes*, either for good or ill. The verb to afford is found in the

> dictionary, but the noun *affordance* is not. I have made it up. I mean by it something that refers to both the environment and the animal in a way that no existing term does. It implies the complementarity of the animal and the environment.
>
> (Gibson 1979: 127)

The telephone as an object in the human environment affords something that is turn-on-able and manipulable by most human hands. A bell of some sort to draw attention to the device and in modern telephones a dialling system to initiate connections are also necessary. The principal affordance of the telephone is the handset, which contains something adjacent to the mouth to speak into and something close enough to the ear for hearing the other party. Although the object contains small loud-speakers and microphones, these devices in other pieces of apparatus provide very different affordances. In the telephone they afford intimacy and privacy for speaking.

By using a telephone, two parties are together in real time, can use ordinary speech levels and respond to each other immediately, even though they may be literally any distance apart. The medium allows interruption, murmurs of affirmation, cries of anger or sadness, laughter, variation in volume and tone of voice as well as communication through spoken language. For most social contexts – a business meeting, a family, a party, a gathering of friends – the intrusion into actual co-presence means the talker on the telephone either has to arrange to postpone the call, leave the social setting or disrupt it. The telephone talker is interacting with someone in a different place which excludes those in the same place. If someone in the same room speaks to us when we are on the telephone there is a risk of confusion – the difficulty of being in two places, two separate interactions at once.[6] Some people like the displacement effect of talking on the telephone as their flow of attention moves from the place they are physically in, to somewhere abstract and a new flow of interaction with the person calling. The telephone call offers an escape from the limitations of the here and now; from the tedium of teenage life in the parental home, from the boredom of standing in a queue or being stuck on a train. As a device used in films to add pace to narrative development, the telephone call puts a character in two places at once, like an intercut, allowing two scenes of the story to develop simultaneously.

The damage to co-present sociability that the telephone threatens can lead to social rules designed to limit its cultural impact. Diane Zimmerman Umble (1992) describes how for the Amish, a religious community in Pennsylvania, telephones are too intrusive to family life to allow them in the home. The need for telephones to do business and to call for assistance in emergencies was solved by having community telephones that are away from the house in 'little buildings that look much like outdoor lavatories' (Zimmerman Umble 1992: 184). The telephones are not listed in the directory, are used mainly for outgoing calls and are shared between six or seven Amish families. The mediating object of the telephone takes up a particular place in this local material culture, channelling it towards business and emergency use and away from personal and intimate use.

In contrast, a study by Jenie Betteridge (1997) of the impact of the telephone on an isolated farming community on an island in the Republic of Ireland showed that the advantages of intimate communication over distance meant that the telephone became firmly established within people's homes. To begin with there was one communal telephone in the post office, which was very important for business purposes as well as keeping in contact with distant relatives. But unlike the Amish community, the inhabitants of Whiddy Island began to install telephones in their own homes and use them to communicate among themselves as well as with those on the mainland, so that it has become 'an integral part of the islander's personal and kinship relationships' (Betteridge 1997: 596). As Betteridge points out, the telephone has a double effect of increasing the amount and frequency of social contact while at the same time reducing the likelihood of face-to-face interaction (Betteridge 1997: 601). This may have reduced the degree of interdependence between islanders but it has greatly increased their contact with wider society, for example by using the telephone to join in phone-in radio programmes.

TEXTS, IMAGES AND SCREENS

Textual objects including books and also letters, labels, lists and so on not only mediate through written language but also take on a distinctive material form which situates them as objects within a culture. Drawing on the writing of Sartre, Benjamin and a number of other sources,

Brenda Danet (1997) describes how books, letters and legal documents can be valued and prized possessions, symbolizing religious, national, familial and personal identity. Their material substance is an integral part of rituals and enactments such as the signing of legal documents. The signed letter or document is a trace of the person whose feelings or actions are attested by the object which can be stored, revered, reviewed and even reinterpreted. The material form of the text is linked to the social relations and interactions with it; lists are acted upon and thrown away, love letters are read and often hidden as a series, the legal document is 'kept safe', often by an agent such as a bank or a lawyer so that it is available for future action.

Computer mediated communication (CMC) dispenses with the material presence of the textual object but Danet comments on the emergence of a new aesthetic, concerned with the look of the text on the screen as opposed to the page: 'some of the aura of texts is being transferred . . . to the computer' (Danet 1997: 27). Colours, sounds, images and a range of typefaces are all cheaply available to those who wish to use CMC and they provide material features of the text object (Danet 1997: 30). However, the disposability of the magnetic form, the difficulty in authenticating origins or provenance, and the dependence on skill, expensive hardware and electricity, limit the power of the computer as a competitor to the written text. Computers have not replaced other forms of textual and image mediation but have provided an additional form – the screen with particular properties.

The screen that we are used to in televisions, video monitors and computers is a flat surface on which the image appears, through the traces of light thrown from behind by a 'modulated scanning beam' (Gibson 1979: 292). The process of display is rapid and continual so the screen can carry images that depict movement as rapid as the eye can perceive. Unlike the projection of film, there is no blurring of each image in a moving sequence of snapshots which the human mind has to accommodate. But the screen image is made up of 'lines' or 'pixels' that are perceptible and do limit the quality of definition of shapes and forms. Fine detail is difficult to see, especially of small objects or objects in the background. If the content of the image is moving – either the object or the camera moves – it is easier to gather visual information on what is there. Unlike the painted canvas, the viewer cannot move closer and further away to improve visual information. Unlike the static object (even one in a glass case) viewers cannot move around it to gain a sense of its mass relative to themselves.

The screen gives a two-dimensional image that shows precise proportions of shape and tones of colour. It can also show movement in real time, both representations of the 'real' (filmed images of 'live', recorded or dramatized human action) and the 'artificial' (cartoons, drawings, graphic designs, text, computer generated images). Gibson (1979: 302) suggests that the moving picture on the screen 'yields something closer to natural visual perception' than the still picture because the human eye developed to register change and transformation; it is unusual for the retinal image to be still in life. The screen can provide an image that is as real as if the screen were a window that looked directly onto the scene that is visible to the camera operator. The screen provides a 'frame', a set of blinkers that limit the direction and field of vision. On the other hand the frame can move, as the camera moves, to show what we could see if we moved our heads either at the neck or by moving the body (Gibson 1979: 297). Progress in the technology of screens suggests that they will become flatter, eventually as flat as the window pane, and that the definition will improve to compete with that of the image drawn, painted, printed or photographed onto paper.

Ruth Levy (1997) describes the emergence of the 'graphical user interface' (GUI) as the visual material form that makes the computer such a distinctive mediating object. She charts the coming together of various technological components to enable the small, personal computer to be usable for design work that led to a GUI in which a pointing device such as a 'mouse' is used to control the computer's operations through icons and menus on the screen that also provide feedback on the instructions. It also led to applications that could draw and represent colours and eventually to the capability to manipulate an image, such as a photograph or a drawing, that had first been 'scanned' into the screen. There was a parallel development of printer technology and the programmes that made the screen image a preview of the printed image. What is remarkable is that these various aspects of what we now take for granted in the most basic home or office computer have been developed since about 1984 when the Apple Mac was launched. The surface of the computer screen is a material *transform* rather than a material form; it is precisely its lack of fixity or continuity that distinguishes it from the art object and the book. The potential for the image on the screen to be changed leads to a way of imaging and viewing the world that Baudrillard calls 'transaesthetics' (Baudrillard 1993b[1990]: 14–19; 1997b: 19–27).

The modern personal computer (PC) makes available to a wide range of people the possibility of producing documents that include chosen design features (type styles, layout, graphic images, photographed images) that have changed the look of documents, reports and letters as well as party invitations, fanzines, political pamphlets, school newsletters and so on. The screen can display and make endless changes to texts, two-dimensional images and even three-dimensional objects, virtually for free, which has made it an indispensable tool in most work situations. It has also brought into many homes (in the developed countries), screens that are used for the production of images and texts, both on paper and increasingly on the World Wide Web.

TELEVISION

The screen of the cathode ray tube as a source of images is more usually associated with the television. Televisions as objects have moved into a central place within many homes and have perhaps become the mediating object *par excellence* of the late twentieth century because of the amount of attention they apparently draw in those cultures that have television. The television is a source of information, education and entertainment that has not seriously displaced any other form of mediation and yet it dominates many living rooms. In the UK 98.4 per cent of households own one or more televisions (ONS 1997: 150), while 82 per cent own a video recorder and 80 per cent of teenagers have a television in their bedroom (ONS 1998: 218). On average British people watch 24 hours of television per week (ONS 1998: 217). As one of the respondents in a study of the domestic use of technology by Sonia Livingstone remarks: 'The television tends to be on.' (Livingstone 1992: 121). But because it has been turned on, that does not mean that it gets the same sort of attention that the telephone does.

McLuhan calls the telephone a 'cool' medium because of its low definition and meagre information: 'so much has to be filled in by the listener' (McLuhan 1994: 23). Surprisingly he also calls television a 'cool' medium. Rather than the generally accepted idea of the television watcher as a passive absorber of whatever emanates from the box, McLuhan points out that the television can 'tend to be on', watched with a partial attention, while the watcher can at the same time take in the newspaper or a conversation, do the ironing or make the tea. The content of television is different from the theatre or film; the television performance is quiet and intimate, it does not require the actors to project or command attention, the close-up is routine and casual and the definition is poor. TV is a 'cool' medium which requires viewers to be participants, to engage; if they do not give their attention to what is going on, then the TV screen becomes a part of the furnishings. Film, on the other hand, is a 'hot' medium that commands complete and continuous attention. In the cinema there is nothing else to do but watch the film; if it fails to capture attention then the only thing to do is to leave. The cinema is dark, the viewers slide down in their seats and give themselves up to the film as if to hypnosis. Barthes (1986) confesses that he likes to *leave* a movie theatre and describes the movie-goer coming to, readjusting to the light, regaining his senses (Barthes 1986: 345). In contrast the object of the television set is familiar and lacking fascination. For Barthes, the film on television is tamed; 'the *eroticization* of the place is foreclosed: television *doomed* us to the Family, whose household instrument it has become – what the hearth used to be, flanked by its communal kettle' (Barthes 1986: 346). In the darkness of the cinema the 'dancing cone' of light projects larger than life images on to the screen. But on the television screen, the image is formed as miniature figures which are projected outwards by the light generated inside the box.

Research into the use of television suggests that 'Presence and absence in front of the set cannot simply be equated with attention (or lack of it) to TV' (Morley 1995: 173). David Morley is interested in how the television as an object fits into domestic space and, while also quoting Barthes, suggests that it is *sound* that is the key attention device of the television. To attend to the television one does not have to be sitting in front of it; the information of news and documentaries, the narrative or plot of drama or films, the jokes of comedy, the songs of variety can all, usually, be enjoyed through the sound channel alone. The television can be on without being watched while other tasks, even in another room, are carried on. Morley recalls an informant who regularly 'watched' television from the kitchen while doing domestic tasks and came into the viewing room to see what was going on when the soundtrack told her that something visually important was happening (Morley 1995: 174). He suggests that early in the development of programming in North America, the model of 'radio with pictures' was adopted rather than that of cinema, so that the housewife could do the housework but still be available to advertisers. Williams (1990[1975]: 25) and Spigel (1992: 30) point out that it was the commercial interests of the radio broadcasters which shaped the medium of television as an extension to radio broadcasting.

Morley's view of the importance of sound as a cue to visual attention is confirmed by experimental studies of television watching by psychologists. Anderson and Burns (1991) review the literature on these studies and point out that 'average viewers do not look at television about one third of the time they are in its presence' (1991: 14). They go on to describe how children have been shown to listen when not watching to identify cues to 'comprehensible and interesting content worthy of full attention' (Anderson and Burns 1991: 15). Most empirical research on attention to television has been with children, presumably because of the fears that children will become passive absorbers of whatever is broadcast. In fact children's attention responds to cues such as the type of voice, the music, movement and scene changes and their attention varies with the viewing environment, programme content and comprehensibility. But what is striking is how little attention is actually paid to the television screen. Between 15 and 19 per cent of the time there is no one in the room in which the television is switched on, and even of those present, attention varies considerably according to the time of day, the type of programme and other activities being undertaken (Anderson and Field 1991: 203–4). 'Online' studies using video recording of those watching television suggest that viewer diaries fairly accurately represent the programmes that were 'watched' but overestimate the programmes that were attended to by a 'watcher'. In general, viewing 'sessions' are short; in one study the median length of viewing sessions was 1 minute, although for adult men 58 per cent of all time spent with TV was in sessions longer than 30 minutes (Anderson and Field 1991: 212). What is more, within the session there is a great variation in the length of 'looks' at the screen; 'most look lengths are of relatively brief duration, with extended looks of greater than 1 minute's duration relatively infrequent' (Anderson and Burns 1991: 6). One of the most interesting findings of these studies was the phenomenon of 'attentional inertia', that is that the longer one looks at a television screen, the more one is likely to carry on looking at it (Anderson and Burns 1991: 6). However, these studies treat 'attention' as an empirical phenomenon traced by eye gaze and the apparent lack of 'attention' to other things. What is not clear is how important the contact with the television is to the person watching, how much their watching of the screen is in fact a 'turning off' or at least an attenuation of their attention to other things.

Television can also be used to block out other interactions (rows, questions, demands for information) and can be switched on merely to give the illusion of co-presence, of someone else being there. Morley argues that the television on in the 'background' provides mainly an aural experience (Morley 1995: 180). But the flickering light, the movement, the play of colours, the presence of figures and other familiar forms are also a soothing co-presence, a sort of moving wallpaper. One of Livingstone's respondents remarks: 'While I work in the living room I usually have the television on without any sound . . . in the background . . . relieving tension' (Livingstone 1992: 121). In my teenage daughter's bedroom it is not unusual to find the television on with the sound turned down, the stereo system playing, while two or three girls chat and dress and also talk to other friends on the telephone. None of these mediating objects has priority over the face-to-face interactions although the telephone seems to command the most direct attention among the objects. All the objects providing their aural and visual information are interacted with in the flow of social action, receiving different levels of attention according to what is going on.

Lynn Spigel argues that the television was seen in the USA as an object around which the family could unite but also as a 'monster that threatened to wreak havoc on the family' (Spigel 1992: 47). One way in which ambivalence towards the television was expressed was by making it into an item of furniture, with doors similar to those of a cupboard that could be shut, hiding the screen. The television was often chosen to fit with surrounding furniture, incorporating the screen not merely in the space but within the ambience of the living room (see Riggins 1994b: 124). As the capability of the television to display images has improved (colour, improved definition, flatter screen) then the outward form of the object has changed towards the 'monitor' style – a plain black or grey box, not exactly square but with no decoration or distinctive style.

Rather than regarding the television as a 'window on the world', linking the private world of the home to the outside world, as early commentators did (Spigel 1992: 102), or as a 'home theatre' in front of which a new set of local, neighbourhood relations would develop (Spigel 1992: 99), the modern television is treated as simply a mediating object for use by those in the household (or bar, or common room).[7] It is a vehicle for a range of programmes and videos that the user can engage completely with or not even switch on – or somewhere in between. Gone are the veneered wooden casings, doors, knobs and cloth grills; the contemporary television is a bald functional object, on a wheeled, cantilevered stand with a video recorder on the lower shelf. Gone is the fear of the 'goggle box' which seduces young children into watching it when it is on and which goggles vacantly at everyone in the room when it is off.

No longer is the screen in the house simply a medium of broadcast; there has been a proliferation of screens for television, video and computer use. George Gilder (1994) argues that broadcast television will soon give way to what he dubs the 'teleputer', which will link the television to the computer and produce interactivity between screen watchers. Instead of broadcasting being controlled by an elite of professionals and determined by the 'lowest common denominators of public interest' (Gilder 1994: 56), all teleputers will be able to send information to each other – much as telephones can now. High definition 'field emission displays' will allow the screens to compete not only with television but also with print on paper. Gilder sees the newspaper as the model for gathering, filtering and presenting information on the teleputer rather than the TV broadcast model of a flow of images and information. The modern newspaper offers a 'jigsaw effect' (Williams 1990: 87) of items set out on the page, organized within sections, with headlines and pictures. The viewer can scan quickly what is on offer and then choose the items to read in more detail. With computer based interactivity and the hypertext and multimedia possibilities that go with it, the screen based newspaper becomes a much more complex and sophisticated medium.

As mediating objects develop they will have to be integrated into an existing material culture within the domestic setting alongside other media (see for example Silverstone and Morley 1990; Hirsch 1992). Higher definition means that the 'readability' of the screen image will soon approach that of the printed page; perhaps the writing is on the screen for paper and print, although all previous death knells for the written and printed text have been hopelessly premature.

CONCLUSION

Objects that do nothing else but mediate, like the telephone and the television, are at the centre of modern material culture in a way that cooking pots and weapons were to past cultures. And of course cooking pots and weapons are still items of major importance in material culture.

Mediating objects enable a form of social interaction, whether between individuals or between broadcasting institutions and masses, that includes information about the real world, the fantasy world, the realm of imagination and the field of emotions. Objects that we can 'turn on', extend or stand in for direct, face-to-face social interaction, enabling communication across time and space. Our interaction with mediating objects, which begins with turning them on, is shaped by their particular form which requires a certain type of attention.

I have argued that certain types of objects mediate, carrying intentional and meaningful messages between people who are not within the same communicative space. The static art work mediates across time rather than space, accessible to whoever will visit and look at it. Its status and value is ascribed through formal features such as the signature and the context of exhibition which situate it in the system of objects. The form of the art work can be utilized either to parody modern consumer culture (Warhol's *Brillo Boxes*) or to exploit the aesthetic properties of an ordinary object (BMW's Z3).

The telephone mediates across spatial distance in the auditory channel. Simultaneous interaction through spoken language including tone and expression are communicated even though there is a loss of definition and background sound. The absence of visual and tactile contact alters the form of the communication; the use of the object transforms and constrains interaction. The telephone's remarkable characteristic as a mediating object is its power to interrupt, to demand complete attention at the expense of any other activity. The video display screen requires attention through the visual channel but unlike the art work, the visual object is transitory. As a computer screen, the image requires attention to the changes as the screen is refreshed and information added. As a television screen, cues in the auditory channel enable us to vary our attention to the screen according to interest. The television as an object has become more a screen which displays images and less an item of furniture that carries coded light. The television screen competes for attention with many other different domestic activities. The location of the mediating object, both within the material environment and the social environment of the home affect the way that the object is used.

Mediating objects have proliferated dramatically in both number and form in the everyday lives of late modernity. As we establish practical relationships with mediating objects like telephones and televisions they are simultaneously engaging us in social relationships, in the exchanging of ideas, values, experiences and emotions. These forms of mediated social exchange are spatially and temporally at a distance from, and in addition to, the flow of direct social interactions and relationships. In this spatial and temporal remove they provide a background sociality that feeds back on the present flow, preparing us for, and enabling us to reflect on, present experience. Our relationships with mediating objects are perhaps the nearest to our relationships with other people. But then there are some things that we become very intimate with, some things which we begin to merge with bodily rather than look at.

NOTES

1 In Wilde's even more famous *Picture of Dorian Gray* the exchange is of the human quality of ageing rather than human vitality itself. A similar theme, the exchange of life between people and their mirror images and shadows, is discussed by Baudrillard (1998: 187–90).
2 Barthes (1973: 88–90) gives an account of the Citroën DS 19 as a mythological object in which it is aesthetics rather than engineering, form rather than functions which are significant.
3 The form is also of course used in art works, most famously Dali's *Lobster Telephone* (1936), but also Joseph Beuys's *Earth Telephone* (1968) in which the shape of the telephone – its mass, the wires coming from it – is mimicked by a piece of earth with straw coming from it. The surface and texture of the manufactured hard black Bakelite telephone contrasts with the messy textured surface of the natural materials in the lump of earth and straw.
4 Jonathan Glancey describes the 'cultural revolution' that the mobile phone is bringing to China's Guangdong province:

> In noodlebars and restaurants at lunchtime, diners yell into their mobile while holding conversations with those seated around them and eating . . . Business men meet in hotel and office lobbies greeting one another with lengthy handshakes while talking to third parties on their mobiles. A young man and his girlfriend ride along the street on their scooter: she receives a call on her mobile. It's for him. As he darts in and out of the traffic, she holds the mobile to his ear.
>
> (*Guardian* 5 June 1998)

5 In Marguerite Duras's novella *Le Navire Night* (1986 [1979]) a passionate love affair takes place entirely through telephone contact: the lovers never meet or see each other.
6 Extensions to the telephone – including hands- free facilities, conference lines and other instruments on the same line – can of course begin to break up the

experience of intimacy and one-to-one co-presence by making the telephonic interaction present to others.

7 In contrast to this view, Roger Silverstone (1994) makes a sustained, if ultimately unconvincing, argument that TV is a 'transitional object' that provides a key element in the ontological security of the modern or postmodern world.

9

WHO'S WHAT? PEOPLE AS OBJECTS ■

> Starting with modernity, we have entered an era of production of the Other. It is no longer a question of killing, of devouring or seducing the Other, of facing him, of competing with him, of loving or hating the Other. It is first of all a matter of producing the Other.
>
> (Baudrillard 1994: 1)

Among the things we make as material objects are other human beings. Baudrillard is referring to the ways in which otherness is produced through a wide range of physical and conceptual strategies which he sums up in the phrase 'plastic surgery'. In this chapter I want to look at some of the ways in which we manufacture human bodies, not through taking the body as raw material but through using the material with which we make objects to make, remake, or alter our bodies. In earlier chapters I have kept to the distinction between humans and objects while exploring how things are included in social relations. Things are things and people are people – up until now. People have been the masters of things, dominating objects which have taken the subordinate (subject!) position.

In this last substantive chapter I shall explore some of

the material overlaps between human beings and objects, the muddy boundaries between people and things, where material is incorporated into bodies. Some objects are taken into the body for clinical, artistic, decorative or other purposes. Sometimes the boundary between body and object is clear, sometimes it is not. When material stuff is made into counterfeit human beings that mimic the outward appearance of human bodies they highlight the boundary between *being* human and *looking like* a human. The making of material stuff to fit into, replace or substitute for human beings or body parts has led to a cultural fantasy about the incorporation of objects – the cyborg (Bukatman 1993: 301–29). The idea of a being who is part human, part object has become a popular myth, celebrated in many science fiction stories and films of the post-industrial age, in which superhuman functionality is blended with human characteristics of emotion and imagination.[1] This myth, which has its origins in the part human, part animal monsters of antiquity (Pan, the centaurs and mermaids) via the myths of constructing nearly-human forms from animals and cadavers (Dr Moro, Frankenstein), provides a cultural space for exploring the boundaries between the human being and the object made by a human. Science fiction is rather like the fantasy life of material culture – even though it is rather a dull sort of fantasy for many people. Its field is the imaginary future in which history is most apparent through the impact of technological development. Some sci-fi concentrates on social and political relationships but the setting is a world that is materially very different from our own. The possibilities for action and the distribution of power are often based on the new capabilities and properties of things to extend human biological abilities.

THE SKIN SUIT

The protective suit is an exemplar of material culture. Made in one place, a physical and cultural environment where the human animal is at home, it allows the wearer to go into hostile and strange environments, literally wearing his or her culture as material as well as symbolic protection. It is for this reason that the body suit has played a central place in science fiction. In Frank Herbert's *Dune* (1968[1965]) the 'stillsuit' of the Fremen cleans and recycles water as it leaves the body so that 'in good working order, you won't lose more than a thimbleful of moisture a day' (1968: 132) – a necessity on a desert planet such as Arrakis where there is no rain and no water. To damage such a suit damages the wearer; as with space suits and pressurized diving suits, the wearer's life is as much in danger as if it were their own skin. Through the rent in the skin, the mainstay of life – whether it be water, oxygen, air pressure or blood – flows till life is lost.

Iain M. Banks's short story, 'Descendant' (1991), is about the only human survivor of a vehicle that has crashed in space. The survivor has descended onto a planet with an atmosphere which cannot support human life, using the anti-gravitational system of the 'smart suit' he is wearing. The suit also used its photopanels like a parachute – just one of a set of fantastic capabilities that include sophisticated senses and the ability to converse in ordinary language with its wearer. But both survivor and suit are damaged; the suit has lost its anti-gravity ability to float, its communications systems (which would have enabled it to call the base for help) is broken and it has a small leak, while the human seems to have internal bleeding, has been unconscious for days and is still in shock. He would have died had the suit not been able to keep him alive.

The story is about the journey across the planet to the base as they take it in turns to walk, the suit carrying the man on its inside, the man carrying the suit on his outside. The suit has consciousness and an independent existence but it is a thing, a tool, designed to support and sustain the man with food, a sewage system, music, images and medical help. The suit is as 'smart' but 20 per cent stronger than the average human, it has similar rights and it has feelings about the war in which they have been involved. This is how it talks to the man:

> Oh, come on; you're a machine too. We're both *systems*, we're both matter with sentience. What makes you think we have more choice than you in the way we think? Or that you have so little? We're all programmed. We all have our inheritance. You have rather more than us, and it's more chaotic, that's all.
>
> (Banks 1991: 55)

There are other differences though. The human masturbates, has dreams and fantasies and is able to annoy the suit by singing made-up songs.

When the suit finally gets to the base it explains to a 'drone' (a sentient machine) that the man had died thirty-four days earlier. Why had it carried the body and not ditched it? The suit shrugs and says: 'Call it sentiment' (Banks 1991: 65). Banks has used the smart suit to explore a human-like relationship between a thing and a human. The suit is not completely independent like a robot (or a drone) and its functions, actions and even shape are oriented to those of human beings. At the centre of the story is the problem of merged identity; these two distinct beings, one human and organic, the other artificial, become so enmeshed in practice that it is not clear to themselves who is who. On the other hand, the material form of the suit expresses sentiment and sensation only when its human charge is no longer able to.

The protective suit provides a fictional device to explore the interconnection between the human body and material culture. But real protective suits become almost part of human subjects. In Chapter 6 we saw how the wetsuit was a part of the windsurf-sailor's equipment, changing not only human capability to be exposed to cold water but also the look and feel of the person inside. As a costume, wearing the wetsuit prepares sailors for the activity of windsurfing; they look and feel the part. The modern 'steamer' is a single garment made out of synthetic rubber lined with knitted nylon, worn close to the skin, with the zip and entry at the back. Unlike ordinary clothes, the wetsuit is worn wet on the inside; its efficacy depends on heating up a thin layer of water next to the wearer's skin which the rubber insulates. It also provides buoyancy and protects the body from light bangs and scrapes. When comfortable, the wetsuit is forgotten during use, and the wearer treats as normal the continual wetness of the body, the slight restriction of movement and the reduction of touch sensitivity. It becomes like a second skin – almost part of the body. The wetsuit provides protection and enables activity in material circumstances that would otherwise be extremely uncomfortable and eventually life threatening. The pressurized diving suit, the spacesuit and the fireproof suit which provide a breathable oxygen supply, go much further in allowing the wearer to enter a strange material environment which would not support human life.

To other people the wetsuit makes the wearer slightly larger and exposes the body form, indicating whether the wearer is male or female, whether childlike or mature, whether large framed or small, whether overweight or slim. But the wetsuit smoothes the line of the body, removing creases, clefts and projections like nipples, removing its genitaled sexuality. It rounds the angles of bones and joints while at the same time acting corset-like to pull in and hold loose flesh. Unlike clothes, which we saw in Chapter 4 form a series of objects that vary in form according to fashion as well as the body, wetsuits and other protective suits look more or less the same. The limits in shape, texture and pattern restrict fashion; the most important distinction they signify is between water sports enthusiasts and others. The protective suit provides a boundary between one cultural grouping and the mainstream which, like all 'dressing up', encourages the wearer to break from everyday routines and habitual behaviours and act differently: this is how the wetsuit contributes to the mimetic activity of playing.

PROSTHETICS

If the material of the protective suit encloses the human body, the reverse happens with many prosthetic devices where the human body encloses material to function as part of that body. Unlike the tool or the mediating object, the medical prosthetic device is not properly an extension of the human body but an artificial object incorporated to replace something that is present in most humans – a leg, an arm, a heart valve, a joint, a piece of bone, an eye, an area of flesh. Dentures or even fillings are very familiar prosthetics that take the place of body material that has decayed or been removed. The material is taken into the body and used as if it is part of the body; it may become indistinguishable to its 'user' from the rest of their body.

The object may work better than the body part it is replacing. It may feel *more* part of the body than the organic and genetically original part. One of my informants[2], Linda, described the immediate change in her life after having a prosthetic hip fitted:

> The first thing I remember after me 'op', waking up, I was lying in bed and thinking 'I haven't got any pain. I've got me leg straight'. Couldn't believe it . . . it's a fantastic operation.
>
> (LL: 128)

Before the operation her own hip had seriously restricted her ability to walk, to move and even to lie straight in bed. But more importantly it had given her continual, deep, nagging pain that could not be controlled by painkillers and which woke her at night. Although there was pain after the operation it was, she said, so much more bearable than 'hip pain'. Linda had observed the operation performed before on someone else; she knew that it involved saws and hammers and chisels to remove the damaged bone and a lump of titanium and cement to replace it. She knew it took four hours and had seen the X-rays showing the metal in her hip. But she was unconcerned about having a 'foreign body' in her body. What was important was the relief from pain and the recovery of the ability to do things that she had been unable to do for years. What had frightened her about the operations, especially when her second hip was replaced, was the long period of dependency on her family and others while her body was recovering from the damage to muscle and other tissue during the operation.

The impact of medical prostheses varies enormously. Linda knew that she had a piece of metal put into her body, but she could not see or feel it. Professionals could spot that she had had a hip replaced by the way she moved, but most people would see the effect as a return to 'normal', to the abilities, movement and a pain-free face that had disappeared as her own hip deteriorated. Some prosthetic devices have no function other than to make the body look or feel complete (the glass eye, the plastic testicle). On the other hand, many prosthetic devices, like the replacement hip, are intended to work as part of the material stuff of the human body. Like the artificial hip, many pins, plates, tubes and pieces of plastic have a functional effect as they are integrated into the material of the body, replacing the structure of damaged flesh or bone, but they do not function in themselves. Other devices like the pacemaker or exterior pump replace bodily mechanical functions without becoming integrated into the structure.

Some prostheses replace both structure and function, they become incorporated into the structure of the body and work within themselves. Lower leg prostheses can include both mechanics and electronics that replicate something of the movement of the original limb as well as the function of the ankle in articulating the foot in relation to the lower leg.[3] The prosthesis not only supports weight but also allows wearers to use their body as they might have expected with their own leg. Most importantly, they will be able to walk confidently on different types of surfaces but some will even be able to do sports that many fully bodied people of the same age would not, such as running, playing basketball, cycling and so on.

The design of modern prosthetic devices is oriented in

two directions. First, it should function as the original organic body part would have.[4] Second, it should 'pass' (Goffman 1990[1963]: 92) or look so much like the original body part that the absence or artificiality is not noticed. These two requirements demand human ingenuity to utilize materials, engineering and design. In wealthy, technologically advanced countries like the USA and the UK, there are many prosthetic devices that make use of advanced materials that combine strength, durability and lightness (carbon fibre, titanium, polymers, silicone, polyethylene, polypropylene) and engineering (pneumatics, motors, radio controllers, microprocessors). Maximizing functionality in prosthetic limbs is judged against a normally functioning limb.[5] Even with the 'hi-tech' prosthetic limb, function and engineering are not the only concerns. A range of artificial materials is used to create a prosthesis that resembles the colour and surface texture of the skin of the wearer.[6] The socket has to engage firmly yet comfortably with the very particular part of the body that, through an accident of birth or life, is foreshortened. Rehabilitating those who have a limb missing, including fitting the prosthesis, involves fitting the prosthesis into the person's life as well as the body.

Steven Kurzman, an anthropologist who has a particular interest in lower limb prosthetics, argues that prosthetic technology enables amputees 'to perform able-bodiedness as an American cultural identity' (1996: 2). Gait, for example, is specific to culture so that the gait that a lower limb amputee wants to reproduce with a prosthesis is the gait of their own culture. The 'normal' gait is the pattern of walking, displaying an efficient use of muscles and joints, most frequently performed by non-amputees. In one culture it is 'normal' to be able to walk down a paved street in leather shoes, in another, it is 'normal' to be able to walk through a paddy field in bare feet (Mauss 1973[1935] provides an early description of the cultural specifity of posture and movement). Function itself is culturally specific so that what a wearer will wish to be able to do in one culture will be different from another culture. There is also a tension between the way that the prosthetist or engineer sees the prosthetic limb (as a tool, as an extension of the amputee's body) and the amputee's view of it as 'functional enhancement' and a 'replication of their limbs' (Kurzman 1997: 4).

Kurzman calls the look of the artificial limb 'cosmesis' and treats it as usually being a desire for the object to look as much like a body part of a non-amputee. Goffman carefully distinguishes the 'perceptibility' of a stigma from knowledge of it (1963: 64–6). It is the degree to which the prosthesis obtrudes into social settings, how noticeable it is, that affects, also by degree, the ability of the wearer to pass as normal. Even those who know about the prosthesis will react differently according to how noticeable it is.

Cosmesis will often be in tension with functionality and Kurzman cites exceptions, people who seek functionality regardless of cosmesis, such as the motorcyclist who prefers flat tread 'feet' for changing gear or the rancher with double, above the knee amputations who chooses to walk on short wooden pegs with no knees and rubber tread 'feet'. In general, however, people who are amputees, or who have been born without a limb, seek the cultural identity of American able-bodiedness which Kurzman says is 'not simply the absence of physical impairment, but is an identity delineated by particular physical appearance and activities' (Kurzman 1996: 5). His interest in prostheses and prosthetic technology is their status as 'boundary objects' (Kurzman 1996: 22) distinctive to a specific culture.

One part of Kurzman's work focuses on the Jaipur ankle-foot prosthesis which, in contrast to the hi-tech materials of prosthetics in the USA, is manufactured out of recycled car tyres, imported aluminium sheeting and cloth. It is made by hammering, wrapping and welding by local technicians rather than by computer controlled machine tools. The prosthesis is made for the individual by the technician using skilled judgements and careful fitting rather than by computer based measurement and design. Technicians from other countries such as Cambodia and Nicaragua are trained by visiting technicians; it is a technology that is dependent on widely available, relatively cheap materials and the refinement of local skills. But what makes the Jaipur foot particularly interesting is that it is appropriate to the cultures in which it is used:

> the Jaipur foot is the only prosthesis currently being used in developing nations which is appropriate to local body movements and geography, such as walking barefoot in wet and muddy climates.
>
> (Kurzman 1996: 27)

ART BODIES

Some medical prosthetic devices are more directly and even exclusively concerned with cosmesis and are the product of art as much as technology. People who have lost parts of their face through trauma, malignant disease or congenital deformity are not able to regain the lost function of eyes, ears, nose, skin and muscle. Where reconstructive surgery is not an option, skilled technicians can create a prosthesis that looks as close as is possible to what has been lost. Wearing their prosthesis, disfigured individuals can go about in the world with their 'spoiled identity' at least partially obscured. Keith Thomas (1994: 30) reports a number of patients who describe their prostheses as directly changing the way they feel about themselves as well as some who actively dislike the prosthesis but still wear it so as not to shock other people. Making the cosmetic prosthesis involves casting, shaping, carving and moulding but its success depends on precisely matching it to its wearer. The technique of shaping material to resemble a human is artistic ('artistic licence' is necessary in carving noses since 'very few of us have the perfect nose': Thomas 1994: 63) and the same techniques and materials are used by artists. The absorption of the body into a cast is, for the prosthetist, part of creating an object that can be tolerably *incorporated* into the body on an everyday basis while the artist casts the body to create a material object that will *embody* something of the particular body.

One artistic use of the cosmetic prosthesis beyond the clinic is to prepare an actor for a part. The temporary prosthesis is designed for the reverse effect of creating a visible stigma which will attract the attention of watchers of a play or film. Often it is intended to shock, as with the cunning device to enable a child actor (or rather her stand-in) to projectile 'vomit' green 'bile' over another character in the film *The Exorcist* (1973). More usually such devices are purely visual such as the additions to human bodies to turn them into beings from other planets in science fiction movies (the television version, *Star Trek: The Next Generation*, has explored a range of variants on the basic human form).

Classical art has always involved figurative representation of the body but they always have features making them distinct from a real human; the cold, hard, smooth material of stone, plaster and bronze sculptures have a colour and texture that does not resemble human skin. Often the sculpture is too small or too large but some life-size statues become eerily lifelike. Even when the material and the stillness of the form are unrealistic, such statues are recognizably human through the interrelated shape of the various surfaces of a body and the presence of a mass equivalent to that of a human body. Some represent gods or mythical figures, others body archetypes (the nubile young woman, the athlete etc.), some, usually just a bust of head and shoulders, represent actual persons of status. It is unusual for statues, such as the Emperor Qin Shi Huangdi's army of 7000 lifesize pottery soldiers, to be actual stand-ins for humans. The mannequin or clothes dummy is a more prosaic and less symbolic stand-in used for making or showing clothes in the west – and of course human beings can be mannequins when they are used for the same purpose.

In the retreat from conceptualism and abstraction towards the figurative, modern artists have developed skills and techniques that overlap with and borrow from those of the prosthetist, both the clinical and entertainment cosmeticist. Taking a mould from the body has provided the possibility of casting a representation as well as a prosthesis. The traditional death mask that preserves the features and repose of the still and lifeless cadaver is perhaps the simplest form. It is a form that recurs in contemporary art; for example, Christine Borland's series of plaster casts taken from mouldings of anthropological and medical skulls (Turner Exhibition, Tate Gallery, London, 1997). The sculpted form that offers a simulacrum, a superficial likeness of the human body, has been incorporated into modern art with mannequins that deviate from the bland body forms in shop windows; the Chapman brothers even retain brand name trainers on their mannequins while the genitals have been exposed and displaced. Charles Ray, Jeff Koons and Abigail Lane also create mannequin style art works that play with posture, size, clothing and decoration to disturb the relationship between the body as object and the body as subject. Mannequins such as Gary Turk's *Pop* (1973), protected in a glass case, are more reminiscent of clothes props in galleries designed to show period costumes or the waxworks that represent famous people. In contrast, a number of Robert Gober's installations are of disembodied legs and torsos that look real apart from their juxtaposition to a wall or their implantation with sheet music, sink drains and candles. The attempt to recover a photo-realist but three-dimensional body image has broken from the limitations of traditional sculpture and ironic mannequins. Ron Meuk's *Dead Dad* (1996–7), lying on a platform almost at floor level at the Sensation Exhibition (Royal Academy, London, 1997) disturbs the normal sense of being viewable in space because the sculpture is three foot long and so looks further away than it is; to move while looking at it is to make one feel like a giant circling a human cadaver. Meuk's skill in attention to detail is close to that of the prosthetist, manipulating materials to represent the form, colour and texture of the body. The effect is of an embodiment that is not a parody or simulacrum of the real but a likeness that lacks life.

Duane Hanson (1925–96) influenced many of those already mentioned and made developing the skills of realistically representing the living body his life's work. His sculptural idiom of casting with silicon moulds was designed to maintain the size as well as the precise proportions of his models. Many of his sculptures are of heavy-set people and capture the posture and expression of individuals going about their everyday business as cleaner, waitress, delivery man, photographer. Each installation uses 'real' clothes to complement the sculptures, which are cast out of polyvinyl acetate with paraffin and oil paints to help get the skin effect. Unlike mannequins that stand stiffly, looking as if they are artificial bodies that have been put into position, Hanson's sculptures stand, sit or lie just as the model did. The weight of flesh is distributed according to the posture so that the effect of skin elasticity and the impact of one body part on another is carefully reproduced. In *Man on a Bench* (1977–8), an elderly man sits leaning forward slightly, his forearms resting on his thighs. The weight of the upper body pushing down through his forearms causes the skin to wrinkle and fold on the underside as it meets the resistance of the trouser material on the top surface of the thigh. Without the resistance, the arms would slide, causing the body to slump forward. The weight of the flesh on the man's face as he leans forward takes up a particular shape, hanging differently than it would if the man was standing or lying on his back. The look of the person and his or her posture withstands close scrutiny without the sculpture revealing its artificiality – except in its immobility. In the gallery it is the absence of breath that distinguishes the artificial art work from the performance artist holding a posture. The effect is a form of embodiment in which the replication of the model is as precise as a photograph – though the techniques are quite different. The sculpture reproduces the model's body as a visible, three-dimensional object caught in a particular moment, a resting posture, that is frozen for much longer than the model's own life.

BODY ART

Performance artists such as Stelarc and Orlan have used their own bodies as a 'canvas' for art whose form they can modify. Orlan has undergone surgery to have plastic inserts under the skin of her face; she calls it 'carnal art'. The finished work is the change to her appearance which, unlike most cosmetic surgery, looks less 'normal' than it did before. The video recordings that show the body opened and bloody seem to be part of the art work too. Stelarc is interested in body modification that is less permanent and more oriented to function. Prosthetic additions such as a third hand or a 'virtual arm' are used to produce drawings. In a series of body suspensions Stelarc used hooks through the skin, ropes and stones as counterweights to make the body itself an object – to make it an 'obsolete body', no longer self-supporting. The sounds of his body were amplified and relayed as part of the art work.

Artists who modify the body are challenging its boundaries, challenging the boundary between what can be *made* by humans and what *is* human.[7] The formation of the body is treated as available for modification in the same way as any other artefact. This challenge of the status of the body may seem at first somewhat heretical – interfering with the distinction between natural bodies and human made artefacts. But body modifications (tattoos, piercings, scarification, implants and suspensions) have long been a part of rituals in pre-industrialized cultures and they have returned to ritual significance in late modern societies among people who do not claim to be artists. In traditional pre-industrialized cultures, body modifications often indicated status (age, gender, social rank) or membership of a tribe or group but in contemporary society they do not seem to have such a coherent meaning.

Piercing, for example, does not arise from cultural pressure or expectation (as circumcision does in both traditional and modern cultures) but is sometimes linked with transitions from one stage of life to another, with life events or affirming individuality and identity. Some piercings are more about how they look to others, some are about how they feel to the wearer but all are an attempt to achieve a variation in the 'normal' body. They are then modifications that operate in exactly the opposite way to medical prostheses which attempt to reclaim function or appearance that is as near as possible to a culturally construed norm. Body piercings most often carry 'ball capture rings' or 'barbells' of surgical stainless steel – the sort of material that will be used in internal, structural, medical prostheses. Through the surface of the body the hard, heavy and shiny material provides a contrast with the soft, pliable, white through black tones of flesh. Body piercing is a form of body modification that cannot 'pass' as a normal body part; it has precisely the opposite aim to the cosmetic prosthesis.

Piercings that can be seen are most often on the face (ear lobes, ear rim, tragus, eyebrow, septum, nostril, lip, labret, tongue) and elicit a reaction from others:

> I had a strange craving. I wanted to put an earring in my lip. I had never seen anyone with this sort of piercing before . . . I wasn't quite sure why I wanted to get this strange piercing, but I knew I needed it . . . For the next few weeks many people notified me that I had a piece of my braces (which I did not have at the time) sticking out of my mouth, and many asked why I was chewing on a paper clip. When I replied that I had a hole in my lip similar to an ear pierce and that the metal was the earring I was wearing in my lip, many were visibly repulsed, which amused me no end.
>
> (Wall 1997: 13–14)

This account, submitted by a teenage woman to an Internet site, describes her enjoyment of the response of others: the piercing was clearly a departure from the usual form of jewellery in this culture. As other parts of the account make clear, the piercing helped her to identify with others who wanted to situate themselves obliquely to the mainstream culture.

Piercings, tattoos and other visible body modifications can be understood as a transgression of and resistance against established values. Paul Sweetman (1999) argues that body modification practices, despite many ambiguities, have the potential 'to act as forms of counter-hegemonic self-inscription, resisting, subverting, or undermining contemporary gendered norms of appearance' unlike other body modification practices such as dieting, keep-fit and aerobics which tend to 'move those involved closer towards, rather than further away from the hegemonic bodily ideal' (Sweetman 1999). What the 'hegemonic bodily ideal' is is clearly in a state of continual change; Sweetman points to comments in the press and elsewhere, and the use of tattooing and piercing in advertisements, as indicators of exotic or unusual people.

Some piercings are not visible in public places – or at least less so. On the body, navel and nipple piercings may be visible depending on dress style. But genital piercings (penis, scrotum, clitoral hood, inner or outer labia: see Clarke 1994 for descriptions and illustrations of the range of piercings) are most likely to be visible only to a lover. I talked to Jeff, who has a number of piercings including ear, tongue, nipple, Prince Albert (ring through penis) and guiche (between scrotum and anus).

Jeff was not part of a group that had visible piercings, neither was he attracted by the 'cultural primitivism' (see Vale and Juno 1989) that enjoys the ritual and even the pain of being pierced. The idea of being pierced came to him in a way he cannot account for; he joked about it being a 'germ' or a 'deformity' that was subconscious and surfaced in his early twenties. At that time there were no piercing studios advertising outside London, but he found a local tattooist who was willing to pierce his nipple. He had rejected the obvious and visible facial piercings at that time in favour of a body piercing which he regards as an 'intimate display' (JR: 328).

Jeff suggested that the importance of piercing for him was not in the experience of getting pierced but in the period after:

> what becomes interesting then is what you do with that hole . . . either the jewellery you put in or whether you stretch it, stretch it to wear larger jewellery or stretch it so that it hangs, so the creativity is actually after . . . after the fact in many ways.
>
> (JR: 340)

The idea of creativity is often linked to piercing and tattooing; it is treated as an expression of individuality in the same way as producing artworks (Vale and Juno 1989; Clarke 1994). Whereas tattoos depend mostly on the artistry of the tattooist, body piercings lead, as Jeff describes, to 'creative' activities by the piercee. There is a personalized ritual of relationship with the pierce – planning the piercing, choosing jewellery, saving up for it, cleaning, changing jewellery, stretching the pierce and so on.

The relation with the pierce and the presence of the object in the body is very physical, especially with intimate piercings:

> there is a whole sort of personal ritual and it's not as if you become blasé about it because it's a different part

> of your body and it's not just the piercing it's also the healing process, which is different, so like when I had my PA done [Prince Albert – ring through urethra and head of the penis], that's quite a bizarre healing process, it's quite worrying at one point because there's a lot of blood involved in it, you know, literally pissing blood is not very, you know, not painful, but not pleasant.
>
> (JR: 391)

As well as pain, such piercings bring bodily pleasures too. Once a new piercing has settled down Jeff described the feeling as being 'really, really good' and lasting for about a year before the sensation becomes as normal as the remainder of body proprioception (JR: 589). Some piercings provide distinctive sensation and he talked of having a ring with a weight in a guiche as 'quite exciting' (JR: 503) and of missing the ring he used to have in his navel because of the way his mug would chink on it when drinking coffee in bed. The pleasure in genital piercings is linked to their effect on sensitive skin, which can lead to heightened sexual pleasure as well as a frequent pleasurable awareness of the body and its sexual parts even when not engaged in sexuality and not aroused. Jeff commented on the extended sensation that derived from jewellery in certain piercings such as his Prince Albert:

> suddenly you realise you have an urethra and it actually has nerves in it, it's actually a really, really exciting feeling.
>
> (JR: 572)

Body (navels, nipples) as well as genital piercings provide a sense of self, of the boundaries of surface as the jewellery in the pierce moves against the skin it is inserted into. The jewellery can also become an extension of the body (see also R.R. Wilson 1995):

> I suppose the PA may have been . . . the prosthetic analogy is there for all to see . . . I have a piece of jewellery, um, that's sometimes known as a megaball, it's like a standard BCR [ball capture ring] but the ball maybe like, you know, um, one and half, two

> centimetres big. And in that sort of situation . . . it provides very sort of, um, very specific and quite bizarre sensations for the wearer but if you are having a sexual involvement then that will literally act as some sort of prosthetic.
>
> (JR: B495)

Jeff also explained how his piercings 'remind' him if he has been over-indulging in late nights, smoking and drinking, by becoming sensitive and uncomfortable. Some piercings never settle down; they may continue to be painful, become infected, migrate to the surface of the skin, or the swelling may never go down. Changing the size, weight and type of the jewellery, playing with it and the rub of clothes against it provide variations in sensation. The jewellery is both incorporated within the body and separate from it. Sensation is derived from the object's transgression of the body's surface and the subsequent effect on nerve endings in that part of the body.

CYBORGS

The cyborg is a mixture of human and machine, in which the machine parts are 'sensate', giving information to the human mind which in turn controls them. Some modern prosthetic limbs provide information directly to the body's nervous system and all prostheses – including body piercings – provide information through their contact with the body's surface nerves. But the cyborg is a modern myth of the extension of human being beyond the normal range of physical capabilities – powers of strength, sense, brain, durability. The mythic 'superhuman', exemplified in the film *RoboCop* (1987), has advanced functionality that comes not from some supernatural or extraterrestial source but from the ingenuity of humans to develop their own species further than biological evolution has managed. The cyborg myth has become a powerful theme in late modern culture, especially in the realm of the Hollywood film (*Six-Billion-Dollar-Man*, *RoboCop*, *Terminator* – see many of the contributions to Featherstone and Burrows 1995; see also Bukatman 1993). The myth involves a reflection on what it is to be human in this culture as well as exploring the practical and moral consequences of breaking down the boundaries between humans and things.

The term 'cyborg' – cybernetic organism – was coined by Clynes and Kline (1960) who were describing 'self regulating man-machine systems' that would be able to cope with different environments for the purposes of space travel (see Tomas 1995: 35). The idea of cybernetics, of feedback systems, was by then at least 12 or 13 years old, having been the subject of Norbert Wiener's (1948) manifesto *Cybernetics: or, Control and Communication in the Animal and the Machine* (see Tomas 1995: 23). The rapid development and miniaturization of a series of technologies that with sensory and feedback systems mimic parts of the human body (robotic arms; servo-systems; memory chips; sensing devices that respond to sight, sound and touch) fuelled the fantasy of the cyborg.

Donna Haraway's 'Cyborg Manifesto' (in Haraway 1991) has been taken to be a key text in exploring the impact of the cyborg on cultural forms (Bukatman 1993; Featherstone and Burrows 1995). Haraway's 'ironic political myth' which treated the 'boundary between science fiction and social reality as an illusion' (1991: 149) used the idea of the cyborg to explore political ideals, historical conditioning and the limits of biological determinism. As a political strategy to encourage thinking beyond existing ideologies and established positions it is a neat textual device (quite how politically effective it is, is far from apparent); but as an analytical device for thinking about human incorporation of objects or machines it is useless. The 'transgressed boundaries, potent fusions, and dangerous possibilities' (Haraway 1991: 154) of Haraway's cyborgs are metaphysical rather than practical; she is not discussing the fusion of metal and skin or electronic sensors and nerves. Her discussion is of subjects in flux rather than subjects being merged with objects; the responsibility for the machines still rests with humans because we make them and as such they are 'an aspect of our embodiment' (Haraway 1991: 180).

The limitations of the cyborg as an idea for understanding the experience of prosthetics is attacked by Vivian Sobchack (1995) whose particular bone of contention is with Baudrillard's (1994[1981]) reading of J.G. Ballard's novel *Crash* (1995 [1973]). Her complaint is that Baudrillard was celebrating the meeting of technology and human body and is somehow aroused by the story, especially its explicit sexual references. But what interests Baudrillard is the reversal of the functionalist model of technology as an extension of man found in Marx and McLuhan, so that in *Crash* it becomes a 'mortal deconstruction of the body . . . the extension of death . . . a body without organs or the pleasure of organs, entirely subjected to the mark, to cutting, to the technical scar' (Baudrillard 1994: 111). Baudrillard is not reading *Crash* as describing a world that is or that ought to be but as 'hypercriticism' in its evocation of a 'mutating and commutating world of simulation and death . . . hypertechnology without finality' (1994: 118–19). Like Haraway (1991), Baudrillard is interested in the mythic, in the world of imagination that arises out of the lived world and will bear back on it but does not claim to be realistic.

Sobchak's anger with Baudrillard's complacency about the real – she refers to his disaffection and disavowal of his own 'lived-body' – is linked to her own real experience of major cancer surgery, amputation and being fitted for a prosthesis. She ironicizes the experience by talking of her status as a 'lean, mean machine', a 'cyborg' reborn through her artificial leg which

> when it or I am working right – almost feels like 'me'. This new socket has also allowed me a kind of experience with 'artificial orifices' that has none of the pain of surgery and all of the erotic play of technology. Every time I put the leg on, I literally 'screw' a valve into a hole in my new thigh, depressing it to let the air out so that the prosthetic sucks my stump into the very depths of its fibreglass embrace.
>
> (Sobchack 1995: 208)

She goes on to describe in a less ironic mode that to use the prosthetic leg, she needed to subjectively feel through her body it's weight and rhythm and to integrate it into her gait. To imagine it as an exteriorized object to be manipulated made using the leg more difficult but such a prosthesis is an object that can be detached and the strength and durability of its modern materials (titanium and fibreglass) do not transfer to its owner/user. Sobchack is clear that, while there was a process of incorporation, it did not amount to a merging; the prosthetic leg was no more than an object, detachable and not integrated into her subjective self:

> what is not true is that I've resigned myself to being a cyborg, a techno-body. My prosthesis has not incorporated me. Rather, the whole aim of my physical

> existence over the last year and a half has been to incorporate it.
>
> (Sobchack 1995: 208)

CONCLUSIONS

Prostheses do not involve the merging of subject with object as in the sci-fi cyborg; the prosthesis remains an extension or an enablement. There is no reason to suppose that taking material permanently into the body, or attaching it routinely, changes the sense of identity of the person. Far more important are the physical limitations of a damaged hip or an amputated leg that lead the person to incorporate some thing into the body, permanently or temporarily. Prosthetics do raise questions about the boundaries and the integrity of the body but there is no reason to regard them as undermining the integrity of the human subject. The prosthetic limb is an aid to using the body in its physical and cultural environment – rather like the protective suit. These material extensions to the body are incorporated on a practical basis, for practical purposes. The impact of being able to walk after amputation, and even to 'pass' as not disabled, must give enormous support to the subjective sense of identity. Like the protective suit, body piercing alters the human form but does not threaten the embodiment of the wearer. Each object serves as an extension to the human body and as such changes not only the range of that body but also the social relations that that person/body can engage in.

The entering of thing into being, or human being into thing does not seem to radically shift the locus of subjectivity. But the *idea* of merging of human and thing remains a fertile site for exploration by science fiction writers, artists, political theorists and film makers. The understanding of human identity can be reappraised and reaffirmed through speculation – in a world bereft of mystical beasts, gods and spirits – about the difference between human subject and material object and the consequences of their co-mingling.

NOTES

1 'The cyborg is the figure born of the interface of automaton and autonomy' (Haraway in *Primate Visions*, p. 139, quoted in Bukatman 1993: 322).

2 In researching this chapter I interviewed a small number of people with direct personal experience of having accepted 'things' to be part of their bodies. Quotations are transcribed from tape recordings of the interviews.

3 'The combination of the Multiflex Ankle and Dynamic Response Foot gives you shock absorption and controlled flexible action at heel strike and a spring action at toe off' (Endolite website 1998 – http://www.oandp.com/commerci/enolite/drfoot.htm). In the UK the Blatchford Intelligent Prosthesis utilizes a microchip to adjust the gait of the artificial leg to variations in the speed of the wearer's pace.

4 The Edinburgh Modular Arm System uses residual movement in the shoulder of its wearer to operate microswitches that control a motorized shoulder, bending elbow, rotating wrist and contracting fingers. 'It becomes so natural that I can do things like tying shoelaces and hammering nails without even thinking', said user Campbell Aird to the *Guardian* (27 August 1998: 5).

5 As one company website puts it: 'we believe the specialized needs of upper extremity patients require a personal focus. These amputees have lost a sophisticated tool of daily life. That's why helping to restore function in people who do not have upper limbs is a primary goal' (Novacare website 1998 – http: //www.novacaresabolich.com/uepp.html).

6 The Edinburgh Modular Arm System is covered in a latex skin 'so life-like that it comes with wrinkles and fingerprints' (*Guardian* 17 August 1998: 5).

7 'in the past, we've considered the skin as surface, as interface. The skin has been a boundary for the soul, for the self, and simultaneously, a beginning to the world. Once technology stretches and pierces the skin, the skin as a barrier is erased' (Stelarc interview in CTHEORY, undated, at: http: //www.ctheory.com/a29-extended_body.html)

10
CONCLUSION

If you have read this book so far, you may have begun to question your own social relationship with it; it is a mediating object that contributes to a material discourse. The book has a biography, linked to the processes of writing, publishing and printing and this particular book might be a second hand copy or one from a library that has been used by other people. It is a thing of its time indicated by its linguistic style, layout and contents, not to mention its publication date and attributed author. As an object it is part of various series – other books on similar topics, other different books in the same bookshop or library, other books from the same print run. The processes of producing the book will have given it an exchange-value and a social use-value and it may have acquired some fetish value through the material discourse of the publisher's blurb, reading lists, reviews and recommendations (I hope so anyway!). Reading involves particular ways of interacting with the object – holding it open in the hands, sitting in an armchair, lying on a bed, sitting at a desk. The eyes have to follow the script, they have to be open and what they see has to be attended to if the activity is to be called reading. The contents of the book will be recycled in essays and conversations, perhaps because it is provocative, perhaps because it deserves ridicule.

Through the course of the book I have introduced a number of different types of objects including the cairn, the mini-strip, teaspoons, shoes and fur, perfume, houses, chairs, stairs, washing machines, dresses, jeans, windsurfers, rigs, a paperweight, petrol pump, art works, a sports car, telephones, computer screens, wetsuits, hip prostheses and penis rings. These things have all been explored as things in social relations; there are particular types of interactions between people and these things which in turn affect relations between people. It is these social relations with things in a modern system of objects that constitute contemporary material culture.

The things I have discussed have rather appeared as if by magic; I have not discussed the design and production process in any depth and, more importantly, I have not discussed the social relations involved in making these things. Besides the economic relations of production there are human activities of work, of repetitively interacting with tools and machines, that produce the plethora of objects to be found in modern, western cultures. I have avoided discussing these sorts of activities, which are important, partly because of space but also because they are so often effaced in the 'living with' relations of material culture. Not only is the worker alienated from their product in modern capitalism but also the product is itself alienated: it seldom bears a trace of who made it or when, carrying at best a brand name and a place where it was manufactured. Many modern artefacts are made in a very different sort of cultural context from the one in which they are used. In using them we interact with the form of the object, which tells us about functional and aesthetic design, materials technology and manufacturing techniques, in the material culture of origin. These features of the material culture are embedded within the object and released as it is used.

There are many types of objects in the material culture of modern societies that I have not mentioned; the things I have mentioned have been chosen to hint at the spheres of contemporary material culture rather than to comprehensively cover the range of objects we live with. I have drawn occasionally on the ideas of anthropologists and historians but I have not attempted to reckon with their analyses of the material cultures of the past or different societies. The artefacts that they are interested in often find their way into museums where they are presented to the curiosity of the general public. As I have hinted, it is in the exhibition and the museum that we come across objects as neophytes, discovering strange objects within the midst or our contemporary culture. I have ignored museums but paid some attention to the exhibited work of artists where it directly addresses the social relations between people and objects. The creator of an ordinary object, that is found and put in a musum, may have made something functional that is not intended to mediate at all. But the art object, no matter what its particular form, *is* intended to mediate and the artist must establish a particular relationship with the viewer through its form.

I have not attempted to present a systematic account of the types of social relations with things that arise through living with them because the fluidity of such relations does not lend itself to systematic analysis. I began by suggesting that the concept of consumption is limited as an approach to material culture, arguing that the ideas of 'living with things' and 'using' them encompass rather better the range of social relationships with objects. Consumption focuses on exchange and the economic processes of the value and choice of commodities. To argue, as Marx did, that commodities are 'fetishized' under capitalism looses the analytic power of the term; I have suggested that social value needs to be understood in terms of use and that the fetish character of objects refers to the ways in which social values are 'overdetermined' or enhanced before and beyond use, through, for example advertising and packaging.

In thinking about the ordinary social relations of 'living with', I began by discussing how we transform a house into a home through *bricolage*, 'keeping' furniture and doing domestic work. Through these activities we achieve dwelling through building. The idea of 'fashion' neatly sums up the fluidity of social relations with objects that link individuals and the culture they live in. However, I argued that fashion is not disembodied as ideas or 'looks' but is realized through a material discourse that involves a series of relations between spoken and written language, the material of clothes as they are worn and even the images of them as objects. To show the complexity of interacting with objects through bodily movement, I explored what is involved in playing with a windsurfer. This is not simply a learnt interaction between individual and thing but one that is part of an actor-network which includes a series of other objects and actors.

Material objects emerge in the context of historical time and then they age, surviving into other times. They reflect something of the particular culture in which they emerged, its forms of industry and the aesthetic values. The temporality of objects can be understood in terms of their 'biography' that affects particular relations with them, revaluing rubbish, collecting things and negotiating their place in an evolving system of objects. All objects mediate at least something of their place in the system of objects but certain objects mediate intentional communications. These objects need to be 'turned on' by receiving attention from humans. At one extreme mediating objects respond with the abstract aesthetic messages of works of art, at the other they are the everyday messages between humans via the telephone. In between, some ordinary objects borrow from the work of art to draw attention to their form while art will parody the commodity to highlight the state of material culture. The reproduction of objects that are more or less identical threatens the singularity of the art object but the play of light on the video screen also threatens the traditional materiality of text and image. The social relations of viewing are adjusted to incorporate the 'transaesthetics' of endless reproduction and instant transformation of the screen.

Finally I discussed the very intimate relations between the thing of the human body and the thing of the artefact. In the form of medical prostheses and jewellery we incorporate inanimate material into living bodies, and through protective suits we increase their resistance to hostile environments. The fascination with bodies as material culture is explored at the level of imagination and practicality by artists who transform their own bodies as so much material or 'make' bodies that might pass as real – if only for a moment.

Science fiction and the predictions of technologists often foresee a world in which objects will take over all our chores and even challenge us for mastery of the world. But worlds such as Ian M. Banks's 'Culture' with its spaceships that have minds, drones with extensive physical and intellectual capacities and human bodies significantly enhanced by manufactured add-ins, are still a long way off. We do have machines that dig roads, wash clothes and build cars – but they all need very careful minding by humans. We do have machines that can remember, manipulate mathematical formulae and visual representations to a degree of complexity that it takes a very skilled human mind to keep up with. But they do not talk or think. These machines have no imagination, political awareness, aesthetic sense, ethical judgement, empathy, emotion, sexuality or wickedness – unless some human has programmed it into them. This means that while the ways in which we interact with objects have changed, we still interact with them as reflections or extensions of ourselves and our bodies or as reflections and extensions of other people – sometimes of those other people collectively as a culture.

Material culture is still human culture; the autonomy of objects is very limited. Things do not have social relations with each other: they are our products and the culture of which they are a part is unequivocally the culture of human society. Modernity, with its rapid development of technology and industrialization, has increased the range and complexity of different things with which we have social relations. The system of objects in a modern industrialized society is vastly greater and more complex than that in a pre-industrialized society. Things are important, although not as important as other people, and their importance increases as they become more intertwined with the way we live our social lives.

In his later work Baudrillard (1990a; 1990b) explores the capability of the object to 'seduce' the subject, to reduce the determinative effect of the social and to lead the subject into the indeterminate realm of chance and the vertiginous, spinning body. Determination, the process of causality, even in the material world, is called into question:

> The reaction to this new state of things has not been a resigned abandonment of old values but rather a mad overdetermination, an exacerbation of these values of reference, function, finality and causality.
>
> (Baudrillard 1990b: 11)

Whereas production was the irreversible, modern process of dominance of subject over object relations, seduction emerges as the reversible, post-modern mode of relationship between subject and object. The result is not the emergence of something new but an excess of the old values; in the face of indeterminacy, overdetermination becomes 'hyperdetermination' (Baudrillard 1990b: 12).

This idea of things as 'seductive' and as sucking us back into our own history, is itself seductive if we try to grasp what is distinctive about material cultures in late modernity. Indeed the fetish quality of objects,[1] where their value is enhanced through the circulation of images and ideas, does make some objects offered for exchange and consumption, fashionable and seductive. For some people, for some of the time, their desire for an object or a series of objects supersedes their desire for engagement in the social world and seems to be a characteristic of consumer societies. But to treat seduction as a dominating principle of modern material culture is to overstate the case. I hope to have demonstrated, even while I have used many of Baudrillard's ideas to reflect on social relations with things, that the forms of things and the social relations in late modernity are much more routine and mundane. The way that material culture connects with the social world is neither a result of consumption choices nor because objects have seduced us. Material culture provides a way of understanding the social world because of the ways we appropriate it, through living with objects in our everyday lives; interacting with them, using them, allowing them to mediate between us and having quasi-social relationships with them. We can, of course, easily put them aside and move on to other types of social action – just as you are about to do with this book.

NOTE

1 The fetish becomes for Baudrillard a representative of the power of the object to determine the subject, to reverse causality (Baudrillard 1990b: 114).

FURTHER READING

As I have argued, material culture is largely absent from sociological discussions but Jean Baudrillard's fascinating (and frustrating!) *The System of Objects* is the nearest thing to a seminal text in this area. Originally published in French in 1968 it has only recently been translated and published in full (London: Verso, 1996). Stephen Riggins has brought together a most unusual collection of sociological studies of material culture in *The Socialness of Things: Essays on the Socio-Semiotics of Objects* (New York: Mouton de Gruyter, 1994). Unfortunately this is currently available only as an expensive hardback book. In Colin Campbell's enormously readable *The Romantic Ethic and the Spirit of Modern Consumerism* (Oxford: Blackwell, 1987) there is a tight and thoroughly sociological argument about the emergence of a modern social order in which fantasy and desire for material objects play a more complex and important part in culture than ever before.

Sociologists have also produced some well argued discussions of consumption in modern societies. Don Slater's *Consumer Culture and Modernity* (Cambridge: Polity Press, 1997) provides a clear account of the theoretical arguments surrounding the significance of consumpton, while Celia Lury's illustrated and accessible *Consumer Culture* (Cambridge: Polity Press, 1996) focuses more on the way consumption practices are linked to social divisions of gender, class, age and ethnicity. Peter Corrigan's *The Sociology of Consumption* (London: Sage, 1997) is organized around consumption practices (magazines, advertising, shops) and considers food, tourism, the home, the body and fashion as spheres of consumption.

Anthropologists have played a major part in bringing the study of material culture from being a resource for studying exotic cultures to making consumption a central issue for the study of modern, western cultures. *The World of Goods: Towards an Anthropology of Consumption*, by Mary Douglas and Baron Isherwood, was first published in 1979 but its republication in 1996 (London: Routledge) indicates its continuing relevance. Daniel Miller's *Material Culture and Mass Consumption* (Oxford: Blackwell, 1987) is also a key text that explores some very tricky but rewarding theoretical issues. Miller's edited collection *Material Cultures: Why Some Things Matter* (London: UCL Press, 1998) provides some very accessible contemporary studies of material culture (including banners in Northern Ireland, paper in the office and furnishings in the home) as well as bringing his theoretical position up to date. Arjun Appadurai's much cited edited collection *The Social Life of Things: Commodities in Cultural Perspective* (Cambridge: Cambridge University Press, 1986) provides a source of very original ideas about the way objects circulate in cultures.

From the perspective of history, Adrian Forty's *Objects of Desire: Design and Society since 1750* (London: Thames and Hudson, 1986) gives a well illustrated and accessible account of the changes in objects in the home and the office and the connections between design, technology and social forms. Asa Briggs's *Victorian Things* (Harmondsworth: Penguin, 1990) is a great source for detail about a period of proliferation and complexity in the world of objects. There is a growing literature about museums as the storehouses of material culture from the past. Susan M. Pearce's edited collection *Experiencing Material Culture in the Western World* (London: Leicester University Press, 1997) covers a variety of topics in this field.

The gendered nature of material culture is brought out in studies of technology such as Ruth Schwartz Cowan's *More Work for Mother: The Ironies of Household Technology from the Open Hearth to the Microwave* (London: Free Association, 1989) and those included in Cynthia Cockburn and Ruža Fürst-Dilić's edited collection *Bringing Technology Home: Gender and Technology in a Changing Europe* (Buckingham: Open University Press, 1994). Pat Kirkham's edited collection on *The Gendered Object* (Manchester: Manchester University Press, 1996) provides a variety of different disciplinary perspectives.

The *Journal of Material Culture* published by Sage has produced three editions a year since 1996 containing articles from a range of mainly social science disciplines on the broad field of material culture. The journal *things*, which takes a more humanities oriented view, has been published since 1994 and is edited by past and present students of the Victoria and Albert/Royal College of Art course in the History of Design.

BIBLIOGRAPHY ■

Adorno, T. and Horkheimer, M. (1979 [1944]) *Dialectic of Enlightenment*. London: Verso.

Akrich, M. (1992) The de-scription of technical objects, in W.E. Bijker and J. Law (eds) *Shaping Technology/Building Society: Studies in Sociotechnical Change*. Cambridge, MA: MIT Press.

Akrich, M. and Latour, B. (1992) A summary of a convenient vocabulary for the semiotics of human and nonhuman assemblies, in W.E. Bijker and J. Law (eds) *Shaping Technology/Building Society: Studies in Sociotechnical Change*. Cambridge MA: MIT Press.

Anderson, D.R. and Burns, J. (1991) Paying attention to television, in J. Bryant and D. Zillmann (eds) *Responding to the Screen: Reception and Reaction Processes*. Hillsdale, NJ: Lawrence Erlbaum.

Anderson, D.R. and Field, D.E. (1991) Online and offline assessment of the television audience, in J. Bryant and D. Zillmann (eds) *Responding to the Screen: Reception and Reaction Processes*. Hillsdale, NJ: Lawrence Erlbaum.

Appadurai, A. (1986) Introduction: commodities and the politics of value, in A. Appadurai (ed.) *The Social Life of Things: Commodities in Cultural Perspective*. Cambridge: Cambridge University Press.

Aragon, L. (1987 [1924]) *The Paris Peasant*, London: Picador.
Ash, J. (1996) The tie: presence and absence, in P. Kirkham (ed.) *The Gendered Object*. Manchester: Manchester University Press.
Ashmore, M., Wooffitt, R. and Harding, S. (eds) (1994) Humans and others: the concept of 'agency' and its attribution, Special issue of *American Behavioral Scientist*, 37(6).
Ballard, J.G. (1995 [1973]) *Crash*. London: Vintage.
Banks, I.M. (1991) Descendant, in *The State of the Art*. London: Orbit.
Barnard, M. (1996) *Fashion as Communication*. London: Routledge.
Barthes, R. (1957) Histoire et sociologie du vêtement: quelques observations méthodologiques, *Annales*, 3: 430–41.
Barthes, R. (1973) *Mythologies*. St Albans: Paladin.
Barthes, R. (1975 [1970]) *S/Z*. London: Jonathan Cape.
Barthes, R. (1977a [1961]) The photographic message, in *Image – Music – Text*. Glasgow: Fontana/Collins.
Barthes, R. (1977b [1964]) The rhetoric of the image, in *Image – Music – Text*. Glasgow: Fontana/Collins.
Barthes, R. (1979) *The Eiffel Tower and Other Mythologies*. New York: Hill and Wang.
Barthes, R. (1986) Leaving the movie theatre, in *The Rustle of Language*. Berkeley, CA: University of California Press.
Barthes, R. (1990 [1967]) *The Fashion System*. Berkeley, CA: University of California Press.
Baudelaire, C. (1995) *The Painter of Modern Life and Other Essays*, trans. J. Mayne. London: Phaidon.
Baudrillard, J. (1981 [1972]) *For a Critique of the Political Economy of the Sign*. St Louis, MO: Telos Press.
Baudrillard, J. (1990a [1979]) *Seduction*. London: Macmillan.
Baudrillard, J. (1990b [1983]) *Fatal Strategies*. London: Pluto.
Baudrillard, J. (1993a [1976]) *Symbolic Exchange and Death*. London: Sage.
Baudrillard, J. (1993b [1990]) *Transparency of Evil: Essays on Extreme Phenomena*. London: Verso.
Baudrillard, Jean (1994 [1981]) *Simulacra and Simulation*. Ann Arbor, MI: University of Michigan Press.
Baudrillard, J. (1995 [1994]) Plastic surgery for the other, *CTHEORY*, http://www.ctheory.com/a33-plastic_surgery.html
Baudrillard, J. (1996 [1968]) *The System of Objects*. London: Verso.
Baudrillard, J. (1997a) Objects, images, and the possibilities of illusion, in N. Zurbrugg (ed.) *Jean Baudrillard, Art and Artefact*. London: Sage.
Baudrillard, J. (1997b) Aesthetic illusion and virtual reality, in N. Zurbrugg (ed.) *Jean Baudrillard, Art and Artefact*. London: Sage.
Baudrillard, J. (1998 [1970]) *The Consumer Society*. London: Sage.

Becker, H.S. (1986) *Doing Things Together: Selected Papers, Part 4: Photography*. Evanston, IL: Northwestern University Press.

Belk, R.W. (1995) *Collecting in a Human Society*. London: Routledge.

Bell, Q. (1992 [1947]) *On Human Finery: The Classic Study of Fashion through the Ages*. London: Allison and Busby.

Benjamin, W. (1973 [1936]) The work of art in the age of mechanical reproduction, in *Illuminations*. London: Fontana.

Benjamin, W. (1985 [1933]) On the mimetic faculty, in *One Way Street and Other Writings*. London: Verso.

Benjamin, W. (1989) Re the theory of knowledge, theory of progress, in G. Smith (ed.) *Benjamin, Philosophy, Aesthetics, History*. Chicago: University of Chicago Press.

Benjamin, W. (1997) *Charles Baudelaire*. London: Verso.

Betteridge, J. (1997) Answering back: the telephone, modernity and everyday life, *Media, Culture and Society*, 19(4): 583–603.

Bloomfield, B. (ed.) (1987) *The Question of Artificial Intelligence: Philosophical and Sociological Perspectives*. London: Croom Helm.

Blumer, H. (1969) Fashion: from class differentiation to collective selection, *Sociological Quarterly*, 10 (summer): 275–91.

Bocock, R. (1993) *Consumption*. London: Routledge.

Bourdieu, P. (1973) The Berber house, in M. Douglas (ed.) *Rules and Meanings: The Anthropology of Everyday Knowledge*. Harmondsworth: Penguin.

Bourdieu, P. (1984 [1979]) *Distinction: A Social Critique of the Judgement of Taste*. London: Routledge.

Bourdieu, P. (1998a) *On Television and Journalism*. London: Pluto.

Bourdieu, P. (1998b) *Contre-feux*. Paris: Liber Raisons d'agir.

Bourdieu, P. (1990) *Photography: A Middle-brow Art*. Cambridge: Polity Press.

Braudel, F. (1992 [1979]) *The Structures of Everyday Life: The Limits of the Possible*. Berkeley, CA: University of California Press.

Briggs, A. (1990 [1988]) *Victorian Things*. Harmondsworth: Penguin.

Bruck, G. vom (1997) A house turned inside out, *Journal of Material Culture*, 2(2): 139–72.

Bukatman, S. (1993) *Terminal Identity: The Virtual Subject in Post-Modern Science Fiction*. Durham, NC and London: Duke University Press.

Buzzaccarini, V. de (1990) Clothing, in C. Pirovano (ed.) *History of Industrial Design, vol. 2, 1851–1918, The Great Emporium of the World*. Milan: Electa.

Caillois, R. (1961 [1958]) *Man, Play and Games*. Free Press: New York.

Callon, M. (1986) Some elements of a sociology of translation: domestication of the scallops and the fishermen of St Brieuc Bay, in J. Law (ed.) *Power, Action and Belief: A New Sociology of Knowledge*. London: Routledge and Kegan Paul.

Callon, M. (1991) Techno-economic networks and irreversibility, in J. Law (ed.) *A Sociology of Monsters: Essays on Power, Technology and Domination*. London: Routledge.

Calvet, J.-L. (1994 [1990]) *Roland Barthes: A Biography*. Cambridge: Polity Press.

Campbell, C. (1987) *The Romantic Ethic and the Spirit of Modern Consumerism*. Oxford: Blackwell.

Campbell, C. (1992) The desire for the new: its nature and social location as presented in theories of fashion and modern consumerism, in R. Silverstone and E. Hirsch (eds) *Consuming Technologies: Media and Information in Domestic Spaces*. London: Routledge.

Campbell, C. (1996) The meaning of objects and the meaning of actions: a critical note on the sociology of consumption and theories of clothing, *Journal of Material Culture*, 1(1): 93–105.

Certeau, M. de (1984) *The Practice of Everyday Life*. Berkeley, CA: University of California Press.

Chabaud-Rychter, D. (1994) Women users in the design process of a food robot: innovation in a French domestic appliance company, in C. Cockburn and R. Fürst-Dilić (eds) *Bringing Technology Home: Gender and Technology in a Changing Europe*. Buckingham: Open University Press.

Clarke, P. (1994) *The Eye of the Needle*. Nuneaton, Warwicks: Pauline Clarke.

Clynes, M.E. and Kline, N.S. (1960) Cyborgs and space, *Astronautics*, September: 26–7, 74–6.

Cockburn, C. and Ormrod, S. (1993) *Gender and Technology in the Making*. London: Sage.

Collins, H.M. (1990) *Artificial Experts: Social Knowledge and Intelligent Machines*. Cambridge, MA: MIT Press.

Corrigan, P. (1994) Three dimensions of the clothing object, in S.H. Riggins (ed.) *The Socialness of Things: Essays on the Socio-Semiotics of Objects*. New York: Mouton de Gruyter.

Corrigan, P. (1997) *The Sociology of Consumption: An Introduction*. London: Sage.

Cranz, G. (1996) The social purpose of chairs: maintaining hierarchy in ancient societies and contemporary institutions. Paper presented at the American Sociological Association Annual Meeting, New York, August.

Critcher, C., Bramham, P. and Tomlinson, A. (eds) (1995) *Sociology of Leisure: A Reader*. London: Chapman Hall.

Csikszentmihalyi, M. (1975) *Beyond Boredom and Anxiety*. San Francisco: Jossey Bass.

Csikszentmihalyi, M. and Rochberg-Halton, E. (1981) *The Meaning of Things: Domestic Symbols and the Self*. Cambridge: Cambridge University Press.

Cullum-Swann, B. and Manning, P.K. (1994) What is a t-shirt? Codes, chronotypes and everyday objects, in S.H. Riggins (ed.) *The Socialness of Things: Essays on the Socio-Semiotics of Objects*. New York: Mouton de Gruyter.

Cuomo, D. (1989) De l'Europe en Amérique et retour: le voyage du jeans, in *Blu Blue-Jeans: Il blu popolare*. Milan: Electra.

Danet, B. (1997) Books, letters, documents: the changing aesthetic of texts in late print culture, *Journal of Material Culture*, 2(1): 5–38.

Dant, T. (1988) Home is 'everything' – the meaning of home for social policy. Paper presented to the Annual Conference of the British Society of Gerontology, Swansea, September.

Dant, T. (1991) *Knowledge, Ideology and Discourse*. London: Routledge.

Davis, F. (1992) *Fashion, Culture and Identity*. Chicago: University of Chicago Press.

Department of Employment (DoE) (1977) *Family Expenditure Survey 1977*. London: HMSO.

Dippert, R.R. (1993) *Artifacts, Art Works, and Agency*. Philadelphia, PA: Temple University Press.

Dittmar, H. (1992) *The Social Psychology of Material Possessions: To Have Is To Be*. Hemel Hempstead: Harvester Wheatsheaf.

Douglas, M. and Isherwood, B. (1996 [1979]) *The World of Goods: Towards an Anthropology of Consumption*. London: Routledge.

Dreyfus, H.L. and Dreyfus, S.E. (1986) *Mind Over Machine*. New York: Free Press.

Duras, M. (1986 [1979]) *Le Navire Night et autres textes*. Paris: Mercure de France, Collection Folio.

Dyson, K. and Humphreys, P. (eds) (1990) *The Political Economy of Communications: International and European Dimensions*. London: Routledge.

Eco, U. (1986) Function and sign: semiotics of architecture, in M. Gottdiener and A. Lagopoulos (eds) *The City and the Sign: An Introduction to Urban Semiotics*. New York: Columbia University Press.

Eco, U. (1987) Lumbar thought, in *Travels in Hyperreality*. London: Picador.

Edwards, D., Ashmore, M. and Potter, J. (1995) Death and furniture: the rhetoric, politics and theology of bottom line arguments against relativism, *History of the Human Sciences*, 8(2): 25–49.

Elias, N. and Dunning, E. (1986) *The Quest for Excitement: Sport and Leisure in the Civilizing Process*. Oxford: Basil Blackwell.

Ewen, S. and Ewen, E. (1992) *Channels of Desire: Mass Images and the Shaping of American Consciousness*. Minneapolis, MN: University of Minnesota Press.

Featherstone, M. (1991) *Consumer Culture and Postmodernism*. London: Sage.

Featherstone, M. and Burrows, R. (eds) (1995) *Cyberspace/Cyberbodies/Cyberpunk: Cultures of Technological Embodiment*. London: Sage.

Fine, B. and Leopold, E. (1993) *The World of Consumption*. London: Routledge.

Finkelstein, J. (1991) *The Fashioned Self*. Cambridge: Polity Press.

Finlayson, I. (1990) *Denim: An American Legend*. Norwich: Parke Sutton.

Fisher, T. (1997) *The Collector Collector*. London: Secker and Warburg.

Fiske, J. (1989) *Understanding Popular Culture*. London: Unwin Hyman.

Forty, A. (1986) *Objects of Desire: Design and Society since 1750*. London: Thames and Hudson.

Forty, A. (1990) Design and mechanization: the standardized product, in C. Pirovano (ed.) *History of Industrial Design, vol. 2, 1815–1918, The Great Emporium of the World*. Milan: Electa.

Freud, S. (1977a [1905]) Three essays on the Theory of Sexuality, in *On Sexuality*. Harmondsworth: Penguin.

Freud, S. (1977b [1927]) Fetishism, in *On Sexuality*. Harmondsworth: Penguin.

Frisby, D. (1992) *Simmel and Since: Essays on Georg Simmel's Social Theory*. London: Routledge.

Gamman, L. and Makinen, M. (1994) *Female Fetishism: A New Look*. London: Lawrence and Wishart.

Genosko, G. (1994) *Baudrillard and Signs: Signification Ablaze*. London: Routledge.

Geras, N. (1976) Essence and appearance: aspects of fetishism in Marx's *Capital*, *New Left Review*, 65: 69–85.

Gibson, J.J. (1979) *The Ecological Approach to Visual Perception*. Boston, MA: Houghton Mifflin.

Giedion, S. (1969 [1948]) *Mechanization Takes Command: A Contribution to Anonymous History*. New York: W.W. Norton.

Gilder, G. (1994) *Life After Television: The Coming Transformation of Media and American Life*, rev. edn. New York: W.W. Norton.

Gilloch, G. (1996) *Myth and Metropolis: Walter Benjamin and the City*. Cambridge: Polity Press.

Godelier, M. (1977) *Perspectives in Marxist Anthropology*. Cambridge: Cambridge University Press.

Goffman, E. (1959) *The Presentation of Self in Everyday Life*. New York: Doubleday.

Goffman, E. (1963) *Behaviour in Public Places*. New York: Free Press.

Goffman, E. (1986 [1974]) *Frame Analysis*. Boston, MA: North Eastern University Press.

Goffman, E. (1990 [1963]) *Stigma: Notes on the Management of Spoiled Identity*. Harmondsworth: Penguin.

Gomez, M.C.A. (1994) Bodies, machines and male power, in C. Cockburn and R. Fürst-Dilić (eds) *Bringing Technology Home: Gender and Technology in a Changing Europe*. Buckingham: Open University Press.

Gordon, C.C. (1996) Artifact and assemblage: notes on knowing and design. Paper presented to the American Sociological Association Annual Meeting, New York, August.

Granö, V. (1997) The collector collector, *things*, 6: 93–9.

Graves, J. (1996) The washing machine, in P. Kirkham (ed.) *The Gendered Object*. Manchester: Manchester University Press.

Gronow, J. (1997) *The Sociology of Taste*. London: Routledge.

Grosz, E. (1993) Lesbian fetishism?, in E. Apter and W. Pietz (eds) *Fetishism as Cultural Discourse*. Ithaca, NY: Cornell University Press.

Haraway, D. (1991) *Simians, Cyborgs and Women: The Reinvention of Nature*. London: Free Association Books.

Hardyment, C. (1988) *From Mangle to Microwave: The Mechanization of Household Work*. Cambridge: Polity Press.

Harvey, D. (1989) *The Condition of Postmodernity*. Oxford: Basil Blackwell.

Haug, W.F. (1986) *Critique of Commodity Aesthetics: Appearance, Sexuality and Advertising in Capitalist Society*. Cambridge: Polity Press.

Hauser, A. (1982) *The Sociology of Art*. London: Routledge and Kegan Paul.

Hawkes, T. (1977) *Structuralism and Semiotics*. London: Methuen.

Hayles, N.K. (1996) Boundary disputes: homeostasis: reflexivity, and the foundations of cybernetics, in R. Markley (ed.) *Virtual Realities and their Discontents*. Baltimore, MD: Johns Hopkins University Press.

Hebdige, D. (1979) *Subculture: The Meaning of Style*. London: Methuen.

Hebdige, D. (1987) The impossible object: towards a sociology of the sublime, *New Formations*, 1 (Spring): 47–76.

Heidegger, M. (1967) *What is a Thing?* Chicago: Henry Regenery.

Heidegger, M. (1977) *The Question Concerning Technology and Other Essays*. New York: Harper Torchbooks.

Heidegger, M. (1978 [1954]) Building dwelling thinking, in *Basic Writings*. London: Routledge and Kegan Paul.

Herbert, F. (1968 [1965]) *Dune*. London: Hodder and Stoughton.

Heywood, I. (1994) Urgent dreams: climbing, rationalization and ambivalence, *Leisure Studies*, 13: 179–94.

Hirsch, E. (1992) The long term and the short term of domestic consumption: an ethnographic case study, in R. Silverstone and E. Hirsch (eds) *Consuming Technologies: Media and Information in Domestic Spaces*. London: Routledge.

Hollander, A. (1993) *Seeing through Clothes*. Berkeley, CA: University of California Press.

Horne, J., Jary, D. and Tomlinson, A. (eds) (1987) *Sport, Leisure and Social Relations*. London: Routledge.

Humphreys, P. and Simpson, S. (1996) European telecommunications and globalisation, in P. Gummett (ed.) *Globalisation and Public Policy*. Cheltenham: Edward Elgar.

Jay, M. (1992) Scopic regimes of modernity, in S. Lash and J. Friedman (eds) *Modernity and Identity*. Oxford: Blackwell.

Jennings, P. (1960) Report on resistentialism, in D. Macdonald (ed.) *Parodies: An Anthology from Chaucer to Beerbohm – and After*. London: Faber and Faber.

Jhally, S. (1987) *The Codes of Advertising: Fetishism and the Political Economy of Meaning in the Consumer Society*. London: Routledge.

Kellner, D. (1989) *Jean Baudrillard: From Marxism to Postmodernism and Beyond*. Cambridge: Polity Press.

Kelly, J.R. (1982) *Leisure*. Englewood Cliffs, NJ: Prentice Hall.

Kinchen, J. (1996) Interiors: nineteenth century essays on the 'masculine' and the 'feminine' room, in P. Kirkham (ed.) *The Gendered Object*. Manchester: Manchester University Press.

Kopytoff, I. (1986) The cultural biography of things, in A. Appadurai (ed.) *The Social Life of Things: Commodities in Cultural Perspective*. Cambridge: Cambridge University Press.

Kreitzman, L. (1999) *The 24 Hour Society*. London: Profile Books.

Kurzman, S. (1996) Research prospectae. http://www2.ucsc/edu/people/kurzman/researchprospectus.htm

Kurzman, S. (1997) Cultural attitudes toward prostheses: an anthropological approach. http://www2.ucsc/edu/people/kurzman/capabilitiesarticle.htm

Latour, B. (1986) The powers of association, in J. Law (ed.) *Power, Action and Belief: A New Sociology of Knowledge*. London: Routledge.

Latour, B. (aka J. Johnson) (1988) Mixing humans and nonhumans together: the sociology of a door-closer, *Social Problems*, 35(3): 298–310.

Latour, B. (1992) Sociology of a few mundane artifacts, in W.E. Bijker and J. Law (eds) *Shaping Technology/Building Society: Studies in Sociotechnical Change*. Cambridge, MA: MIT Press.

Leiss, W. (1978) *The Limits to Satisfaction: On Needs and Commodities*. London: Marion Boyars.

Lévi-Strauss, C. (1966) *The Savage Mind*. London: Weidenfeld and Nicolson.

Levin, C. (1984) Baudrillard, critical theory and psychoanalysis, *Canadian Journal of Political and Social Theory*, 8(1–2): 35–52.

Levin, C. (1996) *Jean Baudrillard: A Study in Cultural Metaphysics*. Hemel Hempstead: Prentice Hall.

Levy, R. (1997) GUI and WYSIWYG: a history of graphic design software, *things*, 6 (summer): 41–59.

Livingstone, S. (1992) The meaning of domestic technologies: a personal construct analysis of familial gender relations, in R. Silverstone and E. Hirsch (eds) *Consuming Technologies: Media and Information in Domestic Spaces*. London: Routledge.

Lunt, P.K. and Livingstone, S.M. (1992) *Mass Consumption and Personal Identity*. Buckingham: Open University Press.

Lurie, A. (1981) *The Language of Clothes*. London: Bloomsbury.

Lury, C. (1996) *Consumer Culture*. Cambridge: Polity Press.

Lyotard, J.-F. (1984) *The Postmodern Condition: A Report on Knowledge*. Manchester: Manchester University Press.

McCarthy, E.D. (1984) Toward a sociology of the physical world: George Herbert Mead on physical objects, *Studies in Symbolic Interaction*, 5: 105–21.

McCracken, G. (1990) *Culture and Consumption: New Approaches to the Symbolic Character of Consumer Goods and Activities*. Bloomington, IN: Indiana University Press.

McLuhan, M. (1994 [1964]) *Understanding Media: The Extensions of Man*. Cambridge, MA: MIT Press.

McRobbie, A. (1989) Second-hand dresses and the role of the ragmarket, in A. McRobbie (ed.) *Zoot Suits and Second-Hand Dresses: An Anthology of Fashion and Music*. London: Macmillan.

Madigan, R. and Munro, M. (1990) Ideal homes: gender and domestic architecture, in T. Putnam and C. Newton (eds) *Household Choices*. London: Futures.

Marcus, G. (1995) *Functionalist Design: An Ongoing History*. Munich: Prestel.

Marx, K. (1973) *Grundrisse: Foundations of the Critique of Political Economy*. Harmondsworth: Penguin.

Marx, K. (1975 [1844]) *Early Writings*. Harmondsworth: Penguin.

Marx, K. (1976) *Capital: Volume One*. Harmondsworth: Penguin.

Matlock, J. (1993) Masquerading women, pathologised men: cross-dressing, fetishism and the theory of perversion, 1882–1935, in E. Apter and W. Pietz (eds) *Fetishism as Cultural Discourse*. Ithaca, NY: Cornell University Press.

Mauss, M. (1973 [1935]) Techniques of the body, *Economy and Society*, 2(1): 70–88.

Mauss, M. (1990 [1950]) *The Gift: The Form and Reason for Exchange in Archaic Societies*. London: Routledge.

Mead, G. H. (1962 [1934]) *Mind, Self, and Society: From the Standpoint of a Social Behaviorist*, edited by C. W. Morris. Chicago: University of Chicago Press.

Mead, G.H. (1980 [1932]) *Philosophy of the Present*. Chicago: University of Chicago Press.

Miller, D. (1987) *Material Culture and Mass Consumption*. Oxford: Blackwell.

Miller, D. (1988) Appropriating the state on the council estate, *Man*, 23: 353–72.

Miller, D. (1995) Consumption as the vanguard of history, in D. Miller (ed.) *Acknowledging Consumption: A Review of New Studies*. London: Routledge.

Miller, D. (1997) Consumption and its consequences, in H. Mackay (ed.) *Consumption and Everyday Life*. London: Sage (in association with The Open University).

Miller, D. (1998) *A Theory of Shopping*. Cambridge: Polity Press.
Mills, C.W. (1953) Introduction to the Mentor Edition, in T. Veblen, *Theory of the Leisure Class*. New York: Mentor.
Moriarty, M. (1991) *Roland Barthes*. Cambridge: Polity Press.
Morley, D. (1995) Television: more a visible object, in C. Jenks (ed.) *Visual Culture*. London: Routledge.
Mumford, L. (1934) *Technics and Civilization*. London: George Routledge and Sons.
Naylor, G. (1990) Great Britain: theoreticians, industry and the craft ideal, in C. Pirovano (ed.) *History of Industrial Design, vol. 2, 1851–1918, The Great Emporium of the World*. Milan: Electa.
Norman, D.A. (1988) *The Psychopathology of Everyday Things*. New York: Basic Books.
Nye, R.A. (1993) The medical origins of sexual fetishism, in E. Apter and W. Pietz (eds) *Fetishism as Cultural Discourse*. Ithaca, NY: Cornell University Press.
Oakley, A. (1976) *Housewife*. Harmondsworth: Penguin.
Oakley, B. (1987) *Windsurfing: Improving Techniques*. Swindon: Crowood Press.
Office for National Statistics (ONS) (1997) *Family Spending: A Report on the Family Expenditure Survey 1996–97*. London: The Stationery Office.
Office for National Statistics (1998) *Social Trends 28: 1998 Edition*. London: The Stationery Office.
Oliver, P. (1987) *Dwellings: The House across the World*. Oxford: Phaidon.
Olszewska, A. and Roberts, K. (eds) (1989) *Leisure and Lifestyle*. London: Sage.
Parker, S. (1983) *Leisure and Work*. London: George Allen and Unwin.
Perec, G. (1992 [1965]) *Les Choses*. Paris: Presse Pocket.
Pietz, W. (1985) The problem of the fetish I, *Res, Anthropology and Aesthetics*, 9: 5–17.
Pietz, W. (1987) The problem of the fetish II, *Res, Anthropology and Aesthetics*, 13: 23–45.
Pietz, W. (1993) Fetishism and materialism, in E. Apter and W. Pietz (eds) *Fetishism as Cultural Discourse*. Ithaca, NY: Cornell University Press.
Poe, E.A. (1986a [1845]) The philosophy of furniture, in *The Fall of the House of Usher and Other Writings*. Harmondsworth: Penguin.
Poe, E.A. (1986b [1845]) The oval portrait, in *The Fall of the House of Usher and Other Writings*. Harmondsworth: Penguin.
Polhemus, T. (1994) *Streetstyle: From Sidewalk to Catwalk*. New York: Thames and Hudson.
Proulx, E.A. (1996) *Accordion Crimes*. London: Fourth Estate.
Putnam, T. (1990) Introduction: design, consumption and domestic ideals, in T. Putnam and C. Newton (eds) *Household Choices*. London: Futures.

Putnam, T. and Newton, C. (eds) (1990) *Household Choices*. London: Futures.

Rakoff, R.M. (1977) Ideology in everyday life: the meaning of the house, *Politics and Society*, 7(1): 85–104.

Rapoport, A. (1969) *House Form and Culture*. Englewood Cliffs, NJ: Prentice Hall.

Read, H. (1956 [1934]) *Art and Industry: The Principles of Industrial Design*. London: Faber and Faber.

Read, H. (1966) The origins of form in art, in G. Kepes (ed.) *The Man-Made Object*. London: Studio Vista.

Rica-Lévy, P. (1989) 1567–1967: du bleu de Gênes au bleu-jeans, in *Blu Blue-jeans: Il blu popolare*. Milan: Electa.

Riggins, S.H. (1990) The power of things: the role of domestic objects in the presentation of self, in S.H. Riggins (ed.) *Beyond Goffman: Studies on Communication, Institution and Social Interaction*. Berlin: Mouton de Gruyter.

Riggins, S.H. (ed.) (1994a) *The Socialness of Things: Essays on the Socio-Semiotics of Objects*. New York: Mouton de Gruyter.

Riggins, S.H. (1994b) Fieldwork in the living room, in S.H. Riggins (ed.) *The Socialness of Things: Essays on the Socio-Semiotics of Objects*. New York: Mouton de Gruyter.

Robbins, D. (1991) *The Work of Pierre Bourdieu*. Buckingham: Open University Press.

Roberts, K. (1970) *Leisure*. London: Longman.

Roderick, I. (1999) Bodies, materials, practice: habiting space and the representational limits of actor-network theory.

Rojek, C. (1985) *Capitalism and Leisure Theory*. London: Tavistock.

Rose, L. (ed.) (1988) Freud and fetishism: previously unpublished minutes of the Vienna Psychoanalytic Society, *Psychoanalytic Quarterly*, 57: 147–66.

Rosen, P. (1993) The social construction of mountain bikes: technology and postmodernity in the cycle industry, *Social Studies of Science*, 23: 479–513.

Rosen, P. (1995) Modernity, postmodernity and sociotechnical change in the British cycle industry and cycling culture. Doctoral dissertation, Lancaster University.

Rubinstein, R.P. (1995) *Dress Codes: Meanings and Messages in American Culture*. Boulder CO: Westview Press.

Rutter, D.R. (1987) *Communicating by Telephone*. Oxford: Pergamon Press.

Sahlins, M. (1976) *Culture and Practical Reason*. Chicago: University of Chicago Press.

Saisselin, R.G. (1985) *Bricabracomania: The Bourgeois and the Bibelot*. London: Thames and Hudson.

Scheuring, D. (1989) Heavy duty denim: 'quality never dates', in A. McRobbie (ed.) *Zoot Suits and Second-Hand Dresses: An Anthology of Fashion and Music*. London: Macmillan.

Schwartz Cowan, R. (1987) The consumption junction: a proposal for research strategies in the sociology of technology, in W. Bijker, T. Hughes and T. Pinch (eds) *The Social Construction of Technological Systems*. Cambridge, MA: MIT Press.

Schwartz Cowan, R. (1989) *More Work for Mother: The Ironies of Household Technology from the Open Hearth to the Microwave*. London: Free Association.

Seamon, D. (1929) *A Geography of the Lifeworld: Movement, Rest and Encounter*. New York: St Martin's Press.

Shaw, F. (1985) *The Homes and Homelessness of Post-War Britain*. Carnforth, Lancs.: Parthenon Press.

Shea, J.G. (1965) *Anatomy of Contemporary Furniture*. New York: Van Nostrand Reinhold.

Shields, R. (ed.) (1992) *Lifestyle Shopping: The Subject of Consumption*. London: Routledge.

Shove, E. (1995) Inside the envelope: building technologies and urban life. Paper presented to the Annual Conference of the British Sociological Association, Leicester, March.

Silverstone, R. (1994) *Television and Everyday Life*. London: Routledge.

Silverstone, R. and Morley, D. (1990) Families and their technologies: two ethnographic portraits, in T. Putnam and C. Newton (eds) *Household Choices*. London: Futures.

Silverstone, R., Hirsch, E. and Morley, D. (1992) Information and communication technologies and the moral economy of the household, in R. Silverstone and E. Hirsch (eds) *Consuming Technologies: Media and Information in Domestic Spaces*. London: Routledge.

Simmel, G. (1950) The metropolis and mental life, in K. Wolff (ed.) *The Sociology of Georg Simmel*. New York: Free Press.

Simmel, G. (1971 [1904]) Fashion, in O. Levine (ed.) *Georg Simmel: On Individuality and Social Forms*. London: University of Chicago Press.

Simmel, G. (1990 [1907]) *The Philosophy of Money*. London: Routledge.

Simmel, G. (1991 [1896]) The Berlin Trade Exhibition, *Theory Culture and Society*, 8(3): 119–23.

Simpson, D. (1982) *Fetishism and Imagination: Dickens, Melville, Conrad*. Baltimore, MD: Johns Hopkins University Press.

Slater, D. (1997) *Consumer Culture and Modernity*. Cambridge: Polity Press.

Smith, G.W.H. and Ball, M.S. (1992) *Analyzing Visual Data*. London: Sage.

Sobchack, V. (1995) Beating the meat/surviving the text or how to get out of this century alive, in M. Featherstone and R. Burrows (eds) *Cyberspace/Cyberbodies/Cyberpunk: Cultures of Technological Embodiment*. London: Sage.

Spigel, L. (1992) *Make Room for TV: Television and the Family Ideal in Postwar America*. Chicago: University of Chicago Press.

Stone, G. (1962) Appearance and the self, in A.M. Rose (ed.) *Human Behaviour and Social Process: An Interactionist Perspective*. London: Routledge and Kegan Paul.

Sudjic, D. (1985) *Cult Objects: The Complete Guide to Having It All*. London: Paladin.

Sweetman, P. (1999) Marked bodies, oppositional identities? Tattooing, piercing and the ambiguity of resistance, in S. Roseneil and J. Seymour (eds) *Practising Identities: Power and Resistance*. London: Macmillan.

Templar, J. (1992) *The Staircase: History and Theories*. Cambridge, MA: MIT Press.

Thomas, K. (1994) *Prosthetic Rehabilitation*. London: Quintessence.

Thompson, M. (1979) *Rubbish Theory: The Creation and Destruction of Value*. Oxford: Oxford University Press.

Tomas, D. (1995) Feedback and cybernetics: reimaging the body in the age of cybernetics, in M. Featherstone and R. Burrows (eds) *Cyberspace/Cyberbodies/Cyberpunk: Cultures of Technological Embodiment*. London: Sage.

Turner, P.A. (1994) *Ceramic Uncles and Celluloid Mammies: Black Images and their Influence on Culture*. New York: Anchor.

Turner, S. (1983) The development and organisation of windsurfing, *Institute of Leisure and Amenity Management Journal*, 1: 13–15.

Vale, V. and Juno, A. (1989) *Modern Primitives*. San Francisco: Re/Search.

Veblen, T. (1953 [1899]) *The Theory of the Leisure Class*. New York: Mentor.

Wall, T. (1997) An anecdotal look at body modification. http://hamp.hampshire.edu/~tawF95/bodmodexp.html

Warde, A. (1994) Consumption, identity-formation and uncertainty, *Sociology*, 28(4): 877–98.

Way, P. (1991) *Windsurfing: Technique, Tactics, Training*. Swindon: Crowood Press.

Wells, D. (1981) *Marxism and the Modern State: An Analysis of Fetishism in Capitalist Society*. Brighton: Harvester.

Wheaton, B. (1997) Consumption, lifestyle and gendered identities in post-modern sports: the case of windsurfing. Unpublished doctoral thesis, University of Brighton.

Wheaton, B. (1999) Culture of commitment, in S. Sydnor and R. Rinehart (eds) *To The Extreme: Alternative Sports Inside and Out*. New York: SUNY.

Whitehead, A.N. (1920) *The Concept of Nature*. Cambridge: Cambridge University Press.

Whiteley, N. (1993) *Design for Society*. London: Reaktion.

Wiener, N. (1948) *Cybernetics: or, Control and Communication in the Animal and the Machine*. New York: Wiley.

Williams, R. (1990 [1975]) *Television: Technology and Cultural Form*, 2nd edn. London: Routledge.

Willis, P.E. (1975) The expressive style of a motor-bike culture, in J. Benthall and T. Polhemus (eds) *The Body as a Medium of Expression*. London: Allen Lane.

Wilson, E. (1985) *Adorned in Dreams: Fashion and Modernity*. London: Virago.

Wilson, R.R. (1995) Cyber(body)parts: prosthetic consciousness, in M. Featherstone and R. Burrows (eds) *Cyberspace/Cyberbodies/Cyberpunk: Cultures of Technological Embodiment*. London: Sage.

Wolff, J. (1983) *Aesthetics and the Sociology of Art*. London: George, Allen and Unwin.

Woodward, V. (1996) Gybing round the buoys, *Trouble and Strife*, 33: 29–34.

Woolgar, S. (1987) Reconstructing man and machine: a note on sociological critiques of cognitivism, in W. Bijker, T. Hughes and T. Pinch (eds) *The Social Construction of Technological Systems*. Cambridge, MA: MIT Press.

Wright, L. (1996) The suit: a common bond or a defeated purpose?, in P. Kirkham (ed.) *The Gendered Object*. Manchester: Manchester University Press.

Wynne, D. and O'Connor J. (1998) Consumption and the postmodern city, *Urban Studies*, 35(5–6): 841–64.

Zimmerman Umble, D. (1992) The Amish and the telephone: resistance and reconstruction, in R. Silverstone and E. Hirsch (eds) *Consuming Technologies: Media and Information in Domestic Spaces*. London: Routledge.

INDEX